STARS ABOVE EARTH BELOW

American Indians and Nature

EDITED BY MARSHA C. BOL

ROBERTS RINEHART PUBLISHERS
for
CARNEGIE MUSEUM OF NATURAL HISTORY

This publication was made possible through the support of the Scaife Family Foundation.

Published by Roberts Rinehart Publishers
6309 Monarch Park Place
Niwot, Colorado 80503
TEL 303.652.2685   FAX 303.652.2689
www.robertsrinehart.com

Distributed to the trade by Publishers Group West

Published in Ireland and the UK by
Roberts Rinehart Publishers
Trinity House, Charleston Road
Dublin 6, Ireland

Published in cooperation with Carnegie Museum of Natural History

Copyright © 1998 Carnegie Institute, Carnegie Museum of Natural History

Cover photographs:
Navajo sand painting, Father Sky and Mother Earth, Juanita Stevens, early 1990s; 35943-1, Carnegie Museum of Natural History
Shield with cover, Crow, collected 1904; 2418-116a, Carnegie Museum of Natural History
Carnegie artifact photographs: Tom Barr
Cover design: Ann W. Douden
Interior design: Pauline Brown

International Standard Book Number 1-57098-198-1
Library of Congress Cataloging in Publication data:
Stars above, earth below : American Indians and nature /
        edited by Marsha C. Bol.
            p.   cm.
        Includes bibliographical references (p.   ) and index.
        ISBN 1-57098-198-1   (hc)
        1. Indian philosophy--North America.   2. Indians of North
    America--Religion.   3. Human ecology--North America.   4. Indians
    of North America--Science.   I. Bol, Marsha.   II. Carnegie Museum
    of Natural History.
    E98.P5S73   1998
    304.2'089'97--dc21   98-5747
                                                                       CIP

10 9 8 7 6 5 4 3 2 1

Printed in the United States of America

Contents

Contents

THE AUTHORS of these essays were chosen for their expertise in their respective disciplines, and we are, indeed, fortunate to have brought together so many authorities to present this overview of the relationships of Native North Americans with the natural world. Among the authors are Native specialists, a folklorist, an astronomer, an ethnobotanist, an ornithologist, a zooarchaeologist, linguists, anthropologists, and an art historian. Together these scholars have created a much-needed interdisciplinary resource in an area where nothing currently exists.

This volume is divided into broad parts: Origin Stories, Astronomy, Animals, Botany, and Nature and Society. Each section is introduced by a general essay that draws upon research on and examples from numerous tribes and groups throughout Native North America. Additional essays discuss the themes from the viewpoint of a specific locale or Native group, allowing the reader a closer view of an individual tribe or cultural region. The essays focus primarily on the ethnographic and historic record to the present day, but also include insights into the archaeological past.

Sky Above, Earth Below: American Indians and Nature expands the theme of the Alcoa Foundation Hall of American Indians, which opened in June 1998. It also complements the exhibition's catalogue, *North, South, East, West: American Indians and the Natural World*, which displays more than two hundred of the most important artifacts.

The Alcoa Foundation Hall of American Indians, its accompanying catalogue, and this comprehensive book of essays offer a special opportunity not only to view artifacts related to these topics but to meet the people who made and used them. Together they give an overview of the connections between Native Americans and their environments.

Publications editor Louise Craft was the guiding hand behind this book. I am grateful to her for shepherding this project to its fruition. Catherine Marshall brought her experienced pencil to the copyediting, Sylvia Keller gave it the final polish, and Tom Barr shot the artifact photographs with a thoughtful eye to the integrity of the objects.

I was most fortunate to have the help of project assistants Melissa Elsberry, Sylvia Keller, and Beth Worstell, who handled research assignments and assisted with a myriad of tasks. Our thanks to Rick Rinehart and Betsy Armstrong of Roberts Rinehart Publishers for their collaboration.

MARSHA C. BOL, PH.D., is an anthropologist and art historian at the Carnegie Museum of Natural History, Pittsburgh, Pennsylvania.

NORA MARKS DAUENHAUER, TLINGIT, is co-editor of several books on Tlingit oral narratives and life stories sponsored by the Sealaska Heritage Foundation, Juneau, Alaska.

RICHARD DAUENHAUER, PH.D., is a linguist and co-editor of several books on Tlingit oral narratives and life stories sponsored by the Sealaska Heritage Foundation, Juneau, Alaska.

CHIEF ADAM DICK (KᵂAXSISTALA), KᵂAKᵂAKAʾWAKᵂ, is a hereditary chief and elder of his nation, presently living at Qualicum, British Columbia.

FRANCES B. KING, PH.D., is an ethnobotanist at the Department of Archaeology, Cleveland Museum of Natural History, Cleveland, Ohio.

SHEPARD KRECH, PH.D., is director of the Haffenreffer Museum of Anthropology and an anthropologist at Brown University, Providence, Rhode Island.

EDMUND JAMES LADD, ZUNI, is an anthropologist at the Museum of Indian Arts and Culture, a division of the Museum of New Mexico, in Santa Fe.

N. SCOTT MOMADAY, PH.D., KIOWA, Regents Professor of English at the University of Arizona, won a Pulitzer Prize in 1969 for his *House Made of Dawn*.

SANDRA L. OLSEN, PH.D., is a zooarchaeologist at the Carnegie Museum of Natural History, Pittsburgh, Pennsylvania.

ALFONSO ORTIZ, PH.D., TEWA, before his death in 1997 was Professor of Anthropology at the University of New Mexico.

AMADEO M. REA, PH.D., is Curator Emeritus of Birds and Mammals at the San Diego Museum of Natural History.

GREGORY SCHREMPP, PH.D., is a folklorist at Indiana University, Bloomington, Indiana.

DAISY SEWID-SMITH (MAYANILTH), Kʷakʷaka'wakʷ, is a recognized historian, language specialist, and author, who works for the Campbell River School District in British Columbia.

NANCY J. TURNER, PH.D., is an ethnobotanist at the University of Victoria, Victoria, British Columbia.

RAY A. WILLIAMSON, PH.D., is Research Professor of International Affairs at the Space Policy Institute, George Washington University, Washington, D.C.

Introduction

Direction

I was directed by my grandfather
To the East,
    so I might have the power
    of the bear;
To the South,
    so I might have the courage
    of the eagle;
To the West,
    so I might have the wisdom
    of the owl;
To the North,
    so I might have the craftiness
    of the fox;
To the Earth,
    so I might receive her fruit;
To the Sky,
    so I might lead a life of
    innocence.

—ALONZO LOPEZ, TOHONO O'ODHAM, SOUTHWEST

1

Native American Attitudes to the Environment

N. Scott Momaday

THE FIRST THING to say about the Native American perspective on environmental ethics is that there is a great deal to be said. I don't think that anyone has clearly understood yet how the Indian conceives of himself in relation to the landscape. We have formulated certain generalities about that relationship, and the generalities have served a purpose, but they have been rather too general. For example take the idea that the Indian reveres the earth, thinks of it as the place of his origin and thinks of the sky also in a personal way. These statements are true. But they can also be misleading because they don't indicate anything about the nature of the relationship which is, I think, an intricate thing in itself.

I have done much thinking about the "Indian worldview," as it is sometimes called. And I have had some personal experience of Indian religion and Indian societies within the framework of a worldview. Sometime ago I wrote an essay entitled "An American Land Ethic" in which I tried to talk in certain ways about this idea of a Native American attitude toward the landscape. And in that essay I made certain observations. I tried to express the notion first that the Native American ethic with respect to the physical world is a matter of reciprocal appropriation: appropriations in which man invests himself in the landscape, and at the same time incorporates the landscape into his own most fundamental experience. That suggests a dichotomy, or a paradox, and I think it is a paradox. It is difficult to understand a relationship which is defined in these terms, and yet I don't know how better to define it.

Secondly, this appropriation is primarily a matter of the imagination. The appropriation is realized through an act of the imagination which is moral and kind. I mean to say that we are all, I suppose, at the most fundamental level what we imagine ourselves to be. And this is certainly true of the American Indian. If you want a definition, you would not go, I hope, to the stereotype which has burdened the American Indian for many years. He is not that befeathered spectacle who is always chasing John Wayne across the silver screen. Rather, he is someone who thinks of himself in a particular way, and his idea comprehends his relationship to the physical world, among other things. He imagines himself in terms of that relationship and others. And it is that act of the imagination, that moral act of the imagination, which I think constitutes his understanding of the physical world.

Thirdly, this imagining, this understanding of the relationship between man and the landscape, or man and the physical world, man and nature, proceeds from a racial or cultural experience. I think his attitude toward the landscape has been formulated over a long period of time, and the length of time itself suggests an evolutionary process perhaps instead of a purely rational and decisive experience. Now I am not sure that you can understand me on this point; perhaps I should elaborate. I mean that the Indian has determined himself in his imagination over a period of untold generations. His racial memory is an essential part of his understanding. He understands himself more clearly than perhaps other people, given his situation in the time and space. His heritage has always been rather closely focused, centered upon the landscape as a particular reality. Beyond this, the Native American has a particular investment in vision and in the idea of vision. You are familiar with the term "vision quest" for example. This is another essential idea to the Indian worldview, particularly that view as it is expressed among the cultures of the Plains Indians. This is significant. I think we should not lose the force of the idea of seeing something or envisioning something in a particular way.

I happen to think that there are two visions in particular with reference to man and his relationship to the natural world. One is physical and the other is imaginative. And we all deal in one way or another with these visions simultaneously. If I can try to find an analogy, it's rather like looking through the viewfinder of a camera, the viewfinder which is based upon the principle of the split image. And it is a matter of trying to align the two planes of that particular view. This can be used as an example of how we look at the world around us. We see it with the physical eye. We see it as it appears to us, in one dimension of reality. But we also see it with the eye of the mind. It seems to me that the Indian has achieved a particularly effective alignment of those two planes of vision. He perceives the landscape in both ways. He realizes a whole image from the possibilities within his reach. The moral implications of this are very far-reaching. Here is where we get into the consideration of religion and religious ideas and ideals.

There is another way in which I think one can very profitably and accurately think of the Indian in relation to the landscape and in terms of his idea of that relationship. This is to center on such a word as *appropriate*. The idea of "appropriateness" is central to the Indian experience of the natural world. It is a fundamental idea within his philosophy. I recall the story told to me some years ago by a friend, who is not himself a Navajo, but was married for a time to a Navajo girl and lived with her family in Southern Utah. And he said that he had been told this story and was passing it on to me. There was a man living in a remote place on the Navajo reservation who had lost his job and was having a difficult time making ends meet. He had a wife and several children. As a matter of fact, his wife was expecting another child. One day a friend came to visit him and perceived that his situation was bad. The friend said to him, "Look, I see that you're in tight straits, I see you have many mouths to feed, that you have no wood and that there is very little food in your larder. But one thing puzzles me. I know you're a hunter, and I know, too, there are deer in the mountains very close at hand. Tell me, why don't you kill a deer so that you and your family might have fresh meat to eat?" And after a

Hopi country in the Southwest. PHOTO BY OWEN SEUMPTEWA

Man has two visions of nature. One is physical; the other, imaginative. The Native American experience of the natural world also includes appropriateness, both morally and naturally.

Northwest Coast Indian country. PHOTO BY MELINDA MCNAUGHER

The Great Plains, home of the Lakota and their neighbors.
PHOTO BY MELINDA MCNAUGHER

Nature is an element in Native American existence.

The Northeast, home of the Iroquois and their neighbors.
PHOTO BY BILL RANDOUR

time the man replied, "No, it is inappropriate that I should take life just now when I am expecting the gift of life."

The implications of that idea, and the way in which the concept of appropriateness lies at the center of that little parable is a central consideration within the Indian world. You cannot understand how the Indian thinks of himself in relation to the world around him unless you understand his conception of what is appropriate; particularly what is morally appropriate within the context of that relationship.

Question: Could you probe a little deeper into what lies behind the idea of appropriate or inappropriate behavior regarding the natural world. Is it a religious element? Is it biological or a matter of survival? How would you characterize what makes an action appropriate or inappropriate?

Momaday: It is certainly a fair question but I'm not sure that I have the answer to it. I suspect that whatever it is that makes for the idea of appropriateness is a very complex thing in itself. Many things constitute the idea of appropriateness. Basically, I think it is a moral idea as opposed to a religious one. It is a basic understanding of right within the framework of relationships, and, within the framework of that relationship I was talking about a moment ago, between man and the physical world. That which is appropriate within this context is that which is *natural*. This is another key word. My father used to tell me of an old man who has lived a whole life. I have often thought of this image. The old man used to come to my grandfather's house periodically to pay visits, and my father has very vivid recollections of this man whom I never knew. But his name was Chaney. Father says that Chaney would come to the house and he would make himself perfectly at home. He would be passing by going from one place to another, exercising his ethnic prerogative for nomadism. But he would make my grandfather's house a kind of resting place. He stayed there on many occasions. My father says that every morning when Chaney was there as a guest he would get up in the first light, paint his face, go outside, face the east, and bring the sun out of the horizon. Then he would pray. He would pray aloud to the rising sun. He did that because it was appropriate that he should do that. He understood. Or perhaps I should say that in terms of his own understanding, the sun was the origin of his strength. He understood the sun, within a more formal religious context, similar to the way someone else understands the presence of a deity. And in the face of that recognition, he acted naturally or appropriately. Through the medium of prayer, he returned some of his strength to the sun. He did this every day. It was a part of his daily life. It was as natural and appropriate to him as anything could be. There is in the Indian worldview this kind of understanding of what is and what is not appropriate. It isn't a matter of intellection. It is respect for the understanding of one's heritage. It is a kind of racial memory and it has its origin beyond any sort of historical experience. It reaches back to the dawn of time.

Question: When talking about vision, you said that the Indians saw things physically and also with the eye of the mind, I think this is the way you put it. You also said that this was a whole image, and that it had certain moral implications. Would you elaborate further?

Momaday: I think there are different ways of seeing things. I myself am particularly interested in literature, and in the traditions of various peoples, the Indians in particular. I understand something of how this works within the context of literature. For example, in the nineteenth century in America, there were poets who were trying very hard to see nature and to write about it. This is one kind of vision. They succeeded in different ways, some succeeding more than others. They succeeded in seeing what was really there on the vision plain of the natural world and they translated that vision, or that perception of the natural world, into poetry. Many of them had a kind of scientific training. Their observations were trained through the study of botany, astronomy, or zoology, etc. This refers, of course, to one kind of vision.

But, obviously, this is not the sort of view of the landscape which characterizes the Indian world. His view, rather, is of a different and more imaginative kind. It is a more comprehensive view. When the Native American looks at nature, it isn't with the idea of training a glass upon it, or pushing it away so that he can focus upon it from a distance. In his mind, nature is not something apart from him. He conceives of it, rather, as an element in which he exists. He has existence within that element, much in the same way we think of having existence within the element of air. It would be unimaginable for him to think of it in the way the nineteenth century "nature poets" thought of looking at nature and writing about it. They employed a kind of "esthetic distance," as it is sometimes called. This idea would be alien to the Indian. This is what I meant by trying to make the distinction between two sides of a split image.

Question: So then, presumably in moral terms, the Indian would say that a person should not harm nature because it's something in which one participates oneself.

Momaday: This is one aspect of it. There is this moral aspect, and it refers to perfect alignment. The appropriation of both images into the one reality is what the Indian is concerned to do: to see what is really there, but also to see what is *really* there. This reminds me of another story. It is very brief. It was told to me by the same fellow who told me about the man who did not kill the deer. (To take a certain liberty with the title of a novel that I know well.) He told me that while he himself was living in southern Utah with his wife's family, he became very ill. He contracted pneumonia. There was no doctor, no physician nearby. But there was a medicine man close at hand. The family called in a diagnostician (the traditional thing to do), who came and said that my friend was suffering from a particular malady whose cure would be the red-ant ceremony. So a man who is very well versed in that ceremony, a seer, a kind of specialist in the red-ant ceremony, came in and administered it to my friend. Soon after that my friend recovered completely. Not long after this he was talking to his father-in-law, and he was very curious about what had taken place. He said, "I wonder about the red-ant ceremony. Why is it that the diagnostician prescribed that particular ceremony for me?" His father-in-law looked at him and said, "Well, it was obvious to him that there were red ants in your system, and so we had to call in a seer to take the red ants out of your system." At this point, my friend became very incredulous, and said, "Yes, but surely you don't mean that there were red ants inside of me." His father-in-law looked at him for a moment, then said, "Not ants, but ants." Unless you understand this distinction, you might have difficulty understanding something about the Indian view of the natural world.

Notes

The poem on page 1 is reprinted from the *South Dakota Review* 7, no. 2 (summer 1969). Used by permission.

This essay was adapted from transcriptions of oral remarks Professor Momaday made informally during a discussion with faculty and students. It is reprinted by permission of HarperCollins Publishers, Inc., from *Seeing with a Native Eye*, edited by Walter Holden Capps, copyright © 1976 by Walter Holden Capps.

Origin Stories

The Creation of the Earth

Earth Magician shapes this world.
Behold what he can do!
Round and smooth he molds it.
Behold what he can do!
Earth Magician makes the
*   mountains.*
Heed what he has to say!
He it is that makes the mesas.
Heed what he has to say!
Earth Magician shapes this world;
Earth Magician makes its
*   mountains;*
Makes all larger, larger, larger.
Into the earth the magician glances;
Into its mountains he may see.

—PIMA, SOUTHWEST

2

Distributed Power: An Overview
A Theme in American Indian Origin Stories

GREGORY SCHREMPP

EVERY SOCIETY has speculated about origins—about how the natural world including all its species and humans with all their customs first came to be. In Native American cultures these speculations take the form of colorful origin stories that, prior to the arrival of Europeans in the Americas, were passed down orally, rather than in written form. Many of these stories have been collected and published, and many continue to be told today.

There is tremendous variety in origin stories among the Native American tribes, and even within particular tribes one finds such an abundance of stories that it is impossible to discuss more than a few of them. Rather than attempting to provide a survey, this essay focuses on one theme that is particularly significant in Native American origin stories and reveals Native American attitudes toward the natural world. This theme of *distributed power* promotes the idea that powers and values available in the cosmos are spread out among the many different species of the universe, rather than restricted to only one or a few species.

It is well known that in the origin stories of most, if not all, societies, humans are portrayed as an especially

Storyteller figurine

In 1962 Helen Cordero created her first storyteller figure, which she fashioned after her grandfather, a respected storyteller.

HELEN CORDERO, COCHITI PUEBLO, NEW MEXICO, CA. 1992 CMNH 35154-7

gifted and favored species; since humans are telling the stories, this is not surprising. And, similarly, we find that the clan, nation, or community that tells a particular origin story frequently portrays itself as an especially gifted and important group, one that deserves to hold a prestigious social and political position. Native Americans are no exception in this regard, for many of their origin stories serve to give status to their tellers.

But equally noteworthy in Native American societies is the number of origin stories that, instead of merely aggrandizing humans, emphasize the positive attributes and abilities of other natural species and the debts that humans owe to them. This focus sometimes takes the form of recognizing ways in which humans are dependent upon other species. At other times it seems to emerge as a desire that humans could share some of the abilities possessed by other natural species. The plots of many Native American origin stories center on attempts by one species—either humans or humanlike heroes—to acquire some of the powers that are distributed among the other species of the cosmos, or to build relationships with those species so that their special abilities can be called upon.

Transformers, Tricksters, and Culture Heroes

The Native American attitude toward nonhuman species is reflected, in part, in the fact that various animal species are treated in origin stories as though they are human. Fish, other animals, and even celestial bodies such as stars are portrayed as living in societies with their own customs and villages, which must be approached with the same degree of caution and respect as would be accorded to human communities. Humans are seen as owing a great debt to the humanlike animal characters that are the central figures in origin stories, for these characters are the ones who first set up the world in such a way that humans are able to successfully live in it.

When a character in an origin story modifies the world in a useful way, that character may be referred to as a *transformer*. Native American origin stories abound with colorful transformers, and many stories imply that there was an entire epoch of transformers and transformations prior to the appearance of humans on Earth. In many accounts Earth is said to be inhabited by hostile monsters until a transformer rids the world of them.

One of the most widely known transformers is Coyote, a figure often credited, especially in western North America, with making the world suitable for human habitation. Coyote is sometimes portrayed as a wanderer who, for example, moves up and down rivers, creating distinctive landmarks while making various modifications in the flow of the water or in the distribution of fish, so that humans will be more successful in obtaining food.

Coyote is sometimes referred to as a *trickster*, because he goes about his work with a childlike innocence, impetuousness, and bravado that leads to many unplanned results of very mixed character. Coyote is both creative and destructive, both serious and buffoonish; his experiments usually aid humans but also sometimes create hardships for them. Of the hardships said to be caused by Coyote, the most notable is the fact that humans must die, rather than live forever. One of the tales told about Coyote is very similar to the Greek myth of Orpheus, who journeyed to the Underworld and attempted, unsuccessfully, to bring his deceased wife, Eurydice, back to the world of the living. When Coyote's wife or children die, he is given directions for bringing them back to life. But because of his impatience Coyote fails to follow the instructions accurately; consequently, his loved ones are not brought back to life, and because of this, humans too must die.

Beaded bottle

The image is of Iktomi, the Sioux spider trickster who plays pranks on humans.

YANKTON SIOUX, SOUTH DAKOTA, COLLECTED CA. 1899 CMNH 1171-35

Many stories about Coyote are full of humor, and certainly such stories are told in part for entertainment. But even in the more foolish of Coyote's doings, important Native American values can be seen. For example, many of Coyote's more humorous adventures are based upon a childish jealousy of the powers or abilities of other animals. Coyote frequently ends up attempting to imitate another animal—for example, making wings for himself and attempting to fly like a bird. His attempts often end in ludicrous failure. In Coyote's intense, childish jealousy of the abilities of other species, we see a humorous reflection on the idea that it might be desirable for one species to be able to acquire some of the powers displayed by other species.

Although this theme is used humorously in Coyote stories, it appears in a more serious form in other Native American origin stories and rituals. For example, some Native American societies practiced a "vision quest," a custom by which maturing tribal members would seek visions—often from animal spirits who would confer special power on the one seeking the vision. The vision quest often seems to involve the same admiration for other species that one encounters in its humorous use in stories of Coyote's adventures.

Coyote is only one of several trickster-transformer figures in Native American origin stories; two other widely known figures are Raven (known especially in the Northwest Coast region) and Hare (known especially in the Midwest and Great Lakes regions). These figures share many characteristics with Coyote, yet they also have some distinctive traits. Raven, like Coyote, is often portrayed as a roving transformer who alters the shape of the world in the course of making a journey, but sometimes a distinct twist is added to Raven's mode of creating. Raven, along with certain other supernatural birds, is sometimes pictured as influencing the world by flapping his wings. With each flap the world is affected in some particular way—for example, a range of mountains could be created. (Tlingit Raven stories are discussed more fully in chapter 3.)

Other transformers are more humanlike, but even these often have some special relationship to a powerful element from the natural universe. Through much of North and South America, part of the transformation of the world is attributed to a pair of supernatural twins, or contrasting personalities, who are frequently said to be born from a human woman but to have the Sun as their father. There are also a number of stories of humans who, scorned and left on their own as children, are adopted by an animal; these adoptees later return to their human tribes and accomplish great deeds for their people.

Besides transformers and tricksters, figures like Coyote, Hare, and Raven, as well as some illustrious human characters, are sometimes spoken of as *culture heroes.* This term designates those characters who first teach humans how to live in a truly human way, that is, according to the values and rules held sacred in a particular society. Besides the numerous stories that tell how such figures have shaped the landscape and rid the world of monsters, there are others that tell how these heroes first taught humans the correct ways to hunt and fish; to take care of animals and game; to make and use fire; to divide up food, perform rituals and other religious duties; and to build and use the tools and implements necessary for carrying on life. In other words the culture hero teaches the people how to establish and maintain a distinct type of culture, a distinct way of life. Stories of culture heroes are found throughout the world, but often—like the Greek Prometheus, who gave fire to mankind—they are humans or gods. The fact that so many Native American culture heroes are animal characters reminds us of the fascination with and sense of indebtedness to the rest of the natural world that are characteristic of Native American origin stories.

Drawing of the Iroquois origin story

This illustration depicts the creation of land, one of a group of stories most commonly referred to as "Earth-Diver" stories. (From J.J. Cornplanter, *Legends of the Longhouse* [Philadelphia, J.B. Lippincott, 1938], p. 21. Used by permission of HarperCollins Publishers)

JESSE CORNPLANTER, IROQUOIS, 1936

One story that tells of such indebtedness is most commonly referred to as "Earth-Diver." It is important because it is so widespread; in fact, it is one of several Native American stories with strong similarities to those found in Asia. "Earth-Diver" tells about the origin of land. Details vary among the many different versions, but the general plot has a group of original beings, usually pictured as animals, attempting to dive to the bottom of an expanse of water that covers everything. After everyone else has failed, the last diver, almost dead from exhaustion, succeeds in bringing a small bit of earth to the surface under its nail or claw. This bit is transformed or unfolds to form the land in its present dimensions. Hence, humans are indebted to the animal hero for the Earth's present landscape.

Cosmic Kinship

In many Native American origin stories elements of the natural world are referred to as though they have a kinship relationship with humans, that is, as though humans are part of a family that also includes nonhuman entities or species. The most obvious examples are instances in which Earth is referred to as a Mother and the Sky or the Sun as a Father. In areas where corn is a particularly important food staple, notably in the North American Southwest, ears of corn used in rituals are referred to as Mothers, and an origin story tells about how Corn Mother first led humans to their present habitation. This is one of several Native American stories in which a living plant is spoken of as a parent to humans.

Other Native American tribes, including those of the Northwest Coast, have origin stories that tell how particular clans are descended from specific animals, which serve as their emblems. Such stories sometimes include an episode in which, during the era of transformations in the distant past, particular animals or birds decide to take off their skins or feathers, revealing humans underneath, who become the founding ancestors of particular human clans. The clan that descends from a particular animal believes that its members have a special relationship with that species. They may dress up to impersonate it on ceremonial occasions, thus complementing what happens in the origin story when the animal first removes its skin to become a human.

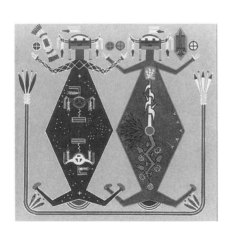

Navajo sand painting: Father Sky and Mother Earth

JUANITA STEVENS, NAVAJO, ARIZONA, EARLY 1990s
CMNH 35943-1

Examples like these illustrate the various ways in which Native American origin stories draw on the image of nature or a particular species as the parent of the human race or of a particular clan. The image of the natural world as the parent of humans is an image that is readily understandable: humans are dependent upon the natural world as children are dependent upon their parents, who give them life and provide for them. It is an image that is found in different forms in origin stories throughout the world. This image has often been noticed and emphasized by European scholars, perhaps

Bear/Raven transformation mask

In part because it is also found in origin stories from Europe—including those about Gaia and other Greek gods—as well as from the Middle East and Mediterranean regions.

In the closed position, this mask represents a bear. When the mask opens, Raven appears on the inside with a human face in the middle.

There is, however, another kinship image prominent in many Native American origin stories that has received less attention by European scholars, perhaps because it has less of a counterpart in European mythology. This is the image of humans related to other branches of the natural universe through intermarriage—in other words, humans having the rest of the natural universe as their "in-laws." A prominent, widespread story in North America, known as the "Star Husband" tale, is based on a human woman, or women, marrying celestial bodies, often stars. The tale often begins with two daydreaming girls wishing they were married to stars. (see story, pp. 47–50). When they awaken, their wish has come true.

They find themselves living in the sky and married to stars, who, in some accounts, are said to have the form of humans. Eventually the girls dig a hole, which turns out to be a hole in the sky, and descend by rope to Earth. Interestingly, there seems to be no *fixed* moral or account of origin connected to this tale. Rather, different tribes have attached many different concluding episodes and origin accounts. The tale is used to account for things as diverse as qualities or characteristics of heavenly bodies or of particular animals, particular ritual ceremonies, or aspects of human nature. It is one of many examples of the same apparent story being shaped in diverse ways by various Native American tribes to account for the origin of different things.

There does not appear to be a single pattern or a predictable outcome for Native American stories about cosmic intermarriage. Some stories, such as "Star Husband," begin with a wish that is fulfilled; others start with a human pursuing for a spouse a being that is thought to be human but turns out to be a member of another species; and in some stories a human is abducted as a spouse by a bear, a jaguar, or some other animal. Sometimes the human ends up leaving and returning to the community of humans at the first possible chance, while at other times an amicable relationship develops, not just between the spouses but between the two species who are related through them. In most cases the human spouse learns or acquires things from living within the animal community that are of value to humans, and brings these positive things back to his or her own human community. In some accounts, for example, this is the way humans acquire cooking fire. In other words, as in the culture hero stories discussed above, things necessary for humans in setting up human society are obtained from other, nonhuman species of the natural universe.

Why should kinship stories based on intermarriage of humans and other aspects of nature be so popular in Native American origin stories? If origin stories based on natural species as *parents* express human dependence on nature, what is expressed in the image of nature as the in-laws of humans? The cosmic in-law theme would seem to be yet another expression of distributed power. Throughout human history intermarriages between different political groups—whether communities, tribes, or nations—have been regarded as important for ensuring cooperation between the two groups and have served as a sign of harmonious inter-dependence between them. Children from such intermarriages are believed to bond the two groups together; through their common children the fates and destinies of the two groups become intertwined. There will be an expectation, on both sides, of reciprocity—the sharing of skills and resources. The members of the two groups will have to be circumspect in their behavior toward each other: they will have to act with generosity and to respect each other's customs and ways of life. The reason that cosmic in-law plots are so common in Native American origin stories would thus seem to lie in the fact that the in-law relation—based on the duty of cooperating and the expectation of sharing—is seen as the ideal way in which humans ought to relate to the other species of the natural universe. Once again, according to the great variety of stories that are told, such relationships do not always work: they sometimes have disastrous consequences. But these failures do not diminish the value of such relationships as ideals, and, indeed, there would seem to be as much risk in foregoing them as there would be in attempting to create them.

The "Emergence" of Humanity

As noted above, some Native American origin stories seem to imply a single great epoch of transformation—a single time in the past when the cosmos was transformed in ways that made it suitable for humans. Not all Native American origin stories imply a single epoch, however. Some suggest, instead, a *series* of stages—most often four—through which the world and human life develop. Examples of this type are the so-called emergence myths found especially in the North American Southwest. These accounts portray humans (or protohumans) as emerging to the present surface of the Earth after living for a time in three other worlds located below the Earth's surface. The decision to migrate from one world to the next frequently follows an outbreak of strife among humans, which sometimes ends in the destruction of one of the worlds. Even in the midst of such troubles, however, the humans learn something new about how to live correctly in difficult circumstances. For example, in one of the previous worlds, Spider teaches people how to weave and thus how to keep warm; in another tale, people learn from ants that they must share food even when it is scarce (it is because ants do this that their waists are so thin).

In most of these stories of emergence, humans are said to arrive at the fourth world by climbing the stem of a plant or vine, perhaps reflecting the agricultural orientation of many of the tribes that tell these stories. Some versions indicate that at the point of emerging into the fourth world, humans split into different Native American tribes, or even into the different Native American and Euro-American identities found in the region of emergence. Many tribes also have accounts of their migration route from their specific point of emergence to their present location. These migration stories include episodes about the origin and unique characteristics of notable landmarks along the way, as well as the mountains and other landmarks that surround the eventual place of settlement. In these migration legends and in numerous other legends, specific lessons and ideals become associated with particular features of landscape, so that anyone encountering the landscape cannot help but recall an important moral teaching.

Blue Corn Maiden Katsina (Sakwap Mana Tihu)

JOHN FREDERICKS, HOPI, CA. 1995
CMNH 36033-1

The journey through the four worlds is sometimes portrayed as a long period of training for enduring a harsh and arid environment. Native American life in the Southwest, where emergence accounts occur in greatest abundance, depends in part upon an attitude of extreme care not to waste food crops, especially corn. In some accounts it is Corn Mother who leads the humans to the fourth world. In another story the people mistreat corn by failing to store it correctly and to value it properly. Because of this, sisters known as the Corn Maidens—the personification of corn—leave the village with the corn from all the storerooms following them. The people then live in hunger and impoverishment until they are able to convince the Corn Maidens to return. The Maidens agree to return each year and fill the corn bins, provided that they are treated properly.

These stories from the Southwest provide a charter—an origin and a set of directions—for the behavior and attitudes that people must maintain in order to live successfully. There are many such stories found in other parts of the Americas. In the Great Plains a story is told about White Buffalo Woman, a culture hero who brings to the people a sacred pipe from which come many of the necessities of life in that area. In the Northwest Coast region, where fishing formed an important source of sustenance, there is a similar story connected with salmon. It sometimes contains an episode in which, after eating salmon, the people fail to reassemble all the bones as ritually required, causing the salmon to depart. There are yet other such stories spread throughout North America. Their central themes focus most often on a woman whose flesh represents the main food source of the region and whose care must be reciprocated by proper treatment. This theme has been adapted through time to a number of different environments.

Many Native American stories of origin are thus accompanied by episodes that express a fear of failure on the part of humans—and a fear that the consequence of failure will be the loss of a world that is habitable by humans. These include episodes in which the whole world is lost

Man's toolbox with story lid

In an endeavor to call upon animals' special abilities and benefits, Inuit hunters decorated their tools, weapons, and related items with images representing the creatures' power. A section of a myth is featured on the lid, perhaps to charm the quarry into giving itself to man.

INUIT, ALASKA?,
COLLECTED 1904
CMNH 3178-114

(as sometimes happens to the three previous worlds in emergence stories); or in which specific plants and animals, or in some cases even implements such as pots and pans, depart or rebel against humans because of mistreatment. An important aspect of the theme of distributed power, in other words, is that various entities of the natural universe, among which the powers of the universe have been distributed, have the prerogative to demand care and respectful treatment from humans if they are to reciprocate with service to humans.

Euro-Americans who have had some exposure to Native American origin stories have frequently expressed the feeling of encountering attitudes toward the natural world that are different from the dominant attitudes found in their own cultural background. Although all life depends upon some degree of self-interested utilization of the natural environment, one can detect many differences in the ways in which humans have envisioned the natural world and their rights and duties regarding it. The human entitlement to the natural world, as portrayed in Native American origin stories, is not unlimited. Humans are portrayed not as possessing the right to unconditional exploitation of nature, but rather as possessing the prerogative to enter into relations of reciprocity with nature. Reciprocity is required by the fact that the powers of the natural world are distributed throughout all of its forms. The ideal relationship is expressed narratively through images of mutuality and interdependence, preeminently in the image of kin or "family ties" between humans and other species. One who challenges the give-and-take character of this ideal does so at one's own risk. The value of this general outlook is, of course, one that seems to be increasingly confirmed by the findings of contemporary studies in scientific ecology. It is an outlook on the natural world that we would all do well to ponder.

Recommended Readings

EMERGENCE/CORN MAIDENS

Benedict, Ruth. *Zuni Mythology*. Columbia University Contributions to Anthropology 21. New York: Columbia University Press, 1935.

Courlander, Harold. *The Fourth World of the Hopis.*
Albuquerque: University of New Mexico Press, 1971.
Waters, Frank. *The Book of the Hopi.* New York: Ballantine
Books, 1963.

TRICKSTERS
Radin, Paul. *The Trickster.* New York: Schocken, 1972.
Ramsey, Jarold. *Coyote Was Going There.* Seattle:
University of Washington Press, 1980.

STAR HUSBAND
Thompson, Stith. *The Star Husband Tale.* Studia
Septentrionalia 4. 1953.

GENERAL WORKS
Bierhorst, John. *The Mythology of North America.* New
York: Quill, William Morrow, 1985.
Erdoes, Richard, and Alfonso Ortiz. *American Indian Myths
and Legends.* New York: Pantheon, 1984.
Vecsey, Christopher. *Imagine Ourselves Richly: Mythic
Narratives of North American Indians.* New York:
Crossroad, 1988.

3

Tlingit Origin Stories

NORA MARKS DAUENHAUER AND RICHARD DAUENHAUER

ORIGIN STORIES are by nature theoretical; they are all human creations after the fact. As one of our clergy colleagues delights in pointing out in his sermons, there were no eyewitness news teams covering the events recorded in Genesis. Or, we would add, of Raven stealing the Sun. These are people's opinion about the origins and meaning of the world and life as we know it. We are dealing with human attempts to codify and transmit a cultural message orally and in writing. Sometimes the versions themselves, as well as the opinions about the versions, conflict. There is no greater unanimity in Native American or other ethnic minority communities than there is in the "dominant culture."

We are opposed to defining or defending the culture of the Northwest Coast Tlingit in terms of Western, Euro-American culture and religion. We think it is spiritually dangerous for Indian identity and pride to be shaped and formulated according to non-Indian concepts, although it is fashionable to do so, giving us such new phenomena as Native American beauty pageants and a Tlingit "national anthem." However, comparisons using familiar Western concepts may be helpful in explaining and understanding less familiar concepts in Tlingit.

The Bible contains two versions of creation. They come from different times and different communities, and were at a later time and place edited into a third version, which is

Genesis as we know it. It should thus not surprise us to find more than one version in Tlingit, and to find these versions evolving. As for conflict in theory and interpretation regarding the text of the story or stories, the entire Judeo-Christian tradition accepts Genesis as canonical, but this has not prevented conflicting interpretations of creation. Judaism, Christianity, and Islam share the same roots, yet are obviously divided from each other and within themselves today. The early Christian church met at several ecumenical councils over the first thousand years of its existence in order to define itself and its beliefs. In 1054 Christianity officially divided into the Eastern (Orthodox, or Greek Catholic) and the Western (Roman Catholic) churches. The Reformation challenged the authority of the Roman Catholic Church, and since that time there has been continuous formation of new churches. Each of these has something different to say about the meaning of Holy Scripture and apostolic tradition. The creation of the world remains an especially sensitive and hotly debated topic.

The main point here is that our interpretation of the past is not static and unchanging, but subject to constant revision and debate. In discussing origin stories, theory is as unavoidable for the Tlingit as it is for Western cultures.

Anyone interested in Tlingit origin stories will eventually encounter theories in two formats. The first is in the written record, now over 200 years old, of comments and analysis by outside observers. Some of these include and discuss the opinions of Tlingit people themselves; others do not. This first category is closed and self-contained and is accessed through a bibliography. The second group of theories is open-ended and consists of the explanations that one will encounter by asking the Tlingit man or woman on the street what he or she thinks about this story or that. The nature and personality of Raven is never far from the center of the debate.

As far as we can tell, it makes little difference whether a theory comes from inside or outside the culture. A native point of view is no guarantee of the "correctness" of that opinion, any more than a thousand years of opinions from within Christianity have resolved the nature and personality of God and how one should worship. The theories cross lines of ethnicity. In the 200-year history of publications about Tlingit Raven, we find Native and non-Native arguing that Raven is God and that Raven is not God. In addition to theological correctness, there is also political correctness. This can easily degenerate into the derogations of anthropologists or linguists by those within the culture, and into denial or dismissal by outsiders of the validity of an intuitive or traditional point of view of those raised within the culture.

A theory proposed by a Tlingit has no greater guarantee of correctness, accuracy, or truth, than a non-Tlingit theory, especially where the topic is so central as the creation of the world and the origins of life and society. This essay combines both points of view. One of the co-authors is Tlingit, raised with the language, culture, and oral literature; the other is non-Tlingit. In the course of the essay, we survey and discuss opinions other than our own, both Tlingit and non-Tlingit, agreeing with some and disagreeing with others. This puts us in the awkward position of disagreeing not only with some Christian missionaries (politically correct) but with some Tlingit points of view (not politically correct).

Whether anthropological, theological, or indigenous folk belief, each generation brings a new personality and point of view to its perception of reality. Thus, the past is always being reviewed and reinvented by insiders as well as outsiders. The Tlingit theoretical tradition has been noticeably susceptible to insider re-evaluation in the last 100 years. This is especially true of Raven stories being reframed in a Christian context.

The concept of Raven as Jesus or the Christian God is implied by the Tlingit storyteller Katishan in 1904.[1] The most recent and most explicit statement we have heard was tape-recorded on January 5, 1995, by a prominent Tlingit village spokesman. In the course of denouncing anthropologists for suggesting an

Raven hat

One of the most popular groups of Tlingit creation stories involves Raven. Raven also plays a social role, different from his mythical one. Society is divided into two halves, or moieties, named the Ravens and the Eagles. Within each moiety are many clans. Every Tlingit belongs to one side or the other. This raven crest hat probably belonged to a clan that owned the right to display Raven.

TLINGIT, EARLY TO MID 1800s
CMNH 3178-60

Asian origin of Alaska Native people, his counter-argument is: "Listen to the stories. Christ was born over here. Christ was what we called Raven, and Raven was God, because the stories tell us that God is the Holy Trinity." He then continues, explaining how one of the well-known elders and storytellers, who died over twenty years ago, "got it all backwards."

We disagree with this particular spokesman. His opinion is not unique, but neither is it shared by all Tlingits. We believe it comes from the social context of the generation that came of age during the period of intense missionization by American Protestants at the end of the nineteenth and beginning of the twentieth centuries.[2] For the Tlingit, this was an era of humiliation and persecution, during which their land was taken and they were denied access to traditional resources, such as salmon streams. The missionaries also attacked their language and culture, with most things Tlingit being defined in negative terms or in terms of cultural deficiency: being without this or that, or this and that is wrong.

The most immediate defense is to demonstrate that "we have that, too." But the process is complex. If one embraces a new religion, one is faced with the problem of how to accept and interpret the past without loss of face. One must reconcile two cultural and religious traditions, the old ways and the new. Sergei Kan was probably the first to examine this new folklore genre in Tlingit, which he admittedly dismissed at first "as a recent invention, a rhetorical 'use of the past' for ideological purposes by elderly Christian Tlingit." He discusses the effort of Tlingit elders to rethink their pre-Christian religion by affirming its validity while acknowledging the greater wisdom and power of Christianity. These interpretations are important because they are "attempts by the colonized people to defend their past against various efforts by Euro-Americans to impose their own, often critical, interpretations on Indian history. To complicate matters even further, some of the key elements of Western ideology, such as Christianity, have been accepted by many Native Americans, so that they now often use Christian concepts to reinterpret their own past."[3]

Kan concludes that "accounts about and interpretations of the past are constantly being reshaped in response to more recent and current events and experiences."[4] This phenomenon of integrating seemingly incongruous or even incompatible material of earlier origin is not new in oral or written literature. In Western tradition, we can see it in the Old Testament, where the editor of Judges comments after relating the gory history of the Levite's concubine (Judges, chs. 19–21) that "In those days there was no king in Israel; every man did what was right in his own eyes" (Judges 21:25). The Christians early on adopted a figural approach to the Old Testament, in which those events are also included in the history of salvation and are interpreted to parallel and prefigure events in the New Testament. In medieval European tradition we see Christian framing in *Beowulf*, the Icelandic Sagas, and Irish literature. Most recently, the Soviet Communists took a similar approach in evaluating and explaining Russian history prior to the Bolshevik Revolution. In all these examples, the effort is to retain the best elements of the past and to affirm their continuing significance, validity, and vitality in terms of the present. With all creation stories, it is best to start at the beginning, and we turn there now.

Types of Tlingit Origin Stories

Tlingit origin stories may be grouped into four broad categories, based on the style, content, and internal relationship of the narratives: (1) early myth time; (2) Raven myth time—Raven as culture hero and Raven as trickster; (3) legendary time; and (4) historical time.[5] These four categories are descriptive and not prescriptive; while not arbitrary, neither are the categories rigid. This type of analytical structure implies concepts of time-depth and genre that may not have been shared by earlier tradition bearers, and this problem has faced all researchers.[6]

Part of the historical process of the shaping of Tlingit oral literature as we know it today seems to have involved flow among the categories. It is probable that over time a personal or family memorate of recent origin (group 4) might attain the status of a community or national legend (group 3). Over an even longer period of time, the historical context may change again, and a legend may acquire the status of distant myth. (We use here the conventional folklore terms: *myth* is that

Raven (left) and Eagle (right)

These two animals, representing the two Tlingit moieties, are painted on the sides of the Naa Kahidi Theater in Juneau, Alaska.

PHOTO BY
MELINDA McNAUGHER

which is sacred and true, usually in the remote past, with divinities, superhumans, or nonhumans as characters; *legend* is that which is historical and true, with human characters; *memorate* is a remembrance of limited distribution, usually personal or family; *folktale* is fiction. Folktales and deliberate fiction are conspicuously absent in Tlingit oral literature.) The Tlingit terms for narratives are *tlaagóo*, specifying a narrative of ancient origin or time; and *shkalneek*, referring to any story or narrative in general.

Early Myth Time

This seems a convenient way to group what are essentially the "odds and ends" of Tlingit creation accounts dealing with cosmic phenomena (Sun, Moon, thunder, earthquakes, winds, and so on), that existed before the birth of Raven. This category may also include various monsters and marvelous creatures that may have existed before or outside of the Raven cycle, such as Gunakadeit (the sea monster), Tl'anaxeedákw (Lucky Lady, Wealth Woman, or Golden Lady), and others; but most knowledgeable Tlingits today would be inclined to place these in group 3, below, to the extent that they are now clan-owned. The significant feature of all the stories in this group is that they are about the origin of cosmic features that existed before Raven entered the scene; more questionably, the category might have historically included other beings in the Tlingit mythological landscape whose origins are ancient and otherwise not explained.

The most interesting and typical stories from this group are about the origins of the Sun and Moon, Thunder and Earthquake. These were among the first Tlingit origin stories recorded by outsiders. Thunder is created by the wings of the Thunderbird, and earthquakes are caused by Old Woman Below, who shakes the column supporting Earth whenever Raven tries to pull her away.[7] Thunder and Earthquake are brother and sister who had to separate forever for unspecified reasons. In another version, this episode is tied in to a larger story in which a chief's daughter has several dog children, one of whom is named Chlkajágo (Lk'ayáak'w in modern spelling), who creates the rainbow (alternatively, his snowshoe tracks create the Milky Way!). He is in love with his sister, but he is discovered when others put pitch in the sister's bed and find it on his buttocks after a liaison. He flees in shame.[8] The Sun and Moon are also brother and sister, but now avoid each other because of shame at the sister's having a lover.[9]

These and the other stories we have placed in group 1 are the most enigmatic in Tlingit oral literature and warrant further study. They may be of ancient origin, or possibly borrowed at a more recent date from other Native American groups. Some of these stories are strikingly "un-Tlingit" in their absence of personal names of characters and clan affiliation. Perhaps as a remedy for this, they seem to be gravitating to group 3. Regardless of origin, many of these stories are alive and well in Tlingit oral tradition today, and the contemporary versions are often more complete than the fragments published by early fieldworkers.[10]

Raven Stories

One of the largest and most popular groups of Tlingit origin stories involves Raven. The most significant feature about Raven is his dual or multiple personality. This has intrigued and confused observers from the earliest accounts to the present day. Since being elusive is part of his personality, this critical frustration should come as no surprise.[11] Following standard practice, we have subdivided Raven stories into two categories, "culture hero" and "trickster." The stories themselves are thoroughly mixed, but it is convenient to separate the personality traits for purposes of discussion. Raven is also often called a "creator," but we do not like this term for a number of reasons. Raven actually creates very little. Most often, he redistributes what is already there. Raven stories of this kind depict him as a rearranger or transformer of the existing world.[12] The most famous examples are Raven's theft and distribution of the Sun, Moon, stars, and daylight, or how he brings fresh water and the salmon run. In all these cases, the natural phenomena already exist, but are being hoarded by one person who refuses to share. Raven manages to steal these and redistribute them to the people. In the process, other features of the world are often created, such as rivers, lakes, and many of the animals.

In many other stories, Raven is a trickster, driven entirely by ego, hunger, and greed, with no evident altruistic motives. These stories often demonstrate how such-and-such animal acquired some physical feature following an encounter with Raven, or how a particular feature of landscape reflects where an event in the Raven cycle happened. But the animals and land already exist prior to their modification. Humans are usually not involved at all, and rarely do the animals that Raven encounters benefit from the experience. The Small Birds are lucky to go away hungry but alive after Raven cheats them out of their share of the King Salmon; Robin is modified by the new red breast, Chickadee by the dark head markings, Jay by the topknot. In contrast, Deer and Brown Bear's Wife die horrible deaths; Cormorant loses his tongue; Bear loses the fat from his thighs in one story, and his genitals in another. Much to the shock of some audiences today (but to the amusement of others), there are several X- and R-rated Raven stories. These deal with Raven's sexual appetite and exploits, and creation of the human body parts. To avoid problems of censorship or public shock, Victorian scholars published these stories in Latin.[13]

Legendary Time

Another large and important category of origin story deals with the acquisition of clan spirits and crests by human ancestors in what might be called legendary time. This genre is extremely important in Tlingit oral literature and world view, because the events happened to the human ancestors and progenitors of today's clans. Thus, the stories are owned by the various clans, and concern over the right to claim, use, and display the crests related to the stories remains central in Tlingit culture today. In this genre, humans are the main characters, and their actions and encounters with the animal, natural, and spiritual worlds have created the physical and intellectual landscapes we know today. In some stories, new animals are created, as when Naatsilanéi carves and creates the Killer Whale for the first time (although a mental or spiritual prototype existed and was revealed to him in an out-of-body experience). In a story from this category (but perhaps

Three Chilkat clan leaders

These men are holding raven rattles, emblems of their prominence, in the correct, inverted position.

PHOTO BY W.H. CASE AND H.H. DRAPER, 1907, ALASKA STATE LIBRARY, 39-443 originally from group 1), Mosquito is created from the ashes of the Cannibal Giant. In other stories, such as the "Woman Who Married the Bear," both bears and humans exist separately before the story, but from this account we know that bears of today are part human, and that humans and bears are related.[14] Stories like this explain the origins of the covenants by which humans and animals interact, and which still govern human behavior. In other stories in this group, spirits of a particular animal or place reveal themselves to a human, or, through the death of an ancestor, a particular place or spirit is claimed by the descendants. For example, the "Glacier Bay Story" is not about the origins of ice and glaciers, but about human history on the land that makes it a sacred space for certain clans. Stories in this group also explain the origins of important cultural things such as copper and fish traps, describing how the Tlingit or other people first acquired them, often from another group. These stories typically involve physical journeys or out-of-body experiences.

Raven on top of a totem pole at the University of Alaska in Juneau

Totem pole images allude to origin stories that everyone in the community generally knows.

PHOTO BY
MELINDA MCNAUGHER

This group of origin stories is very important because it provides the cultural, intellectual, and spiritual contexts for the totemic art depicted in carving, painting, and weaving that are commonly displayed in museums. It is incorrect to say that a totem pole or other visual art object *tells* a story; rather, it *alludes* to a story that everybody already knows, and it identifies the group membership of the owner. The Christian cross similarly does not tell a story, but alludes to one we know from other sources and identifies the relationship of the bearer to those events. Contextualizing the objects on display is the biggest challenge in museum education.

Songs may also refer to these legendary events, and many Tlingit narratives include songs that commemorate the events of the story and are ritually performed at certain times to call those events to mind. These, too, are difficult for those outside the culture to understand, much as an outsider might not appreciate the difference between "Dixie" and "Yankee Doodle."[15]

It is interesting that Katishan explains at the end of his Raven cycle that since the time of the Raven stories "everything is about spirits."[16] We take this to mean that spirit acquisition stories had been gaining in popularity over time, and that the Raven stories were diminishing in significance. It also implies a concept of time-depth, with the spirit and crest acquisition stories being more recent than the Raven stories, and increasingly capturing the popular imagination. This would also explain the tendency for older myths that do not fit the new system to be subsumed into it and reshaped through association with a specific clan.

Tlingit Raven: What Raven Isn't; What Raven Is

Let us consider what and who Raven is not. We begin with the most important issue: Raven is not Jesus. Raven is not God or a divinity in the Judeo-Christian tradition. In our opinion, Raven is not a god at all, in anybody's tradition, including Tlingit. Raven is not a creator, although he is often labeled as such. Raven enters into the created world; he does not create it, he does not bring it from nonexistence into being. One can expect to hear differing and opposing opinions within the Tlingit community. Some Tlingit Christians reject Raven stories and other aspects of Tlingit folklore as demonic; others try to synthesize

Raven rattle

Raven rattles conventionally depict a complex scene in which a human reclines on the back of a raven while his tongue connects with the tongue of a frog. Meanwhile a second bird's head, formed from the raven's tail, holds the frog.

HAIDA?, MID 1800s
CMNH 3178-2

Raven and Christianity. To suggest a negative approach, Raven stories can also be made compatible with the new Christian point of view by simply regarding them as a separate tradition and not attempting to explain it in Christian terms.

It is important to clarify that Tlingit people do not and did not worship Raven (or totem poles). The danger today is that if we define Raven in Judeo-Christian terms, then we have to accept or reject or understand him on those terms. The usual reactions are confusion, shock, denial, and rejection. For example, the raucous humor of Raven stories often makes White readers, listeners, or viewers uncomfortable. Especially in an age of anxious political correctness, many liberal Whites feel that by laughing they may be showing disrespect for Natives. Some Tlingits, particularly those most acculturated and remote from Tlingit oral tradition, react to the more salacious escapades of Raven with shock or denial. We have heard monolingual, English-speaking, middle-aged Tlingits angrily deny that some of the stories exist, saying "I've never heard this." They may have never heard them, but the stories are in the "canon."

These reactions are the cumulative effects of a century of language loss, cultural change, and Victorian Protestant missionization and education, all of which have contributed to a gradual replacement of the traditional Tlingit world view with a Western world view as a principal frame of reference. As long as we think of Raven in the context of Christian divinity, we can only defend or deny him in those terms. And in those terms, at best, his actions are undignified, and at worst, unacceptable. But, in fact, we *should* be shocked by Raven's actions; we should find them unacceptable, but for different reasons. Not because Raven fails to live up to the image of anyone's divinity, but because he falls short of accepted standards of human social and spiritual behavior. Raven is a negative example. He is an example of how *not* to behave. This is part of what a trickster is. In some traditions he is a sacred clown.

Despite Christ's exhortations to "rejoice," Christianity has a reputation for being joyless, and joylessness seems to have been an occupational hazard for Victorian missionaries.

Through the distortions of humor, Raven helps us look into ourselves, to laugh at ourselves rather than at others, and perhaps to blame ourselves rather than others. Raven should shock us from our complacency and acceptance of unacceptable behavior. The message is double-edged: we should be able to laugh at ourselves at times and not take ourselves too seriously; we should also be able to fear our "dark side" and learn to take ourselves with deadly seriousness.

What is Raven, if not a god or creator? As described above, he is on the one hand a rearranger and perfecter of the natural, created world; and, on the other hand, he is a negative example of human imperfections. He redistributes and modifies most of creation to human advantage by destroying monopolies and distributing to the common people the necessities for human survival that were formerly hoarded by rich, remote, and powerful creatures and people. These are admirable achievements. But, through his negative examples, he demonstrates those human frailties that tend to weaken and destroy human society and spiritual growth. Among these are greed, gluttony, and, above all, manipulation and lying. In the Tlingit language, the stem for *Raven* and the stem for *liar* are the same. In his sexual adventures Raven is immature, boorish, greedy, and manipulative. As a transformer or culture hero, his achievements are admirable, but as a trickster he is cruel at worst and ambivalent at best. He has been called "the personification of ambivalence."[17] One deals with Raven and enters into partnership with him at the risk of life and limb, as Deer, Bear, Cormorant, Bear's Wife, and others learn the hard way.

The Meaning and Importance of Raven and Other Origin Stories Today

As hackneyed as some Tlingit stories have become, they remain popular and powerful because they address psychological and spiritual anxieties that continue to haunt us today. Two of the most serious events in the Raven cycle treat the sharing and passing of power across the generation gap: the

Birth of Raven sequence addresses the uncle/nephew relationship, and in the Theft of the Sun sequence, it is the relationship of grandparent and grandchild. Both of these remain high-anxiety situations in Tlingit society today. In the story about the Sun, we often tend to overlook the grandfather who refuses to share his light and we focus instead on Raven who must resort to stealing it. On the cultural level, many grandchildren feel that the older generations have withheld and are still hoarding information. We are witnessing among the younger Tlingit generations the rise of "pan-Indian" healing ceremonies imported from other Native American cultures and the creation of new spirit robes to be worn for healing, perhaps because the younger people feel that they are denied access to Tlingit tradition and must create their own, or that the traditions are too encumbered by various constraints. On the political level, shareholders of Sealaska Corporation are still divided almost evenly over the question of issuing new stock to those born after December 18, 1971, and who are currently disenfranchised under the Alaska Native Claims Settlement Act. To issue new stock would be to distribute and share the wealth and power more widely. In all social and political interactions, Raven is still alive and well, lurking in the shadows of the human psyche, whether in the clan house or the boardroom, whether in our homes or workplace. We need to hear the stories. The Earth is very old, but the stories of its origins remind us how we as humans face the same problems every generation as we continue to live in it.

According to some Tlingit tradition bearers, Raven first created or shaped the world as a culture hero and then fell and entered the world, to walk around as trickster. When asked where Raven is now, one Yukon storyteller explained that he's "tired" and decided "just to live as Crow." As an original transformer, Raven's work is done. But as a trickster, he is alive and well, ideally to help us work through our own "dark side" as we create our own present. As for the other heroes of Tlingit legend and origin stories, ideally we live according to the covenants they established with the spirits of animals and the land. Raven and other originators, transformers, and shapers of the world as we know it, are all around us in the natural world—the world of ecology and natural history. They also surround us in Tlingit visual art: the hats, the robes, the totems—the artwork that W. B. Yeats called "the artifice of eternity."

Notes

1. John Swanton, *Tlingit Myths and Texts* (1909; reprint, New York, Johnson Reprint Corporation, 1970).
2. See Nora M. and Richard Dauenhauer, *Haa Ḵusteeyí, Our Culture: Tlingit Life Stories* (Seattle: University of Washington Press, 1994).
3. Sergei Kan, "Shamanism and Christianity: Modern-Day Tlingit Elders Look at the Past," *Ethnohistory* 38 (1991): 364.
4. Ibid., 381–82.
5. The fourth category, historical accounts, includes precontact clan migration histories and more recent oral histories of contact (and conflict) with other Native people and with the arriving Europeans. In this group we also include contemporary personal memorates. These genres are as important as the others discussed above in explaining how the world as we know it today came into being historically and socially, from the Tlingit point of view. This group comprises a major section of contemporary Tlingit oral literature. The stories in this group share equally with those in other groups in being subject to and shaped by the processes and dynamics of folklore and oral literature, but this group is not central to our discussion in this essay.
6. See Frederica de Laguna, *The Story of a Tlingit Community: A Problem in the Relationship Between Archeological, Ethnological, and Historical Methods,* Bureau of American Ethnology Bulletin 172 (Washington, D.C.: U.S. Government Printing Office, 1960), 128; Catharine McClellan, *My Old People Say: An Ethnographic Survey of Southern Yukon Territory,* Publications in Ethnology 6 (Ottawa: National Museum of Man, 1975), 70–72.
7. Ivan Veniaminov, *Notes on the Islands of the Unalaska*

District, trans. Lydia Black and R. H. Geoghegan, ed. Richard Pierce (Fairbanks and Kingston, Ontario: Limestone Press, 1984), 411–12 (originally published in Russian in 1840). In other versions, lightning comes from the blinking of Thunderbird's eye, and the Old Woman chops away the support with an ax.

8. Aurel Krause, *The Tlingit Indians: Results of a Trip to the Northwest Coast of America and the Bering Straits,* trans. Erna Gunther (Seattle: University of Washington Press, 1956), 183–84 (originally published in German in 1885).

9. Veniaminov, *Notes on the Islands,* 412; also cited in Krause, *The Tlingit Indians,* 185. This is a widespread motif in world folklore, A736.1.1 in the Thompson Index: Sun and Moon as brother and sister who separate as the result of incest. See Stith Thompson, *Motif-Index of Folk-Literature,* vol. 1 (Bloomington: Indiana University Press, 1966), 146–47.

10. From the living tradition, details of the stories are that lightning is created when the Thunderbird blinks his eyes, and that the Milky Way was created from the tracks of the snowshoes of Lk̲'ayáak'w. Because Lk̲'ayáak'w talked a lot, a talkative person is referred to in Tlingit today as "Lk̲'ayáak'w."

11. The two most recent and comprehensive studies of the trickster figure are Barbara Babcock-Abrahams, "'A Tolerated Margin of Mess': The Trickster and His Tales Reconsidered," *Journal of the Folklore Institute* 9 (1975): 147–86, and Robert D. Pelton, *The Trickster in West Africa: A Study of Mythic Irony and Sacred Delight* (Berkeley and Los Angeles: University of California Press, 1989). Both writers include a detailed survey and critique of earlier theories about trickster. Babcock-Abrahams emphasizes trickster as an elusive linker operating as a liminal figure at the margins of boundaries. Pelton's approach is spiritual and ultimately theological, emphasizing the idea of sacred joy in human creativity and self-realization; a trickster figure is usually not regarded as a god or as divine, but the trickster helps humans become aware of their own potential for divinity.

12. Two commonly used technical terms are *culture hero* or *demiurge*. The former refers to the person responsible for establishing the shape and norms of a given culture. The latter derives from two Greek words, *demos*, meaning "people," and *ergos*, meaning "worker," hence somebody who works for the people. The term is used in religion and folklore to describe the personality who creates the material world out of chaos. In many cultures, the roles of transformer, culture hero, and trickster are distinct; in Tlingit, they combine in the person and personality of Raven.

13. Swanton, *Tlingit Myths and Texts*, 7, 16, 18, 365; Franz Boas and George Hunt, *The Jesup North Pacific Expedition*, Memoir of the American Museum of Natural History, vol. 10, pt. 1 (1906; reprint, New York: AMS Press, 1975), 171–72, 175–77. The most recent book about Raven is Peter Goodchild, *Raven Tales: Traditional Stories of Native Peoples* (Chicago: Chicago Review Press, 1991); Goodchild uses the Tlingit Raven cycle as the departure point for his comparative study because he considers it among the most fully developed. The most complete source of Tlingit Raven stories is in Swanton. The classic comparative study is Franz Boas, *Tsimshian Mythology* (1916; reprint, New York: Johnson Reprint Corporation, 1970).

14. This particular story is extremely popular in Tlingit oral tradition. It is well documented in publications beginning with Veniaminov, *Notes on the Islands*, 413–14; Katishan incorporated it into his Raven cycle (Swanton, *Tlingit Myths and Texts*, 126–29); and Catharine McClellan devoted a substantial monograph to it, *The Girl Who Married the Bear: A Masterpiece of Indian Oral Tradition*, Publications in Ethnology 2 (Ottawa: National Museum of Man, 1970). See Nora M. and Richard Dauenhauer, *Haa Shuká, Our Ancestors: Tlingit Oral Narratives* (Seattle: University of Washington Press, 1987), for two versions in Tlingit and English.

15. See the works by the Dauenhauers cited above, and *Haa Tuwunáagu Yís, for Healing Our Spirit: Tlingit Oratory* (Seattle: University of Washington Press, 1990).

16. Swanton, *Tlingit Myths and Texts*, 154.

17. Paul Radin, *The Trickster: A Study in American Indian Mythology*, with Commentaries by Karl Kerényi and C. G. Jung (1956; reprint, with an introduction by Stanley Diamond, New York: Schocken Books, 1972), xiii. The content and pagination of the main text is identical with earlier editions.

4

The Girls Who Married Stars (Lakota, Great Plains)

THERE WAS A BAND OF INDIANS encamped at a certain place. Two very pretty maidens were sitting out in the cool evening to pass the time away. Looking up toward the sky they saw the stars shining and one of them said, "How pretty the stars are this evening! I wish that big one were a human being and I would marry him!" The other said, "I wish that little star were human and I would marry him." After a few moments two men appeared, one a good deal older than the other, who was young and small. They said, "Rise, young maidens, and we will go home. You have just promised to marry us." The girls assented and went with the two men, intending to accompany them home. Soon they noticed that they were leaving the earth and were on their way to the stars.

When they reached Star-land they found it a beautiful place. The people were good to them. Each maiden went to the home of the parents of her new husband. But after some time the maiden of the older man looked down on the ground and saw wild turnips growing thick. She was fond of them and one day mentioned to her husband that she would dig some to eat. Now the two girls, although not related by blood, had made friends in Star-land, so the girl went to her friend to accompany her. The husbands warned them that some of the turnips were female and some male and they must not dig any of the male turnips. The maidens [promised to] observe this caution, but on their way they came to some plants and the older girl said, "I wonder why they told us not to dig a male turnip. I believe I will dig one just to see if they will know!" She dug and dug right through the sky and fell through to the earth. She was at that time pregnant and she fell through to her own people like a shooting star back to the earth.

Now when this maiden caved in from Star-land to earth she gave birth to a child. Various animals like bears and badgers came there to see [what had fallen] and found a live child with the dead mother. The animals assembled discussed which one should take and rear the child. The bear chose the badger, the badger the birds, and so on. Finally all agreed that the badger should rear the child because she was adept at digging into the earth. So she took the child to her den. It was not large enough, so she made it wide and deep and gathered straw and grass and soft weeds to make the child a bed, and laid it there. She paid strict attention to the child, turning it first on one side and then on the other. While she nursed her little ones the badger nursed the child with the others.

After the child had reached a certain age, the badger had to go out and hunt for the child with bow and arrows. Often when she returned the bear would take away the game by force. Time and again the bear had done this. In the meantime the child grew up to be a strong boy. The badger explained to the boy the story of his birth and the difficulty she had had in rearing him. She said, "The kinship that I claim for you is that of grandson because I reared you. And because of the way you were born I will name you Shooting Star!" As the badger spoke, the bear called her to come out to kill game, for the buffalo were near; then the bear claimed all the game. The next time the bear did this Shooting Star said, "Grandmother, let me brave the bear," and he went out to face the bear and defied him. The bear started to run, but Shooting Star shot an arrow through the bear's kidney and killed him. He said, "Grandmother, go over to the Bear's den and take all the meat he has taken away from you."

Badger said, "Grandson, I am going to wish for a fortune for you. I am going to wish for you to own some buckskin leggings and some moccasins trimmed with porcupine quills," and every time that she wished fortune for him, it came.

Shooting Star asked his grandmother, "Are we the only ones in existence on this earth?" The grandmother said, "There are some other nations like the bear, the beaver and the birds." Shooting Star grew more inquisitive and asked, "Are there others besides those you have mentioned?" The grandmother said, "Yes, yonder toward the sun-setting where you see those high mountains there is another nation of men living." Shooting Star said, "I am going over there to see them." The grandmother said, "Be very careful on the way and do not let anyone deceive you." His grandmother gave him a bow and arrows and he set out toward the sun-setting.

On the way he saw men and women peeping out all around him and saying, "Here comes a woman imitating a boy!" but when he threatened them with his bow and arrows they went away. When he had come near to the band and had reached a high point overlooking the village, night overtook him. Looking toward the village he noticed four white tipi and a summoner was announcing, "Ho-o-o-o! Shooting Star is coming." The four tipi were for the first-born maidens of four prominent families. All these maidens now said at the same time, "Father, when Shooting Star comes I want to marry him." As Shooting Star, having descended from the hill, was approaching the village the announcer cried again "Here comes Shooting Star!" One of the girls invited him to her tipi and the family insisted that he should marry her, but he was determined to see them all first and make his selection. When he finally chose one all the others began to weep.

Iktomi [the trickster spider, see page 17] learned why they were weeping and said, "Let us

Illustration from The Girls Who Married Stars *storybook in Alcoa Foundation Hall of American Indians, Carnegie Museum of Natural History*

DRAWING BY
NANCY PERKINS

arrange now to kill Shooting Star." He put up two poles near together and captured Shooting Star and tied a hand and foot to each pole. He advised everyone to have a sharp knife ready to cut Shooting Star in pieces. His wife warned him what the people were going to do and he told his wife to tell her father and mother to move camp to a high peak away from the band. When he was fast bound he said, "My kinsmen, before you kill a human being, is it not right that he should say his last words?"—"Let him say what he has to say!" sneered Iktomi. So he called out, "My father, remember that I am here helpless. Come from the four winds with your invasion to save me!" They heard a loud roar from the winds.—"Hurry up! hurry up! cut him up!" said Iktomi, but the knives would not cut into his body. At this moment came a strong wind with thunder, so strong that it blew away the people and Iktomi, and the thunder loosened the bonds that bound Shooting Star. So he returned to his father-in-law and they came back to the village and he lived there with them.

The Woman Who Fell from the Sky
(Seneca, Northeast)

A long time ago human beings lived high up in what is now called heaven. They had a great and illustrious chief.

It so happened that this chief's daughter was taken very ill with a strange affliction. All the people were very anxious as to the outcome of her illness. Every known remedy was tried in an attempt to cure her, but none had any effect.

Near the lodge of this chief stood a great tree, which every year bore corn used for food. One of the friends of the chief had a dream, in which he was advised to tell the chief that in order to cure his daughter he must lay her beside this tree, and that he must have the tree dug up. This advice was carried out to the letter. While the people were at work and the young woman lay there, a young man came along. He was very angry and said: "It is not at all right to destroy this tree. Its fruit is all that we have to live on." With this remark he gave the young woman who lay there ill a shove with his foot, causing her to fall into the hole that had been dug.

Now, that hole opened into this world, which was then all water, on which floated waterfowl of many kinds. There was no land at that time. It came to pass that as these waterfowl saw this young woman falling they shouted, "Let us receive her," whereupon they, at least some of them, joined their bodies together, and the young woman fell on this platform of bodies. When these were wearied they asked, "Who will volunteer to care for this woman?" The great Turtle then took her, and when he got tired of holding her, he in turn asked who would take his place. At last the question arose as to what they should do to provide her with a permanent resting place in this world. Finally it was decided to prepare the earth, on which she would live in the future. To do this it was determined that soil from the bottom of the primal sea should be brought up and placed on the broad, firm carapace of the Turtle, where it would increase in size to such an extent that it would accommodate all the creatures that should be produced thereafter. After much discussion the toad was finally persuaded to dive to the bottom of the waters in search of soil. Bravely making the attempt, he succeeded in bringing up soil from the depths of the sea. This was carefully spread over the carapace of the Turtle, and at once both began to grow in size and depth.

After the young woman recovered from the illness from which she suffered when she was cast down from the upper world, she built herself a shelter, in which she lived quite contentedly. In the course of time she brought forth a girl baby, who grew rapidly in size and intelligence.

Clan animals on great Turtle's back

The nine clan animals are (*clockwise from the turtle's head*) the hawk, snipe, wolf, beaver, turtle, eel, deer, heron, and bear (*center*).

WAYNE SKYE (1949–),
SIX NATIONS RESERVE,
ONTARIO, CANADA, WOLF
CLAN, CAYUGA, 1996
CMNH 36182-1

When the daughter had grown to young womanhood, the mother and she were accustomed to go out to dig wild potatoes. Her mother had said to her that in doing this she must face the west at all times. Before long the young daughter gave signs that she was about to become a mother. Her mother reproved her, saying that she had violated the injunction not to face the east, as her condition showed that she had faced the wrong way while digging potatoes. It is said that the breath of the West Wind had entered her person, causing her conception. When the days of her delivery were at hand, she overheard twins within her body in a hot debate as to which should be born first and as to the proper place of exit, one declaring that he was going to emerge from the armpit of his mother, the other saying that he would emerge in the natural way. The first one born, who was of reddish color, was called Othagwenda; that is, Flint. The other, who was light in color, was called Djuskaha; that is, the Little Sprout.

The grandmother of the twins liked Djuskaha and hated the other; so they cast Othagwenda into a hollow tree some distance from the lodge.

The boy that remained in the lodge grew very rapidly, and soon was able to make himself bows and arrows and to go out to hunt in the vicinity. Finally, for several days he returned home without his bow and arrows. At last he was asked why he had to have a new bow and arrows every morning. He replied that there was a young boy in a hollow tree in the neighborhood who used them. The grandmother inquired where the tree stood, and he told her; whereupon then they went there and brought the other boy home again.

When the boys had grown to man's estate, they decided that it was necessary for them to increase the size of their island, so they agreed to start out together, afterward separating to create forests and lakes and other things. They parted as agreed, Othagwenda going westward and Djuskaha eastward. In the course of time, on returning, they met in their shelter or lodge at night, then agreeing to go the next day to see what each had made. First they went west to see what Othagwenda had made. It was found that he had made the country all rocks and full of ledges, and also a mosquito which was very large. Djuskaha asked the mosquito to run, in order that he might see whether the insect could fight. The mosquito ran, and sticking his bill through a sapling, thereby made it fall, at which Djuskaha said, "That will not be right, for you would kill the people who are about to come." So, seizing him, he rubbed him down in his hands, causing him to become very small; then he blew on the mosquito, whereupon he flew away. He also modified some of the other animals which his brother had made. After returning to their lodge, they agreed to go the next day to see what Djuskaha had fashioned. On visiting the east the next day, they found that Djuskaha had made a large number of animals which were so fat that they could hardly move; that he had made a sugar-maple tree to drop syrup; that he had made the sycamore tree to bear fine fruit; that the rivers were so formed that half the water flowed upstream and the other half downstream. Then the reddish-colored brother, Othagwenda, was greatly displeased with what his brother had made, saying that the people who were about to come would live too easily and be too happy. So he shook violently the various animals—the bears, deer, and turkeys—causing them to become small at once, a characteristic which attached itself to their descendants. He also caused the sugar maple to drop sweetened water only, and the fruit of the sycamore to become small and useless; and lastly he caused the water of the rivers to flow in only one direction, because the original plan would make it too easy for the human beings who were about to come to navigate the streams.

The inspection of each other's work resulted in a deadly disagreement between the brothers, who finally came to grips and blows, and Othagwenda was killed in the fierce struggle.

Coyote Obtains Fire
(Jicarilla Apache, Southwest)

When the people came up on earth, Coyote was the very last one of the animals to emerge.

When this world was made the trees wouldn't burn. The people were living without fire.

The coyote was running all over. No one knew where he would be the next day. He was running from place to place.

One time he found a place with great rock cliffs all around.

In the bottom was a hollow place. A great spruce tree was standing there. The people who lived there were the fireflies. They came up in the cliffs by means of rock steps, so that no one could see their footprints and know the way to enter. The stones were laid one ahead of the other, so that the people, when they came out, could step on these rocks.

Coyote saw some little children playing on the other side of the cliff. He asked them, "Where is the entrance to this place?"

The children paid no attention to him, however.

He thought and thought, "What will these children like?"

He picked some cedar berries. He made beads out of these. He took four strings of these beads to the children. He colored them four colors, the first black, the second blue, the third yellow, and the fourth all colors. He went back to the children with them. He started to speak to them, but they paid no attention to him. They acted as if they didn't understand what Coyote was talking about.

He was trying to make a game for the children so that he could draw them to him. He wanted them to talk to him and laugh at him too.

Finally they noticed him. He said to them, "Now I'll give you these beads, but you have to show me the way to get in. I want to see the inside of this cliff place. If you show me the way, I'll give you these beads."

He put the beads around the necks of two girls and two boys. He said, "How pretty you are! You look nice now. You have on pretty necklaces."

The four children were pleased then and led Coyote to this entrance. They showed him the stones and said, "Right here is where you go down. Right at this tree is the door. We live beyond the cliff. This is the way we get in; this is the way we get out."

They spoke to the tree and said, "Come, bend down to us."

Then the tree bent down to each of the children.

"Now bend away from us," they said, and it took them across the cliff.

But Coyote didn't go in yet. He just learned how. The four children got on the other side and then had a tree which was standing there throw them on the outside again in the same way. Both were spruce trees. Now coyote saw how to do it, but he didn't go in yet.

He asked the children, "What's going on down there?"

"We have great fun every night," they told him. "We have a big fire there each night and we dance around it."

Now Coyote knew all about what was going on on the other side. That's what he wanted. He wanted to get that fire and take it to his people. He wanted his own people to have good times at night too.

In the Beginning Coyote Created the Universe

PAINTING BY HARRY FONSECA, MAIDU, 1982

He went back to the people and told the chief. The chief gave commands to all fast birds and fast animals to help.

Coyote said, "Now I'm going to go to those people. When I get fire I'm going to hand it to one of you, and the one who takes it should run, and when he tires he should give it to another fellow."

Now everything was arranged. The fast running birds were notified too. They were told to stand all around the world and to be prepared to run. "The fireflies might prove to be good runners," Codi[1] said. That is why all these helpers were picked out. These people were all around the world waiting. If the fireflies were not good runners, Coyote was not going to pass it on, but if they proved to be good runners he was going to do so. He explained all this to them.

Coyote then went and got some dry cedar bark. He shredded it and tied it around his tail. He made a regular torch.

When night came he went over to the place of the cliff. He went to the young spruce and spoke to it, and it put him over on the other side.

He saw the fireflies dancing with the deer and antelopes, with the white-tailed deer too. Flicker was there too. They were all having a good time dancing.

Coyote came up. He asked permission to join the dance.

Mountain-lion was chief there. Mountain-lion told him, "If you won't be too rough I'll let you join the dance."

"I'll try," said Coyote.

Coyote danced. He tried to dance close to the fire. But some were suspicious of him. Every time he got too close to the fire, someone got in between him and the fire.

After a while the people got tired of watching him and relaxed their vigilance. Then he approached even nearer to the fire and pushed his tail with the cedar bark into the flames.

Someone called to him, "Codi, your tail will be burned!"

"No, I always do that without any trouble. I am a wonder worker."

He watched his tail. When it was ignited he started to run.

Someone called, "Codi is running!"

Everyone started to run after him. He lost his way. They all tried to circle around him, but he ran between them whenever he saw a space. Then he remembered where the place of exit was. He started to run that way.

He ran to the tree, crying, "Come, bend to me!" It bent down. Then he said, "Now you turn the other way with me." It did.

The people from that place were coming close behind him. They were gaining on him. He dodged about among the trees. Some trees he hit with his tail while he was running, and those are the ones which burn well today, like the oak and the pine. But he did not hit the rocks with his tail, and that is why they can't be made to burn now.

The fireflies and others were running after him still. Codi began to run around the world. On his way he set many things on fire; he spread it all over. Those who were running after him grew tired when they got about half way. They gave up, thinking, "Let him keep the fire."

The fireflies came back to one place. They had a council. They asked, "Who was it who told the coyote how to come in?"

Then the other children told on the four who had taken the beads from Coyote and given him the information. They said, "Coyote paid those beads for the fire."

The parents of those children got after them, but it was too late then.

Coyote had run far. He was tired by the time they gave up the chase. He fell right in the·shade, his tail still burning. He rested and started running again. He went on until he had circled the world.

He meant to touch every kind of tree with his tail, but he missed one which was standing to the east. So all wood but this one kind will burn. Even if you put this one into the stove it will not burn.[2]

Coyote came back to the Indian camps. He said, "Now you can use this fire."

The people were all glad now they had fire.

When Coyote ran around the world he went the way the sun goes. He headed for the east and then for the south, and so on. But he didn't run straight. He zig-zagged all around. The others took no part in the run. They stood around and just watched him.

Raven Makes the Aleutian Islands and the Alaska Peninsula (Tlingit, Northwest)[3]

[Raven is falling.]
That's then he's wishing,
"I hope I fall on a
bunch of tan-
gled kelp.
I hope I fall
on a bunch of
tangled kelp."
This is what Raven's wishing for.
"Let me fall on a bunch of tangled kelp."
But as he's wishing,
his nose falls off.

Raven mask

HEILTSUK, BRITISH COLUMBIA,
COLLECTED 1904
CMNH 3178-30

He starts to fall down.
[Mary Pelayo: What's a bunch of kelp?]
Well, that's the one out there,
bull kelp,[4]
bull kelp.
When bull kelp gets tangled up,
it gets like a boat.
It gets hard on the surface of the sea.
It has a knob, or head.
There's hair on it.
It grows up from the bottom of the sea.
Raven fell on this.
My, he's trying to catch his breath back.
He's lying there for a long time.
He hears this sound beside him:
phhhhhht, phhhhht.
Exhaling.
Gosh, he's looking for it.
What's that—what's that breathing?
At one point it popped up
exactly where he's watching a sea otter.[5]
It's a sea otter.
They call it "sea otter,"
yáxwch',
sea otter.
Look!
Then Raven calls him,
"Hey, pardner, come over!
Come on over, you sweet guy.
Come over,
come on over, hon.
Isn't there any way you can help me?
Do you get down to the bottom?"
"Yes," the sea otter says to him.
"I reach the bottom."
Gasp!
"Cousin, good buddy,"
(how he addresses him like his kin)
"Bring me up some gravel.
It's lying on the bottom.

Bring me up some gravel.
Get me some gravel
from down there."
So he dove down,
the sea otter dove.
After a long time
Raven heard him breathing again.
He surfaced.
He swam over.
When he hands him the gravel—
ah haa!—
when he puts it in his hand,
how good Raven feels!
They say this was out past the Aleutian Islands.
There's a rocky peninsula.
This is where Raven fell.
Then Raven tosses the gravel—these pebbles—
toward the mainland.
As he threw them,
each became an island.
Wow! They became islands.
Then he flies to one
and he sits there
to catch his breath.
While he's catching his breath there for a long time,
he tosses another one.
It becomes another island.
It's another island again.
He tosses another pebble toward the mainland.
Then he flies to it.
Gosh! He's having a hard time flying.
Now and then he sits on one of the islands.
While he's catching his breath again like this,
all the while he's doing this,
he's throwing pebbles ashore over there.
This is what became the long peninsula,
the peninsula
on the other side of the
Aleutian Islands.

Notes

"The Girls Who Married Stars" was told by Susie Hollowhorn, Manderson, June 27, 1926 and is reprinted by permission of the American Folklore Society from Martha Warren Beckwith, "Mythology of the Oglala Dakota," Journal of American Folklore 43, no. 170 (Oct.–Dec. 1930): 408–11. Not for further reproduction.

"The Woman Who Fell from the Sky" is reprinted by permission from J. N. B. Hewitt, ed., Seneca Fiction, Legends, and Myths, part 1, Thirty-second Annual Report of the Bureau of American Ethnology (Washington, D.C.: Government Printing Office, 1918), 460–62.

"Coyote Obtains Fire" is reprinted by permission of the American Folklore Society from Morris Edward Opler, Myths and Tales of the Jicarilla Apache Indians, Memoirs of the American Folklore Society 31 (New York, 1938), 269–72. Not for further reproduction.

"Raven Makes the Aleutian Islands and the Alaska Peninsula" was told in Tlingit by Susie James (1890–1980), Sitka, September 1972. It was recorded by Mary Pelayo and transcribed in Tlingit and translated into English by Nora Marks Dauenhauer.

1. Coyote addresses the other animals and birds and is addressed by them as Codi in these tales. The word cannot be translated but has the force of "friend."

2. The informant did not know the name of this tree. According to P. E. Goddard ("Jicarilla Apache Texts," Anthropological Papers of the American Museum of Natural History 8 [1911]: 209), this was petrified wood.

3. This Raven story is an example of a Tlingit etiological story with Raven as demiurge, culture hero, creator or rearranger. Such stories are designed to be read orally; therefore, a short-line format, in which the line-turnings reflect pauses in oral delivery, is used.

Tlingit storytellers change tenses for dramatic effect. To reflect this in English, the past tense has been used for completed or historical action or to show distance from the events. The present represents "live action." This distinction also helps the stories to be read orally, because most people tell informal jokes and funny stories in English in the present tense.

Raven stories are often told in a sequence, with one episode flowing into another. Here, we pick up the Aleutian story at the "cliff hanger" ending of the previous story, "The Birth of Raven," and "Raven and the Flood," where Raven is left falling over the ocean. In turn, the present story flows into how Raven gets fire.

4. Bull kelp (geesh) or ribbon kelp, *Nereocystis luetkeana*, is a long, tubular seaweed with a pod or air bladder at the end. From one end of the pod hang ribbonlike blades of kelp, and from the other end extends a tube or stipe (stalk) up to thirty or forty feet long resembling a bull whip, from which the popular name derives. It is one of the most common seaweeds from California to Alaska.

5. Sea otter (yáxwch'), *Enhydra lutris*, now rare, was widely hunted during the Russian period.

Astronomy

Song to the Pleiades

Look as they rise, rise
Over the line where sky meets the
earth;
Pleiades!
Lo! They ascending, come to guide
us,
Leading us safely, keeping one;
Pleiades,
Teach us to be, like you, united.

—PAWNEE, PLAINS

5

American Indian Astronomy: An Overview

RAY A. WILLIAMSON

SOMETIME IN THE DISTANT PAST, long before Europeans set foot on North America, Native Americans learned to organize their lives around the cyclical appearances and motions of the Sun, Moon, and stars. They learned to read the apparent yearly journey of the Sun, following its daily position rising or setting along the horizon to schedule their ceremonies, planting, and harvest, or to predict the best times to gather wild foods, fish, or hunt. The constantly changing face of the Moon provided a different cycle, one that Native peoples used to parse the slowly changing year into manageable parts. Finally, Native Americans closely watched the stars to assist in finding direction, timing ceremonies, and supplementing the solar calendar. Some Native American groups maintain and use their knowledge of the sky actively today. Others have virtually lost those traditions; for these groups, the only available record was collected years ago by anthropologists and other scholars who thought to inquire about tribal views of the sky.

The original inhabitants of North America developed an elaborate lore to explain and interpret the celestial sphere. These myths and stories, which are passed down from generation to generation, have helped American Indians make sense of the sky and relate its varied appearances to their lives. To Indians in a traditional setting, the celestial bodies are living beings, related directly both morally and spiritually to life on Earth.

Ancestral Pueblo petroglyph panel in central New Mexico

Rock art along the Rio Grande fairly frequently depicts starlike symbols.

PHOTO BY
RAY A. WILLIAMSON

Generalizing about the Native American view of the sky and how it relates to life on Earth can lead to oversimplification, because each tribe, sometimes even different groups within a tribe, hold different views of the meaning of the cosmos. Nevertheless, the notion that parts of the cosmos are deeply interconnected is widespread in Native North American philosophy. As most American Indians view the world, rocks, rivers, trees, animals, sea creatures, people, Sun, Moon, and stars are all related and interact with each other in significant ways. Thus, in Native American stories, sky beings descend to Earth and humans travel to the sky. Yet the two worlds are quite different in kind. Looking at the sky realm, we see regular motion, while the Earth supports a superficial stability that is always poised to break into chaos.

In most stories, celestial beings are part of the sacred realm and intercede in human affairs beneficially. For example, in Southwestern Navajo and Plains Pawnee lore and practice, the stars aid in healing.[1] For the Southwestern Pueblos, the Sun brings health and prosperity. Yet sky beings also show a dark side; the California Chumash, for example, feared Sun, who they said might swoop down to Earth from his sky path and grab up the weak and unprotected. As they said, when Sun finally reached his crystal home in the west after grabbing one or two humans, he and his daughters would pass his victims "through the fire two or three times and then eat them half cooked."[2] The stories, which are part of a vibrant oral tradition, take their power from grafting eternal truths onto everyday experiences, imparting philosophies that sustain the tribal group. In general, by watching the stars, the Sun or Moon, Native North American groups learn important lessons about both Earth and sky and their own place in the cosmos; these lessons give them laws and principles by which to live. Their stories provide daily inspiration for life on Earth.

The study of ancient celestial practices, which may be revealed in archaeological remains, is generally termed *archaeoastronomy*; scholars term the study of astronomical knowledge and traditions within a living society, *ethnoastronomy*. Although throughout the years a few insightful archaeologists and ethnographers have collected information about the astronomical practices of the peoples they have studied, only recently have astronomers, archaeologists, ethnographers, and others worked together systematically with Native American collaborators to comprehend the extent and depth of Native North American sky knowledge. This essay sketches some of the results of this research.

Shield with cover

Astronomy and the Calendar

Native Americans developed what we might term a deeply practical knowledge of the sky. Agricultural peoples understood, for example, that the cyclic patterns of the Sun and Moon, the stars and planets, provide signs by which to plant and harvest.[3] Indeed, scholars have been aware for

When a Plains warrior dreamed of an image such as this one, a man inside the sun, he painted it on the cover of his shield.

CROW,
COLLECTED 1904
CMNH 2418-116a

many years that Native American agriculturalists watch the regular motions of the sky to time their activities. More recently, scholars have realized that peoples who make their livelihood by gathering wild foods and hunting animals must also follow the progression of celestial patterns with care. The tribes of southern California, for example, practiced little or no agriculture in the eighteenth century when the Spanish moved in and began to displace the Indian tribes. Nevertheless, they had a well-developed calendar that relied on close observations of the Sun, Moon, and stars, as well as the behavior of animals and birds. As one member of the Cahuilla tribe in southern California described the astronomical observations of his tribe:

They studied the north star, how it turns about, and the seven stars [the Big Dipper] and the morning star—all this helped to know when to go and gather their food. The month that the road runner flies means certain things, and the habits of many animals all meant something to these older people who studied the signs of the Sun and the Moon and the stars and the animals.[4]

Acoma Pueblo woman dressed for the Fiesta de San Esteban, held each year on September 2

Note the four painted lines across her hands, which probably represent the four cardinal directions—north, south, east, and west—and the *tableta* with star, cloud, and rainbow symbols.

SMITHSONIAN INSTITUTION NATIONAL ANTHROPOLOGICAL ARCHIVES, 74-659

The need to sustain or improve food production must certainly have aided the development of a calendar. However, the calendar also served ritual needs. The more accurate the calendar, the more closely ceremonies matched the natural rhythms of the world, making them more powerful. Closer celestial observations for ritual purposes thus aided Native American groups to refine the calendar.[5] Whether agriculturalists or hunters and gatherers, consistent observations of the celestial bodies enabled Native North Americans to participate fully in their environment and provide for their needs.

The "Fixed" Stars

Urban dwellers seldom experience the full splendor of the night sky, for urban skies are generally polluted by the all-night glow of the city. Indeed, so rarely do most people see a clear night sky that when they do they may lose even the most familiar patterns—the Big Dipper, the Pleiades, and Orion—in the thousands of fainter stars that crowd a fully transparent night sky.

Early Greek astronomers called the stars "fixed" because, over a few generations of human observers, they appear to maintain their positions relative to one another. During any night, stars appear to rise along the eastern horizon and move from east to west through the sky, providing a useful timing device. The Hopi Indians of Arizona time the stages of their ceremonies by watching the movement of Orion and the Pleiades from their ceremonial room, the kiva.[6] The Klamath Indians of northern California watched the changing position of Orion to determine time in the winter.[7] To follow time's flight, the Mescalero Apaches in central New Mexico watch any star or constellation in the south-southwest, noting its movement through the night sky against the backdrop of the horizon or an artificial structure.[8]

The fixed stars as a whole seem to rotate slowly throughout the year, individual stars and their constellation patterns appearing to rise four minutes earlier each morning. Over a month these small changes add up to a full two hours. For instance, in late June the Pleiades rise just before the light of dawn overwhelms them. By late September they rise at midnight, and by late December they are readily visible in the eastern sky just after dark. Each summer night the familiar western constellation Cygnus passes overhead, and Scorpio's curving pattern is visible in the southern sky. By contrast, the constellations of Orion and Taurus are seen most readily in the winter sky, when they appear nearly overhead in

Star quilt

The Morning Star dominates Lakota quilt design. Lakota quilters learned the technique from Euro-American women in government schools and church guilds, and most likely singled out the star of Bethlehem pattern as a favorite because of its resemblance to their traditional Morning Star design.

NELLIE STAR BOY MENARD, SICANGU (BRULÉ) LAKOTA, ROSEBUD RESERVATION, SOUTH DAKOTA, 1994
CMNH 35882-1

December and January. Cygnus and Scorpio have disappeared from view by early December.

This small daily shift of the stellar background makes it seem that the Sun moves eastward among the stars each day. As the Sun moves through the stellar background, stellar patterns that had been blotted out by its brilliance for a month or so become briefly visible in the first faint light of dawn before they fade in the light of the rising Sun. As the Sun works its way further eastward among the stars each day, they appear to rise earlier each morning and move ever higher in the sky before dawn.

The first time a star or star pattern appears in the east in association with sunrise, is called an *heliacal rise*, after the Greek word for Sun, *helios*. This first appearance can be highly effective in setting a yearly calendar, because it happens over only a few days, depending on sky conditions and the observer's visual acuity. Some Navajo singers, or medicine men, use this phenomenon to determine the beginning of each month. The first appearance of Old Man with Legs Spread

Drilled depressions in a sandstone boulder in Chaco Canyon, New Mexico

This pattern, probably of Navajo origin, seems to represent the Navajo constellation Revolving Male (Ursa Major). Similar constellation patterns are found on sacred rattles and in sand paintings.

PHOTO BY
RAY A. WILLIAMSON

Apart (Corvus), for example, marks the beginning of the Navajo month corresponding to November. When First Big One (part of Scorpio) is visible after sunset for the last time in the year, December has arrived.[9] This phenomenon—the last time a star or constellation is seen in the year is called an *heliacal setting*. Some Navajos have also used the heliacal setting of First Slender One (Orion) in the spring at twilight as a signal that it is time to begin planting.[10] The Skidi Band of the Pawnee, who had an extremely detailed knowledge of the stars, used to watch for the heliacal rise of the pair of stars called the Swimming Ducks to signal the start of their spring Thunder Ritual.[11]

Throughout the year, the so-called circumpolar constellations remain visible in the northern hemisphere.[12] The most familiar of these, the Big Dipper, was used in northern countries as a nightly clock and a guide to the seasons.[13] Navajo farmers watched the position of Revolving Male (the Big Dipper) around the pole to schedule planting. When Revolving Male stands straight up at about nine P.M. early in the spring, they know the time has arrived to prepare the fields for the first crops. When, in May and early June, Revolving Male lies on his side in the west, they can complete their planting of corn, beans, and squash.[14] Members of the Zuni tribe in western New Mexico used the position of the Seven Ones (the Big Dipper) to determine when to begin their spring corn planting, work-

ing "by the light of the seven great stars which were at that time rising bright above them . . . looking at the stars they saw how they were set, four of them as though around a gourd like their own, and three others along its handle!"[15] The California Pomo Indians, who gathered wild foods, hunted, and fished, rather than growing crops, observed the position of the Big Dipper to determine the best times for fishing.[16]

*Robe with
Ursa Major*

The Arapaho call Ursa Major (the Big Dipper) the "Broken Backbone." About the painting on this robe, collector Cleaver Warden, an Arapaho, noted: "Designs surrounding this broken backbone are shapes, colors of mountains, hills, rivers, ravines, valleys, creeks, two bears' claws" (CMNH Accession Notes, 3179-294, 1903).

ARAPAHO, COLLECTED 1903 CMNH 3179-294

Although American Indians followed many noncircumpolar star groups throughout the year, the Pleiades have remained of particular interest, perhaps because they are easy to pick out in the winter sky. The Zunis call them the Seed Stars and relate them to the growing season, perhaps because they first appear in the early morning sky during the height of summer when seeds would be forming.[17] The Cayuga Nation of the Iroquois set the time of their important Midwinter Ceremony by watching for the position of the Pleiades following the first new Moon in January. When the Pleiades appear directly overhead just after sunset, the officials in charge of the ceremony count five days before beginning the Stirring Ashes Rite of the Midwinter Ceremony. This generally takes place between late January and mid-February.[18]

By watching very carefully through several generations it becomes apparent that the stars change position slowly over time. For example, today the North Star (Polaris) lies less than a degree from Earth's geographic North Pole, yet in A.D. 1200, when large agrarian villages flourished along the Mississippi, it circled a full seven degrees from the pole. This extremely slow stellar movement, which is called *precession*, results from a slow rotation of Earth's axis as it spins. Over 26,000 years, Earth's North Pole traces a broad circle through the stars, making it seem that Polaris has moved away from the pole and back again. The constellations move with Polaris, causing a slight shift in periods of heliacal rise and set over the years. Structures built hundreds of years ago to align with the rise or set of certain stars would today align to different stars or to none at all.

Bighorn Medicine Wheel, summer solstice sunrise

The Bighorn Medicine Wheel lies in an excellent location for sky watching at an altitude of nearly 10,000 feet near the summit of Medicine Mountain in Wyoming's Bighorn Mountains. It was made by piling up thousands of stones in a wheel-like pattern oriented to the sun and stars.

DRAWING BY
SNOWDEN HODGES

For example, the early Plains people constructed the Big Horn Medicine Wheel in Wyoming in part to follow the yearly calendar. The Big Horn Medicine Wheel, along with a number of other so-called medicine wheels in the Northern Plains, is revered by members of the Plains tribes. First built hundreds of years ago by ancestors of the current Plains peoples, the medicine wheels were formed by gathering stones from the local landscape and laying them out along lines radiating from a center rock cairn, like spokes of a wheel. The medicine wheels probably served as sacred structures, and they also appear to have been deliberately designed to mark important dates in the yearly calendar, including the summer solstice, and times announced by the rise or set of certain bright stars.[19] At the Big Horn Medicine Wheel, for example, eight hundred years ago the star

Aldebaran would have made its first appearance along one of the spokes in late June just before the summer solstice. By watching this appearance, an astute observer would know that the summer solstice had almost arrived. Yet today, because of precession, Aldebaran appears for the first time in the year in late July, well after the solstice.

According to one Navajo creation story, the Milky Way, that vast collection of stars that appears like a hazy path cutting across the summer sky, was created by Black God who sprinkled stars through the Dark Upper after carefully placing the named constellations one after the other to create regular patterns. Roughly 10° wide[20] in the Northern Hemisphere, the Milky Way is best seen on late summer evenings when it crosses nearly overhead. Many Indian groups interpret the Milky Way as a sacred path through the sky, whether a Path of the Dead, as among many California groups and the Pawnee, or one along which a dog scattered corn meal, as the Southeastern Cherokee tell.[21] Because the Milky Way is so diffuse and stretches across the sky, it is not used to signal a specific date in the calendar, yet Native American groups generally saw it as celebrating the arrival of summer, the growth of crops and wild foods, and comfortable nights.

Sun

As the brightest object in the sky, the Sun was generally the most important being of the celestial sphere, an object of veneration and sometimes of fear. He (or she, depending on the tribal belief) provides heat and light, promotes crop growth, and provides a sense of direction and time in the daylight hours. In the summer, the Sun can also be a tyrant, causing the crops to wither and dry up; in the winter, the Sun withdraws and Earth grows cold.

When the French explored the Mississippi during the late 1600s, they encountered the Natchez, a people who cultivated corn, built large temple mounds, and worshiped the Sun. According to the Natchez, from the Sun came a being who gave them their customs, their arts, and creation stories. The spirit of their celestial benefactor then entered a stone, which the Natchez preserved in a temple built atop one of the mounds. Within the temple, the Natchez continually preserved a fire devoted to him. Four temple guards, one for each of the four directions, watched over the fire and kept it going. The temple door opened to the east; every morning before sunrise and at sunset they built a fire to the Sun before the door of the temple.[22] The Natchez considered their chief, who wielded great power in the tribe, to be the earthly manifestation of the Sun, called "Great Sun."

Conveyance of the Great Sun of the Natchez Indians (after Du Pratz, who was in Louisiana from 1718 to 1734)

Natchez chiefs were thought to have been descended from the sun. Their dwellings were built on top of artificial earthen mounds. Here Great Sun, the chief of the Natchez, is being carried to the harvest festival.

Many of these practices and the celestial observations that supported them disappeared soon after contact with the Europeans, who openly opposed such "idolatry" and made every attempt to convert the Indians to Christianity and force them out of their native customs and habitat. Yet, despite these losses, the Sun's daily and yearly motions remained a constant source of interest and information to many Native Americans, in part because knowledge of the calendar is so basic to human existence.

Compared with the stars, each of which rises and sets in the same positions night after night for many years at times that vary with the season, the Sun appears to rise and set at a different place each day. Beginning with the winter solstice near December 21, which is the shortest day of the year and the traditional New Year's day for many tribes, the Sun rises in the southeast and each day afterward moves a little northward. Day after day, it picks up speed in its northward journey, and the days lengthen until around the first day of spring (the vernal equinox on March 21 or 22) the daily movement along the horizon equals a full diameter of the Sun (one-half degree arc). At that point in its cycle, the Sun rises due east and sets due west, and day equals night. As it continues northward, the Sun's motion slows imperceptibly each day until it nears its northern-most position along the horizon. Finally, at the summer solstice, near June 21, the Sun's northward journey slows to a halt and we experience the longest day of the year.

We call the days of reversal in summer and winter the *solstices*, after the Latin term meaning "Sun *(sol)* standstill," because the Sun appears literally to stand still for a short time on its yearly journey along the horizon. Traditionally, the Pueblo Indians say that the Sun stays in one place for four days, a number that also equals the four sacred directions.[23] After the Sun turns around and heads south, it again appears to pick up speed in its yearly journey until it reaches a position on the celestial equator, when it once again rises in the east and sets in the west at the autumnal equinox (about September 21). Its southward motion slows as it nears the winter solstice, when it appears to stop once again and turn around to repeat the yearly cycle.

For the Pueblo people, like many peoples of the Northern Hemisphere, the turnaround at the winter solstice is of singular importance, for it promises the coming of longer days, spring, and the world's renewal, despite three or more months of cold weather. The Zuni Indians of New Mexico, for example, celebrate the winter solstice with a New Fire Ceremony, in which they extinguish all the fires in the village and rekindle the year's new fire with prayers and hope for a bountiful harvest.[24]

Because of the slow apparent motion of the Sun along the horizon near the solstices, observers find it extremely difficult to determine the exact day the solstice arrives. Accuracy requires practice and a convenient place from which to observe, year after year. Therefore, Pueblo observers, at least, would choose a place that allowed a good view of the horizon and from which they could clearly pick out positions along the horizon at which the Sun rose or set days or even weeks prior to the solstice. Because the Sun's day-to-day motion is fast enough at that time to detect daily changes in horizon position, it was possible for them to anticipate the arrival of the solstice.[25] Announcing the coming solstice well in advance gave celebrants ample time to prepare for solstice rituals. The historic Pueblo practice had significant roots in Anasazi times as well. The Anasazi, in what is now southwestern Colorado and southeastern Utah, constructed some of their buildings to support calendar watching. At Hovenweep National Monument, for example, thirteenth-century builders constructed three buildings with small ports in their outside walls that allowed observers within to determine the arrival of the solstices and equinoxes with considerable accuracy.[26]

Although the equinoxes were observed, they were less important than the solstices to most Native American groups, perhaps because at equinox the Sun does not turn around to mark a reversal, but simply appears to move either north or south rather quickly. Traditionalists in the Southwest Pueblos still observe the Sun regularly to set their

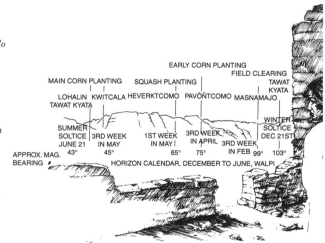

Sunrise horizon planting calendar from the Hopi pueblo of Walpi

When the sun reaches the appropriate place along the horizon, the Hopi know it is time to plant certain crops.

DRAWING BY SNOWDEN HODGES AFTER DARYLL FORDE, "HOPI AGRICULTURE AND LAND OWNERSHIP," *JOURNAL OF THE ROYAL ANTHROPOLOGICAL INSTITUTE OF GREAT BRITIAN AND IRELAND 61* [1931]: 357-405

agricultural and ritual calendars.[27] However, most groups also make allowances for the demands of modern society and wage earners by planning major observances when a majority of tribal members can attend. The Mescalero Apaches of central New Mexico, for example, schedule their major girls' puberty ceremony, which used to be held on the summer solstice, on the July Fourth weekend to accommodate the many tribal members who now live far away from the reservation.[28]

Precession, which significantly alters the location of the stars, has less effect on the Sun's position with respect to the horizon. Its position at the summer and winter solstices changes very slowly over the centuries, making it possible today to witness the play of light and shadow on architectural features nearly as the builders might have seen them one or two thousand years ago. Thus it is that visitors to Chaco Canyon National Historical Park in New Mexico can witness the arrival of the summer solstice at Casa Rinconada, a prehistoric Pueblo ceremonial building. Casa Rinconada is a circular structure some sixty feet across and about twelve feet deep. Originally, it was roofed over and could have held several hundred worshipers. Built in the eleventh century by ancestors of the Pueblo people generally called the Anasazi, Casa Rinconada seems to have been designed not only to hold ceremonies, but also to serve as a kind of model of the world. It is round like the horizon, was built on an accurate

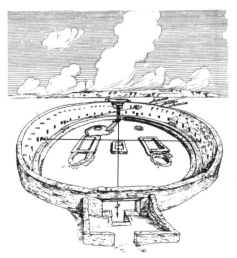

Casa Rinconada, Chaco Canyon National Historic Park

This structure, which is about sixty feet across and nearly twelve feet deep, was constructed in the late eleventh century and is aligned along the cardinal directions. It also has an alignment to the summer solstice sunrise.

DRAWING BY
SNOWDEN HODGES

north-south axis, and contains architectural features that emphasize the four directions. A door or window opening in the northeast of the building allows the light of the Sun to stream through at the time of the summer solstice and light up a large, low niche on the opposite wall.[29]

Like their descendants, the Pueblo Indians, the Anasazi were agricultural people who depended heavily upon the cultivation of corn, beans, squash, and leafy vegetables. Their need for an accurate calendar is relatively obvious. Groups whose survival depended on strategies of gathering, hunting, and fishing, rather than horticulture, have also paid close attention to the Sun. For example, the Mescalero Apache, who lived by hunting and gathering until this century, still observe the solstices closely.[30] At the beginning of the century, Native American hunter/gatherer groups throughout California watched the Sun for the arrival of the solstices and celebrated these events with considerable investment of time and effort. Until the latter part of this century, observing the solstices and equinoxes was still important among the Ajumawi of northeastern California, who marked the beginning and end of the storytelling season by the autumnal and vernal equinoxes. The mountain the Ajumawi call Simloki commands a prominent place on the western horizon of Ajumawi territory. At sunset, Simloki casts a dramatic shadow across the Fall River Valley in which the Ajumawi live. At the equinoxes and solstices, the shadow reaches across the valley to areas considered sacred by the Ajumawi. At one time the Ajumawi celebrated the arrival of the equinoxes or the solstices by racing Simloki's shadow across the landscape to the sacred areas, a ceremony suggested by one of the Ajumawi creation myths in which Jamul, the Silver Fox Man, who gave the people good laws, and Kwahn, Coyote Man, who changed them, raced each other across the landscape to determine who would lead the people.[31]

Moon

The monthly transformation of the Moon from a tiny sliver of light following the Sun below the horizon, to a fully illuminated globe and back, provides yet a third means of measuring time. As the second brightest object in the sky, the Moon is also easy to observe. Its changeable form, its close relationship to the Sun, and the approximate equality of its monthly cycle to a woman's menstrual period have made it the subject of myth and folklore for Native Americans, and for groups throughout the world.

The lunar month lasts 29.5 days, starting with the Moon's first appearance as a thin crescent just after sunset, with cusps that face east, away from the Sun. As the Moon grows to fullness, it pulls farther and farther to the east from its brighter companion each night. By the time the Moon is fully lit, it rises opposite the Sun, as the latter body is setting. It continues to rise later each night, declining in brightness as darkness spreads across its face from west to east. Soon it rises just before the Sun and diminishes to a thin crescent before disappearing in the Sun's glare as both rise together. A day later the cycle of lunar rebirth begins again.

The lunar phases make possible a simple calendar, used in virtually every society of the world. Although 29.5 days divides the year into about twelve and a third parts, an inconvenient multiple of months, many cultures have used the lunar month as a basic unit of time. Indeed, the lunar month provides the basis for the Western, twelve-month European calendar we live by today. The Europeans settled the problem of incommensurability of the lunar and solar calendars by ignoring the progress of the Moon entirely and force-fitting six months of either 30 or 31 days into each half year.[32]

Several Native American groups solved the problem in a simpler way by adding an extra month every three years. The Hopi, for example, keep both a solar horizon calendar and a lunar calendar to determine when to hold their ceremonies and adopt this approach to reconcile the two calendars.[33] California groups kept track of the days, months, and years by using counting sticks and knotted cords in concert with careful observations of the Moon.[34] They too faced the inherent mismatch of the solar and lunar calendars. The Tolowa of northern California, for example, tell a humorous tale suggesting that the trickster Coyote had something to do with creating a fractional month. According to the story, there used to be fifteen moons, but Coyote worried that this made the year too long. "This needs to be fixed," he thought. So Coyote hid outside their sweathouse one day, and when the months emerged, he pounced on them, managing to kill two of the fifteen. The thirteenth month he only wounded by stabbing it in the rump. From thenceforth the thirteenth moon was only one-third its normal length each year.[35]

The Moon's motions along the horizon are much more complicated and swifter than the Sun's. Each month, the Moon covers about the same distance that the Sun moves in an entire year. Taking for simplicity a month starting on the vernal equinox, the new Moon will set with the Sun, within a few degrees of the equator.[36] Seven days afterward, when the Moon is one-half full, it sets about midnight near the summer solstice position. When it turns full another seven days later, the Moon rises and sets near the equator again. Yet a further seven days later, the Moon will set near the winter solstice position. However, in the northern fall and winter, when the Sun stays low in the sky, the new Moon rises near the Sun, but moves to the Northern Hemisphere by the time it turns full. If a full Moon occurs near the winter solstice, it will travel a path near that of the summer solstice Sun. The full Moon high in the sky causes a snowy winter landscape to sparkle with particular intensity. In contrast, near the summer solstice, the full Moon shines low in the sky, as it follows close to the path of the winter Sun.

These subtleties of the Moon's motions, hardly noticed by most people today, were well known to Native American observers. The Navajos, for example, tell a story that accounts for the Moon's quirky behavior. When the First People climbed up from the underworld and found the surface dark, they endeavored to make two celestial bodies to bring light to the world—

Rattles

These doughnut-shaped rattles represent both the sun and the moon. Arapaho boys and men belonged to a series of age-related societies throughout their lives. Young men who advanced to the Star Company, the second level of the societies, used this type of rattle.

ARAPAHO,
COLLECTED 1903
LEFT: CMNH 3179-201
RIGHT: CMNH 3179-287

one that would bear heat and light, and a second that would carry coolness and moisture. Both were made from crystal. The first was given a mask of turquoise, the second a mask of white shell. Both were decorated with twelve eagle feathers to guide them on their journeys. When they were ready, Sun rose from his position on the eastern horizon and began to light the world, following a path indicated by the twelve feathers. Then, when Moon began his path, Wind Boy tried to help with a push, inadvertently causing the eagle feathers to obscure Moon's view of the right path. Ever since, Moon has followed strange paths across the sky.[37]

Because the Moon does not quite follow the yearly solar path called the *ecliptic*, but appears to travel a course that extends both above and below the ecliptic by about five degrees, its extreme points of rise and set fall both within and beyond the solstice extremes over a cycle of 18.6 years. Following this cycle and making predictions according to it requires extremely careful, long-term observations of moonrise and moonset. There is little doubt that some Native American observers developed the skills necessary to observe and predict this cycle. The prehistoric record at Chimney Rock Pueblo some 1,200 feet above the valley floor in southern Colorado suggests that the Anasazi who constructed the pueblo may have followed the lunar cycle. Astronomical evidence from the site is supported by archaeological research showing that the pueblo had been reconstructed after seventeen years. These architectural changes were of the right nature to accommodate changes in the Moon's position over that period.[38] However, confirmation of this hypothesis awaits further investigation both at Chimney Rock and at other contemporary Anasazi sites. Ethnoastronomical studies in the historic period have turned up no clear evidence that Native Americans actually followed the Moon's motions with such care.

Planetary Movements

Native American observers of the night skies must have been especially intrigued by the planets, which look like bright stars but move among the stellar background, most often toward the east, but sometimes in the opposite, or retrograde, direction toward the west.

The planets follow paths nearly along the ecliptic, completing a full celestial circle over different periods. Venus and Mercury always appear as either morning or evening stars. Mercury stays very close to the Sun and is thus difficult to pick out in the Sun's glare; in its cycle, Venus swings through a wide arc on either side of the Sun. Because Venus is brighter than any star or planet, it is particularly noticeable, especially when the waxing or waning crescent Moon wanders nearby. In Mesoamerica, the Maya followed the cycles of Venus intently and based a complicated calendar on its motions. In

Pawnee earth lodge

Buffalo and Lance Dances were held inside. The Pawnee considered their earth lodges to be models of the cosmos. Traditionally, the roof of the lodge was supported by four large posts representing the stars of the four directions. The circular roof represented the sky, and the doorway opened to the east and the Morning Star.

contrast to Venus and Mercury, the other visible planets—Mars, Jupiter, and Saturn—appear anywhere near or along the ecliptic.

We know relatively little about Native American observations of the planets, perhaps because most early ethnographers had little knowledge about the motions of the planets and did not know what to ask. Many groups recognized morning and evening stars, but the available data seldom make clear whether they applied the designation only to Venus or Mercury, or whether it also applied to other planets or sometimes to bright stars. For example, the Zuni certainly used observations of "morning star" to time the beginning and ending of several ceremonies. Yet the data suggest that they used any convenient starlike object that might appear in the early morning sky.[39] Saturn, Jupiter, and Mars also occasionally appeared as the morning star when their paths took them near the Sun.

The Skidi Pawnee, who considered the stars holy beings, were astute observers of the starry heavens and extremely well versed in the motions of the planets. They considered Morning Star, who they apparently associated with the planet Mars, as one of their most important deities.[40] Evening Star, probably associated with Venus, was of secondary importance. The Skidi Pawnee timed their Morning Star sacrifice, in which they periodically sacrificed a captured maiden or young boy, to occur just as the Morning Star appeared. In carrying out this ceremony, the Skidi Pawnee reenacted part of the story of Morning Star and Evening Star from the creation of the world. In addition to bringing blessings to the Pawnee, this ceremony was considered by the Skidi Pawnee to be an enactment of the myth of Morning Star and Evening Star, when Morning Star overcame many obstacles to reach Evening Star and marry her.[41]

Among the California Indians, Venus was an important celestial object and was differentiated from the other planets.[42] For some groups, morning and evening star was a single being, associated with Venus. Others, like the Pomo, considered the two as different, closely related beings.[43]

Irregular Appearances

Generally, Native American groups find the regular appearances and movements of the celestial objects of deep interest. Yet, the order and predictability of the sky is occasionally upset by irregular, unpredictable appearances of eclipses, meteors, and comets, as well as unusual atmospheric phenomena. Most tribes understood these appearances as portents, which might signal hard times for the individual or group.

Lunar and solar eclipses are especially impressive and can be frightening because they alter the appearances of these important celestial bodies so dramatically. During a lunar eclipse, which occurs only when the Moon is full and the earth comes between the Sun and the Moon, the lunar face gradually darkens as Earth's shadow moves across it, taking on a disturbing, deep blood-red shade in full eclipse. The Moon remains darkened for about half an hour, after which the shadow gradually moves off, leaving the surface bright again. Although the Moon recovers its normal appearance, the effects on the human psyche of a gradual darkening of the full Moon are strong, even in this rationalized age.

A total solar eclipse inspires even more awe, in part because it is so rare. As the eclipse advances, the Sun loses progressively more of its light as a dark disk appears to cut away more and more of the Sun's face. After more than half of the Sun is covered, the sky begins to darken, turning an eerie gray-blue color. Finally, the Sun turns totally dark and the stars become visible overhead. Surrounding the vanished solar disk is a glowing white corona. After a few seconds or minutes, the total eclipse ends as a blindingly bright crescent Sun reappears. Even outside the path of totality, daylight assumes an uncomfortable aspect as the sky darkens.

Few people will experience more than one total eclipse of the Sun in a lifetime, if that. Although an average of four solar eclipses occur each year, as viewed from somewhere in the world, the Sun, Moon, and Earth need to be lined up just so to produce a total eclipse; most observers will see only partial eclipses. It is much more common to witness a total lunar eclipse, because Earth casts a shadow much larger than the diameter of the Moon.

Nothing in the written record suggests that Native Americans had developed the ability to predict eclipses, yet they were certainly affected by them and generally took them as evidence of an imbalance in the world that would lead to danger and death for the tribal group. The Tewa of the Rio Grande, for example, dreaded the eclipse of the Sun. They took it as a sign that Sun Father was displeased with them and was retiring to his house in the underworld. A solar eclipse would reportedly occasion a prayer to the Sun that illustrates how important it was to them:

Let the earth be covered with all things beautiful.
All trees, plants, flowers. Let the deer, antelope,

mountain sheep and turkey roam over the earth that we may have food in plenty for our children. Let the eagle soar over the earth that we may have plumes [feathers] to offer to our gods. Refresh our mother earth with rains that she may be happy.[44]

The Yokuts of central California viewed solar and lunar eclipses as caused by the wings of a giant condor, which periodically covered the Sun or Moon. Although we have no direct information about how the California Chumash viewed and responded to solar eclipses, several Chumash rock art paintings seem to represent the circumstances of a solar eclipse.[45] The Pawnee told a tale citing their fear "that when the time came for the world to end the Moon would turn red; that if the Moon should turn black it would be a sign that some great chief was to die."[46]

The brief appearance of meteors and fireballs has also elicited interest among some Native American groups, as they considered them falling stars. The Skidi Pawnee, who kept careful watch on the movements and appearances of the night sky for guidance in their lives, considered meteors and fireballs as children of Tirawahat, their supreme being, who were coming down to Earth. They especially revered meteorites, meteors that had survived the fiery descent to Earth, and kept small ones wrapped in their medicine bundles. As the ambassadors of Tirawahat, meteorites brought wisdom and advice to the tribe. The Skidi Pawnee told stories and sang songs about meteors that had come to Earth.[47] They looked forward to the Perseid and Leonid meteor showers that occur during August and November, respectively, during which many thousands of meteors fill the sky over the course of a night.

Conclusions

This brief account can only point to the richness and complexity of Native American sky knowledge and use. Because they depended in part on their understanding of the sky and its lessons to survive a sometimes hostile world, Native Americans had considerable incentive to learn and pass on this knowledge. At one time much of it was broadly shared, even if certain, more esoteric aspects were reserved for specialists.

The rhythms of the sky are deeply ingrained in Native American life, even among individuals who no longer follow tribal religious beliefs. Upon entering a tipi, the Sioux will walk around to the left, in a sunwise direction. The proper way to enter a Navajo hogan is also to the left. Traditionally, the door of both the tipi

Floor plan of a Navajo five-log hogan

The form of the five-log hogan, one of the principal hogan designs, is specified by the origin myths of the Navajo. This hogan has major supporting beams in the south, west, and north. The door, which according to the origin myths should face to the east, is framed by two smaller logs. When one enters a hogan, the proper way to proceed is in a sunwise direction around to the left.

DRAWING BY
SNOWDEN HODGES

and the hogan should face toward the east. Ritual structures are commonly oriented along the four cardinal directions. For example, the Southeastern Creek Green Corn Ceremony was held on a ceremonial ground that was oriented to the four directions.[48] The Iroquois League of Nations used as their political symbol the Iroquois longhouse, oriented east-west. The longhouse stretched from the eastern door, guarded by the Mohawks, to the western door, guarded by the Seneca. The Onondagas in the middle were keepers of the fire and hosted the grand councils of the Iroquois.[49] Other vestiges of sky knowledge are evident in tribal emphasis on the number four or six, symbolic of the four or six directions (including zenith and nadir), and even in the way tribal political or social activities are organized.[50]

Today's non-Indian society tends to view knowledge of the sky principally as a specialized activity accessible only to experts with years of training, so most people are surprised at how much can be accomplished by careful, patient observations, even using only the naked eye, the horizon or a simple artifice, and a bit of ingenuity. Upon reflection, it is hardly surprising that Native Americans would be aware of the rhythms of the sky and would incorporate them into their lives. They were close observers of the natural realm because

Zuni hunting charms

This set of Zuni hunting charms, popularly called fetishes, depicts the animal guardians of the six directions. Clockwise from upper left, these animals are: Bear (West), Badger (South), Eagle (Above), Mountain lion (North), Mole (Below), and Wolf (East).

DINAH GASPAR, ZUNI, NEW MEXICO, 1991
CLOCKWISE FROM UPPER LEFT: CMNH 35154-3 a–f

their lives depended on their skills at interpreting the signs around them, including the celestial sphere.

Sadly, much Native American sky knowledge has been lost—the victim of acculturation, neglect, or death. Fortunately, sparked in part by the interest of scholars outside the tribes, a few intrepid tribal members have begun to stem the loss of celestial knowledge by seeking out the elders and others who have retained some of the old stories and information about tribal observations of the sky. Some are collecting this information for tribal archives, to pass along to the young. Others have incorporated these traditions in new songs, plays, and stories, and are making them once again a living part of Native American life.

Notes

1. Fr. Berard Haile, *Starlore Among the Navaho* (Santa Fe, NM: Museum of Navaho Ceremonial Art, 1947), 17–23; Von Del Chamberlain, *When Stars Came Down to Earth* (Los Altos, CA: Ballena Press, 1982), 45.

2. Thomas C. Blackburn, *December's Child* (Berkeley and Los Angeles: University of California Press, 1975), 93.

3. Anthony Aveni, ed., *Native American Astronomy* (Austin: University of Texas Press, 1977), and *World Archaeoastronomy* (Cambridge: Cambridge University Press, 1989); Ray Williamson, ed., *Archaeoastronomy in the Americas* (Los Altos, CA: Ballena Press, 1981).

4. Francisco Patencio, *Stories and Legends of the Palm Springs Indians* (Los Angeles: Times-Mirror Press, 1943), 113.

5. Ray Williamson, *Living the Sky: The Cosmos of the American Indian* (Norman, OK: University of Oklahoma Press, 1987), ch. 13.

6. Alexander M. Stephen, *Hopi Journal of Alexander M. Stephen*, ed. Elsie C. Parsons, Columbia Contributions to Anthropology 23 (New York, 1936).

7. Leslie Spier, "Klamath Ethnography," *University of California Publications in American Archaeology and Ethnology* 30 (1930): 218.

8. Claire R. Farrer, *Living Life's Circle: Mescalero Apache Cosmovision* (Albuquerque: University of New Mexico Press, 1991).

9. Aileen O'Bryan, "The Diné: Origin Myths of the Navaho," *Smithsonian Institution Bureau of American Ethnology Bulletin* 163 (1956): 16–17.

10. Sallie P. Brewer, "Notes on Navaho Astronomy," in *For the Dean: Essays in Anthropology in Honor of Byron Cummings* (Tucson: University of Arizona Press, 1950), 136.

11. Chamberlain, *When Stars Came Down to Earth*, 139.

12. Stars considered circumpolar vary with latitude. As viewed from within the Arctic Circle, for example, nearly the entire Northern Hemisphere could be considered circumpolar. As an observer moves south from the Arctic Circle, the diameter of the circle of stars diminishes until one reaches the equator where the North and South Poles are both along the horizon.

13. Richard H. Allen, *Star Names: Their Lore and Meaning* (1899; reprint, New York: Dover, 1966).

14. Brewer, "Notes on Navaho Astronomy," 134.

15. Frank H. Cushing, *Outlines of Zuni Creation Myths*, Thirteenth Annual Report of the Bureau of American Ethnology (Washington, D.C.: Smithsonian Institution, 1896), 392.

16. Edwin Loeb, "Pomo Folkways," *University of California Publications in American Archaeology and Ethnology* 19(2) (1926): 228–29.

17. M. Jane Young, and Ray A. Williamson, "Ethno-astronomy: the Zuni Case," in Williamson, *Archaeoastronomy in the Americas*, 190.

18. Frank G. Speck, *Midwinter Rites of the Cayuga Long House* (Philadelphia: University of Pennsylvania Press, 1949), 49–50.

19. John A. Eddy, "Medicine Wheels and Plains Indian Astronomy," in Aveni, *Native American Astronomy*, 147–70.

20. To give an idea of scale, the Moon and the Sun both extend across about one-half degree.

21. Travis Hudson, "California's First Astronomers," in *Archaeoastronomy and the Roots of Science*, ed. E. C. Krupp (Washington, D.C.: American Association for the Advancement of Science, 1984), 44; Chamberlain, *When Stars Came Down to Earth*, 112; James Mooney, *Myths of the Cherokee*, Nineteenth Annual Report of the Bureau of American Ethnology (Washington, D.C.: Smithsonian Institution, 1900), 259.

22. John R. Swanton, *Indians of the Southeastern United States* (1946; reprint, Washington, D.C.: Smithsonian Institution Press, 1979), 779.

23. Four days is a reasonably good reflection of the period any observer might estimate without benefit of instruments.

24. Matilda Cox Stevenson, *The Zuni Indians*, Twenty-third Annual Report of the Bureau of American Ethnology (Washington, D.C.: Smithsonian Institution, 1903).

25. Michael Zeilik, "Anticipation in Ceremony: The Readiness Is All," in *Astronomy and Ceremony in the Prehistoric Southwest*, ed. J. B. Carlson and W. J. Judge, Papers of the Maxwell Museum of Anthropology, no. 2 (Albuquerque: Maxwell Museum Press, 1987), 25–41.

26. Williamson, *Living the Sky*, ch. 6.

27. Stephen C. McCluskey, "The Astronomy of the Hopi Indians," *Journal of the History of Astronomy* 8 (1977): 174–95.

28. Farrer, *Living Life's Circle*. This ceremony can be held at any time after a girl has begun to menstruate. However, many families wait until the July Fourth weekend in order to take part in the more public ceremony that makes it possible for more family members to attend.

29. See Williamson, *Living the Sky*, ch. 6, for a detailed description of Casa Rinconada and its astronomical significance. The term Anasazi is a Navajo word that means "ancient people who are not Navajo." Scholars have adopted the term to refer collectively to all the ancestors of the Pueblo tribes, though archaeologists also recognize that differences of geography, language, and custom existed among the many Anasazi groups, just as they now do among the Pueblo tribes.

30. Farrer, *Living Life's Circle*.

31. Although Kwahn always won these races, Jamul always contested them, calling for another trial, so the contest between order and disorder continues. See Jack M. Broughton and Floyd Buckskin, "Racing Simloki's Shadow: The Ajumawi Interconnection of Power, Shadow, Equinox, and Solstice," in Ray A. Williamson and Claire R. Farrer, eds., *Earth and Sky: Visions of the Cosmos in Native American Folklore* (Albuquerque: University of New Mexico Press, 1992), 184–92.

32. Except, of course, for February "which alone has twenty-eight," and except for the extra day of February each four years. The extra February day every leap year results from the fact that the solar year is nearly 365.25 days long, requiring a correction every four years.

33. McCluskey, "The Astronomy of the Hopi Indians," 174–95.

34. Hudson, "California's First Astronomers," 44.

35. Phillip Drucker, "The Tolowa and their Southwest Oregon Kin," *University of California Publications in American Archaeology and Ethnology* 26 (1937): 240.

36. The Moon's apparent orbit is tilted by a few degrees with respect to the ecliptic, the Sun's apparent yearly orbit.

Hence, depending on its position along that apparent orbit, it could be in line with the Sun or slightly displaced from the Sun. When the Moon is exactly in line with the Sun at new Moon, a solar eclipse would occur somewhere on the Earth.

37. Franc Johnson Newcomb, *Navaho Folk Tales* (Albuquerque: University of New Mexico Press, 1990), 81–82.

38. J. McKim Malville and Claudia Putnam, *Prehistoric Astronomy in the Southwest* (Boulder, CO: Johnson Books, 1989), ch. 5.

39. Jane Young, "Morning Star, Evening Star: Zuni Traditional Stories," in Williamson and Ferrer, *Earth and Sky*, 79.

40. Although this identification is far from certain, astronomer Von Del Chamberlain has shown that it fits well with the celestial circumstances surrounding the only Pawnee Morning Star sacrifice for which we know the date with sufficient accuracy to link the event with the sky. See Chamberlain, *When Stars Came Down to Earth*, 71–90.

41. Natalie Curtis, *The Indians' Book: Songs and Legends of the American Indians* (reprint, New York: Dover, 1968), 91–144.

42. Hudson, "California's First Astronomers."

43. Loeb, "Pomo Folkways," 228.

44. Matilda Cox Stevenson, Notes, National Anthropological Archives, Washington, D.C., n.d.

45. Travis Hudson and Earnest Underhay, *Crystals in the Sky: An Intellectual Odyssey Involving Chumash Astronomy, Cosmology, and Rock Art* (Socorro, NM: Ballena Press, 1978), 53.

46. George Dorsey, "The Pawnee: Mythology," *Carnegie Institution of Washington Publications* 59 (1906): 134–37.

47. See, for example, Chamberlain, *When Stars Came Down to Earth*, 144–45.

48. John R. Swanton, *Religious Beliefs and Practices of the Creek Indians*, Forty-second Annual Report of the Bureau of American Ethnology (Washington, D.C.: Smithsonian Institution, 1928), 182.

49. Paul H. Wallace, *The White Roots of Peace* (Port Washington, NY: Ira J. Friedman, 1968).

50. Farrer, *Living Life's Circle*.

Animals

I Sing for the Animals

Out of the earth
I sing for them,
A Horse nation
I sing for them.
Out of the earth
I sing for them,
The animals
I sing for them.

—LAKOTA, PLAINS

6

Animals in American Indian Life: An Overview

SANDRA L. OLSEN

IT WOULD BE DIFFICULT to overestimate the value of animals in the daily lives of Native Americans, both past and present. Before plants and animals were domesticated in North America, people relied solely on wild plants and animals for their survival. Since only the dog and turkey were domesticated before the arrival of European colonists, hunting continued to be a crucial part of the economy even after corn, beans, squash, and other cultigens were common. Beyond the obvious nutritional value provided by meat as a source of protein, calcium, fat, and other essential elements of the diet, animals yielded a wide variety of useful by-products. Hides, with or without the fur attached, served as necessary raw material for clothing, footwear, thongs, tents, bedding, and bags. Before metals and plastic became available, bones, antler, and teeth were important sources for both tools and ornaments. Tendons were used to make sinew thread—helpful in making bows more elastic, for securing arrow points and other tools to wooden shafts, and for sewing leather. Even hooves and horns could be used to make rattles, containers, and glue. Bird feathers functioned

Turtle necklace

For special occasions Plains people wear parts of animals whose abilities they desire. A necklace made of turtle femurs represents the turtle's longevity.

PLAINS, COLLECTED CA. 1899 AT YANKTON AGENCY, SOUTH DAKOTA CMNH 1171-38

Sandra L. Olsen

Horse dragging a travois on the Plains, 1895–1899

After the introduction of the horse, Plains people could more easily move their tipis and other possessions to follow the herds.

as elaborate ornamentation, warm cloaks and blankets, and to fletch arrows. It was possible to use virtually every part of an animal either for food or as raw material for functional objects.

In prehistoric North America, only the dog was used as a means of transporting supplies. Through the attachment of a wooden frame known as a *travois*, the Plains Indian dogs were employed to drag small burdens. With the arrival of horses in the sixteenth through eighteenth centuries, Native Americans had a method of rapid transit for riders and for carrying heavy goods. The horse was an important aid in hunting large game like bison and made an enormous impact by escalating intertribal warfare.

We know that trade and exchange between groups were conducted over long distances because marine shells from the Pacific, Atlantic, and Caribbean have turned up inland, hundreds of miles from their origin. Shells were also used as currency on both coasts.

The close ties between humans and fauna generated by the need for meat and by-products meant that animals played an important role in Native American religion and society. Many tribes are divided into clans or moieties whose namesakes are animals like the eagle, owl, bear, badger, and wolf. The behavior of certain animals contributes to the attribution of human personality traits to them, such as the cowardly but clever coyote. The rich oral traditions—

including origin myths and folktales—often focus on one animal and its interaction with others. Hunts were preceded and followed by rituals designed to communicate reverence for the prey species and to insure that successful yields would continue.

Whole volumes have been written on the roles of animals in societies. In this essay, some key examples are highlighted to illustrate the diversity of species and their uses that have been documented among North American tribes.

PHOTO BY JESSE H. BRATLEY

Dream of Plenty

The Inuit believe that hunting and fishing require not only prowess on the hunter's part but the animal's willingness to give itself to man. Thus, hunters call upon animal spirits in dreams, asking for their cooperation in the hunt.

MABLE NIGIYOK, HOLMAN ISLAND, NORTHWEST TERRITORIES, CANADA, INUIT, 1992
CMNH 35412-8

Invertebrates

Insects, spiders, scorpions, and the like must have been a great annoyance or even danger to Native Americans. There are historic accounts of people in the Eastern Woodlands rubbing bear grease on their bodies to deter mosquitoes from biting. Close contact with animals exposed hunters to fleas and ticks that carried such diseases as Rocky Mountain Spotted Fever. Like all preindustrial societies, until recently, Native Americans had to cope with lice by cutting their hair, shaving their heads, applying herbal medicine, and grooming. Wooden lice-crushers were used by the Hopi, and bone picks were worn in the hair by men of most of the southwestern tribes, including the Apache, Pima, Hopi, and Zuni.

Some insects bore far more positive connotations, however. Bees furnished honey that could be harvested for food and beeswax that could be used to haft arrow points and tools into wooden shafts and handles. One of the most fascinating uses of insects is the making of a brilliant red dye from a scale insect (*Dactylopius coccus*); this pigment, known as cochineal dye, is still made to paint hides and dye textiles. The females of the insect are dried to make the dye.

A wide variety of insects are edible and have furnished Native Americans with a ready source of calories. Most of the records of eating insects come from the Plains or the West. In the central prairies, the Great Basin, and California, roasted, boiled, or dried grasshoppers were an important part of the diet. They were collected by setting forest or brush fires, organizing communal drives toward a central pit, or by the use of nets. Other insects that were eaten include crickets, ants, lice, caterpillars, flies, and the larvae of many species. In times of famine, cultures that lived in marginal environments, like the Pima and Tohono O'odham (Papago) of southern Arizona, relied heavily on insects to stave off hunger.

Insects and spiders, like most animals, were often associated with particular powers. The Oglala Lakota, for example, saw a connection between moths and the wind, because of the wind generated by their wings. A cocoon encapsulated the wind and all its power. The spider could tap into the power of the wind because its web stretched outward toward the four directions, the homes of the four winds.

Mollusks, particularly marine and freshwater species, were extremely important to certain cultures. Miles of shell middens along the coastlines attest to the significance of clams, oysters, scallops, and other types of shellfish in the diet of coastal peoples. The Lakota and many other inland tribes depended to a small extent on freshwater bivalves, and the California Indians ate some land snails, but marine mollusks were of much greater importance where available. Snails and some bivalves were collected by first locating their trails, holes, or "squirts" in the sand along the beach and then digging them up. Some of the most commonly consumed shellfish on the East Coast were the quahog (*Mercenaria mercenaria*), conchs (*Busycon carica* and *B. canaliculatum*), the surf clam (*Spisula solidissima*), the soft-shell clam (*Mya arenaria*), periwinkles, and moon snails. Native Americans on the West Coast harvested limpets, abalones, snails, littleneck clams (*Prototheca staminea*), Olympia oysters (*Ostrea lurida*), basket cockles (*Clinocardium nuttalli*), bent-nose clams (*Macoma nasuta*), butter clams (*Saxidomus giganteus*), along with other invertebrates like barnacles, urchins, crabs, chitons, and octopuses.

Mollusks provided not only food; their shells were raw material for making beads. Strung together in long strands, shell beads served both as ornamentation and as currency. *Wampum* is the generic term for standard-length strands of these shells used by tribes in eastern North America to trade for other products. The word is a shortened form of the Narragansett *wampompeag*, meaning "white string," used to refer to white shell beads of inferior value. White beads came from the conch shell, each of which would yield several beads. The more valuable purple shell currency was manufactured from the quahog, or hard clam, from which only a single bead could generally be made per shell. The Powhatans used pearls from freshwater mussels as beads to decorate earrings, headdresses, clothing, and moccasins.

California Indians like the Miwok used the purple olive shell, Washington clam, red abalone, and other shells for necklaces, headdresses, money, and gambling chips. The Miwok also used strands of clam shell beads to trade for furs, baskets, bows and arrows, fish, and other commodities that could be obtained from other tribes like the Pomo. A hundred dollars worth of shell money was worth two women, two grizzly or cinnamon bear skins, or three ponies.

Feather presentation basket

This type of ornate basket, adorned with feathers as well as clam and abalone shells, was presented as a valuable gift to honor the recipient.

POMO, CENTRAL CALIFORNIA, LATE 1800s OR EARLY 1900s CMNH 7851-205, GIFT OF MISSES MATILDE AND DOROTHEA W. HOLLIEDT

Fish

Seasonally at least, fish have provided an important element in the diet of many Native American cultures. For some, like those living along the coasts, fish are at the center of their economy. The Northwest Coast tribes and those residing along the coast of Alaska have long depended on the arrival of Pacific salmon (*Oncorhynchus* spp.) to their rivers every summer to supply them with large quantities of food. Other migratory species, like the eulachon (*Thaleichthys pacificus*)

TOP: *Kʷakʷaka'wakʷ family spearfishing for salmon at Quatsino, North Vancouver Island, British Columbia, date unknown*

PHOTO BY BENJAMIN W. LEESON. VANCOUVER PUBLIC LIBRARY, 14059

BOTTOM: *Scooping eulachon*

Tlingit fisherman scoops up hundreds of eulachon with dip nets during the fish's annual migration from the sea to freshwater rivers to spawn.

PHOTO BY LOUIS SHOTRIDGE, DATE UNKNOWN. UNIVERSITY OF PENNSYLVANIA MUSEUM, 14766

and the Pacific halibut (*Hippoglossus stenolepis*), also provided the Northwest Coast tribes with a rich supply of fresh and dried fish. The eulachon also yielded high quantities of fat that could be used in lamps and was high in vitamin A. The availability of so many fish traveling upriver, even for a brief period each year, led to the concentration of human populations in the most productive locations.

On the East Coast, the Atlantic salmon (*Salmo salar*), Atlantic cod (*Gadus morhua*), Atlantic herring (*Clupea harengus*), and several species of shad (*Alosa* spp.) and menhadens (*Brevoortia* spp.) were highly valued food resources for the Native Americans. Some of the first European colonists in Virginia and North Carolina recorded the smoking of large yields of fish on racks in Algonquian villages.

Little in the area of technology can compare to the variety seen in Native American fishing tackle and techniques. Fishing equipment and strategies are closely linked to the behavior of the prey species. It is known from archaeological, historic, and ethnographic accounts that Native Americans manufactured nets, fishhooks and lines, boats, traps, leisters, spears, bows and arrows, harpoons, plant poisons, and weirs of various designs. Some fishhooks were of simple design; others were complex composites of wood, bone, and sinew or twine. When fishing with bow and arrow, to compensate for light diffraction, the tip of the arrow was placed just under the water to align it better with the approaching target. Spears and leisters were obviously most effective where the water ran clear. Harpoons were generally used on large species of fish, as well as on sea mammals. One of the most common kinds of trap used by Native Americans was a conical basket placed in the river current so that the fish would swim into the large end and not be able to turn around and exit. By varying the dimensions, the hunter could control the size of fish caught: larger fish would not enter the trap and smaller ones could easily escape, leaving only medium-sized fish in the trap. Fish weirs were linear or V-shaped structures built across rivers or inlets by stacking stones into piles at close intervals or by placing vertical sticks very close together to form a fence. This allowed fish to be "herded" into traps or "corrals" where they could then be retrieved. Weirs took advantage of the natural flow of the water, but could only be used in relatively shallow areas. Many remains of prehistoric stone weirs can still be seen on the rivers of Virginia and elsewhere in the Eastern Woodlands.

Halibut hook

Tlingit fishermen used a specially carved hook, suspended downward so the halibut would see the decoration and be influenced by it. In selecting the image to carve on the hook, fishermen often chose a powerful creature, perhaps itself a good fisher, whose spirit would entice the fish to the bait.

TLINGIT, PRE-1898
CMNH 638-13

Typical fish weir found in Virginia and North Carolina

Stone walls funnel fish into a wicker trap, shown here, or a net.

DRAWING BY
SANDRA L. OLSEN

Amphibians and Reptiles

Native Americans utilized this group of animals less than any other type of vertebrate. They ate Bullfrogs (*Rana catesbeiana*) and various kinds of turtles and tortoises, but because the skins of toads are often poisonous they were not consumed. Nor would Cherokee ball players eat frogs before a game, because the brittleness of frog bones might be transferred to the human athletes. In southern Arizona and California, the Desert Tortoise (*Gopherus agassizii*) was at least seasonally important. The local people came to know where burrows containing as many as eight tortoises at a time were located, so collecting them was relatively easy. Various tribes caught Snapping Turtles (*Chelydra serpentina*) and other aquatic species by lowering a piece of meat on a line into the water. Deadfall traps placed just underwater near the shore were used by eastern tribes like the Cherokee. The Hopi, Zuni, and others wore turtle shell rattles on their legs for dances. The widespread Eastern Box Turtle (*Terrapene carolina*), which has a hinged lower shell that closes tightly, was often made into a hand-held rattle by attaching it to a wooden handle. Lizards were eaten by the Pima and Tohono O'odham in southern Arizona, as well as by other desert-dwelling people. Lizard effigies are common in prehistoric and recent jewelry in the Southwest.

Frog mask

Several clans of the Raven moiety use the frog as one of their crests. This forehead mask could have been made for any of them. Although called a frog, this image is likely that of the Boreal Toad *(Bufo boreas boreas)*, common in the Tlingit region.

TLINGIT, COLLECTED 1904
CMNH 3178-25

Rattlesnakes (*Crotalus* spp.) are probably the most significant reptiles in terms of Native American symbols. Because of their habits and their poison, they were both revered and feared as potent spirits in many cultures. Among the Cherokee, the bite of a poisonous snake was given little verbal attention, so as not to offend the snake. The victims would instead blame other creatures like the toad, or say they were only scratched by a brier. A great variety of medicinal plants could be used to treat the wound. The Cherokee, for example, prescribed Seneca snakeroot, horehound, wild plantain, St. Andrew's cross, basswood bark, or starry campion.

Birds

Birds have served a variety of purposes for Native Americans over the millennia. Although they have rarely been the dominant food resource for any tribe, they have contributed to the diets of most cultures as seasonal or occasional meat sources. Moreover, their plumage provided warmth and comfort when woven into blankets and offered unlimited possibilities for ornamentation. The exquisite mantles of the priests and noble women of the Powhatans were often made by weaving turkey or other birds' feathers into a twined cloak. The Virginia colonists remarked on how some of the mantles resembled deep purple satin and that the feathers completely concealed the underlying weave. Across North America, Native people manufactured whistles, beads, and awls from hollow limb bones and wore the talons of large raptorial birds as pendants. Costumes and ceremonial paraphernalia were sometimes adorned with bird skins, wings, and heads. Certain greatly revered raptors like Bald (*Haliaeetus leucocephalus*) and Golden (*Aquila chrysaetos*) Eagles, hawks, and owls often served as clan symbols.

Large game birds like the Wild Turkey (*Meleagris gallopavo*) and the Canada Goose (*Branta canadensis*) were consumed throughout North America. People living near coasts and lakes supplemented their diets with aquatic birds. Seasonal migrations of flocks of various species from Canada to Mexico provided a diverse selection of avifauna.

Headdress and trailer

Feathers from the Golden Eagle, Great Horned Owl, and American Crow adorn this headdress and trailer. Until the close of the Plains Indian Wars in 1891, only men who had carried out brave deeds in battle were entitled to wear feather headdresses. Later elaborate bonnets assumed more generalized roles and were, and still are, frequently worn at community events as badges of honor and recognition.

LAKOTA, PINE RIDGE RESERVATION, SOUTH DAKOTA, CA. 1910
CMNH 35153-16 & 18, GIFT OF ALBERT MILLER

Hunting techniques practiced by historic aboriginal cultures probably differed little from those methods used by their ancestors. In addition to snares, nets, and traps, communal drives were employed by some cultures. The Shoshone drove American Coots (*Fulica americana*) and ducks from the water to people on shore, who then killed the birds with sticks or by wringing their necks before the birds could conceal themselves in tall grass.

Nets were commonly strung across trails or in trees to capture birds. Wearing antelope disguises, a group of Shoshone hunters would herd Sage Grouse (*Centrocercus urophasianus*) and rabbits toward a large net that would then drop or tighten to entrap the animals.

Several North American tribes made duck decoys. Remarkable preservation at Lovelock Cave, Nevada, has led to the recovery of 3,000-year-old decoys of American Coots, Common Mergansers (*Mergus merganser*), Greater White-fronted Geese (*Anser albifrons*), Canada Geese (*Branta canadensis*) and Ring-necked Ducks (*Aythya collaris*) that were made by stretching a bird skin over a tule reed form. Many ethnographic reports describe hunters putting duck skins or gourds on their heads as they swam right up to live ducks. They captured the ducks by grabbing their feet and pulling them underwater, so as not to disturb other nearby fowl.

Pit-trapping is a well-known method of capturing eagles and hawks. The pit containing the hunter was camouflaged with twigs and grass; bait, such as a live rabbit, was placed on top. When the raptor approached the bait, the concealed hunter seized its legs. Eagles were caught in this manner in the Southwest by the Apache, Hopi, and Navajo; in the Plains by the Arapaho, Blackfeet, Cheyenne, Nez Percé, and Hidatsa; and in the East by the Seneca, Cherokee, and others. The eagles, which were prized for their feathers, were usually partially plucked and released.

Decoy

Duck hunters fashioned decoys out of tule growing in the marshes. They camouflaged these figures by covering them with actual duck skins, complete with feathers.

PAIUTE, NEVADA, CA. 1980
CMNH 31588, GIFT OF DR.
CRAIG C. BLACK

Occasionally young birds were taken from their nests and raised as pets. The Thompson Indians and certain southern California tribes reared eaglets in captivity. Hopis kept hawks and eagles by tethering them to their rooftops until they killed the birds ritually. The Shoshone are reported to have kept mockingbirds and magpies in cages as household pets.

Wild Turkeys were first domesticated in Mexico, and in the United States there is evidence of their domestication in southwestern Colorado as early as the Basketmaker III period (circa A.D. 450–750). There is debate about whether turkeys were kept primarily for their plumage or also for their meat. Early Spanish reports about the Zuni support the theory that they were only used for their feathers; however, the large numbers of turkey bones found in refuse deposits in southwestern sites throws suspicion on this idea. In the eastern half of North America, Wild Turkeys were hunted, but apparently never tamed. Turkey feathers were used in weaving blankets and for fletching arrows. Across North America, their hollow limb bones were also modified into whistles, tubular containers, beads, and other objects.

Scarlet Macaws (*Ara macao*) were an important trade item in Arizona and New Mexico from A.D. 1100 to 1375. Mexican trade centers, like Casas Grandes, in Chihuahua, Mexico, apparently distributed these parrots to populations as far north as the northern borders of Arizona and New Mexico. Their vibrant plumage provided elaborate ornamentation. As evidence of their significance, they were buried in individual graves or even in the arms of humans, their bones were not made into artifacts, and they were apparently not eaten. Following European intrusion, the Rio Grande Pueblo revived the use of macaw feathers. Among the Hopi, there is evidence of continual use of macaws from the 1100s through the 1960s at least. Padre Luis Velarde recorded, in 1716, that the Pimas of southern Arizona plucked the brilliant red feathers in the spring to wear as personal adornment.

Painted parrot pot

The parrot design is a trademark of Acoma and Laguna Pueblo pottery. Parrot feathers and even live parrots were imported from the tropics of Latin America as early as A.D. 1100.

ACOMA PUEBLO, NEW MEXICO, CA. 1880–1900
CMNH Z-9-306

In the eastern United States and Canada, the Passenger Pigeon (*Ectopistes migratorius*) was second only to the Wild Turkey in significance as a game bird. The nestlings were either eaten fresh with vegetables or could be smoked and dried over the fire. The fat from these pigeons was collected and stored in containers in massive quantities and was spread on bread like butter.

Because Passenger Pigeons nested in large colonies in the same parts of the forest year after year, Native Americans could gather together each spring to collect them. This seasonal event led people to congregate from miles around and was thus important in bringing neighbors together. Among the Winnebago, the chief would invite the whole tribe to a pigeon feast. The Seneca held a pigeon dance, and offerings were presented to the nesting place. The Delaware, Dakota, and others would not allow anyone to harm the adult birds, for fear of driving them away from their nesting area permanently.

So successful were Native Americans at hunting Passenger Pigeons that accounts of taking between 800 and 1,500 a day were recorded for the Onondaga, Cornplanter Seneca, and other tribes. In their most common habitats Passenger Pigeons could be caught with nets, but most were killed as squabs that were dislodged from their nests. With long poles, the women popped the young out of their nests to be retrieved on the ground, eviscerated and smoked over a fire in vast numbers. Arrows tipped with large blunt points were also used to shoot the young nestlings. In addition to pushing the young out of their nests, whole groves of trees were often felled with axes so the squabs could be collected. Nets, though less efficient, could still produce large yields. The Cayuga, Ojibwa, and other groups were reported to have killed 200 to 300 birds at a time with various kinds of nets.

Although Native Americans took advantage of the colonial nature of Passenger Pigeons and sometimes killed the birds in numbers exceeding their needs, this species was not driven to extinction until European Americans began paying Indians to kill them and started a campaign of hunting them for themselves. Originally, millions of these birds existed in North America, but the last documented sighting of a Passenger Pigeon occurred in 1900.

Plains Indians used bird skins stuffed with grass or hemp in ceremonial medicine bundles or as individual fetishes. The religious or magical powers attributed to these fetishes depended upon the type of bird used and the culture making them. The Arikara, for example, used the Swainson's Hawk (*Buteo swainsoni*), Long-eared Owl (*Asio otus*), Arctic Loon (*Gavia arctica*), the now extinct Carolina Parakeet (*Conuropsis carolinensis*), Peregrine Falcon (*Falco peregrinus*), Cooper's Hawk (*Accipiter cooperii*), Western Grebe (*Aechmophorus occidentalis*), Burrowing Owl (*Athene cunicularia*), and others. Members of the mystic Owl Society hung a prepared owl skin symbolizing night on the wall of their sacred lodge whenever they met. Its eyes, made from bison horn, represented the Morning Star, while its feathers represented trees and bushes. Individual fetishes were often buried with their owner, whereas medicine bundles and other stuffed birds that were clan or society symbols were passed on for generations. Tribes known to have used bird skins in a ceremonial manner include, in addition to the Arikara, the Osage, Omaha, Pawnee, Blackfeet, and Assiniboine.

The symbolic associations between birds and other elements of nature can often be explained by the ethology of a particular species. For example, nocturnal birds like owls, Common Poor-wills *(Phalaenoptilus nuttallii)*, and Common Nighthawks *(Chordeiles minor)* were associated with the dusk, night, and the moon by Pueblo Indians. The Horned Lark *(Eremophila alpestris)* and bluebirds *(Sialia* spp.) move down from the mountains to lower elevations in the winter, so they are linked to that season symbolically. Other associations are less direct, however, like the

Shield

The design on this unusual Crow man's shield is constructed from the three-dimensional body and wing feathers of a Cooper's Hawk with two-dimensional painted legs and feet. Reality and illusion merge into a single bird of prey. Painted zigzag lines of lightning, representing power, emanate from the bird's eyes.

CROW, COLLECTED 1904
CMNH 2418-119 a

classification of the hummingbird as a rain symbol by the Pueblos because its iridescent feathers resemble a rainbow.

Mammals

Although other animals figured in the lives of Native Americans, mammals were the predominant group in most

cases. They were obviously critical to the diet of North American Indians, but their importance goes well beyond their use as food. Because mammals seem more human in their behavior and appearance than other animals, there is a greater tendency to anthropomorphize, or assign human characteristics, to them. This results in closer attention to hunting rituals where mammals are involved, more inclusion of mammals in folktales, and more use of mammals as moiety or clan symbols.

Wolf katsina (Kwewu)

HOPI, ARIZONA, COLLECTED 1904
CMNH 3165-150

Rabbits and Hares

In archaeological collections, especially from the western half of North America, the bones of rabbits and hares are often the most frequently encountered food remains. It is clear that these small, but easily obtained animals were important in the diet of many tribes. They were stalked individually by all members of the society, or they could be hunted communally by beating the bushes and surrounding them, or by driving them into a natural cul-de-sac. Rabbits were sometimes trapped in a burrow, pulled out by twisting their fur around a barbed stick, and shot with an arrow or clubbed. The Hopis, the Indians of Baja California, and other southwestern tribes regularly used

Hopi man with rabbit stick, ca. 1912–1922

Men and boys used this type of curved throwing stick.

PHOTO BY EMRY KOPTA.
SMITHSONIAN INSTITUTION
NATIONAL ANTHROPOLOGICAL
ARCHIVES, 4742

rabbit sticks to hunt rabbits. Acting like nonreturning boomerangs, they were thrown along a low, straight trajectory, striking the animal with surprising force. The Catawba Indians in North Carolina used a straight throwing club to dispatch rabbits. Great Basin tribes, like the Paiute, drove rabbits into nets. A variety of deadfalls and snares were also used.

Rodents

Rodents were probably more of a nuisance than an aid to Native Americans. Rats and mice took up residence around middens and constantly tried to enter food storage containers and areas. Many species were eaten, however, with squirrels, prairie dogs, woodchucks (*Marmota monax*), and beavers (*Castor canadensis*) being the most desirable.

The pelts of many of these species, like the beaver and muskrat (*Ondatra zibethicus*) were highly valued by Native Americans as well as by early European explorers. The French in the northern United States and Canada set up strong trade networks with many local tribes to obtain furs. The European demand for pelts led to a rapid escalation in the killing of various fur-bearing species and sped up encroachment by European trappers into various regions of North America.

The quills of the porcupine (*Erethizon dorsatum*) were especially important to tribes throughout much of North America. Quillwork is one of the most beautiful media for decorating leather headdresses, clothing, bags, and sheaths, as well as pipes and birch-bark containers. The quills are plucked, flattened by drawing them through the teeth, dyed, and sewn onto pieces of leather or bark in complex designs. The porcupine's native range includes most of Canada, the Great Lakes region, and the Rocky

Moccasins

A Lakota woman applied porcupine quills to decorate this elaborate pair of men's moccasins. The horseshoe motifs may indicate the wearer's prowess in acquiring horses.

LAKOTA, CA. 1890s
CMNH 9955-25A a & b,
GIFT OF HENRY P. WALKER

Mountains down to Arizona. As European trade beads began to appear in quantity in North America about 1800, fine quill-work diminished in frequency. Even today, however, there are still talented artists continuing the tradition.

Carnivores

North American carnivores include such species as the mountain lion, lynx, bobcat, bear, wolf, coyote, domestic dog, raccoon, badger, and a variety of weasel-like animals. These playful and ferocious animals provided a rich resource for a large repertoire of fables, tales, and stories in Native American oral traditions. They were competitors of human hunters, pests, vermin control, and in some cases fearsome attackers. Some, such as bears and raccoons, could provide meat. Here we can only provide two brief examples of their roles in the life of Native Americans.

Wolf? mask

Bears and wolves look similar in Northwest Coast carvings. However, this mask probably represents a wolf, because wolves are usually carved with a more slender snout.

TSIMSHIAN, COLLECTED 1904 CMNH 3178-28

The coyote (*Canis latrans*) assumes a dual personality in most Native American mythology and folklore. Throughout its range, there is a recurrent pattern of classifying the coyote on the one hand as a creator, great hunter, and sacred overseer; and on the other as a trickster, thief, and coward. Among many tribes, particularly in the Plains, it is esteemed as the creator of the sun, moon, and stars. According to some beliefs, the coyote bestowed fire on mankind, but also introduced death. Most frequently it is renowned as the creator of animals and the one who may determine the success or failure of a hunt.

The negative aspects of the coyote's image may, in part, be attributed to its habit of eating nearly anything, stealing other animals' prey, and darting away at the first sign of trouble. The coyote is a central character in tribal folktales which are aimed at teaching children not to be foolish or greedy. The Pima, Tohono O'odham, Navajo, Apache, Zuni, Paiute, Hidatsa, Arapaho, and Crow tribes have extensive folklore about the coyote. All these tribes regard him as a trickster, a bungler, a coward, and one who is envious, greedy, and easily duped. At the same time, these tribes view him as a powerful spiritual entity. The Cheyenne consider the coyote's howls to be forewarnings of approaching enemies. To the Zuni, the coyote is the god of the west. The Tohono O'odham tribe is divided into the Coyote and Buzzard moieties and the coyote plays an important role in their Creation Myth.

Among certain tribes the coyote is closely linked to illness and witchcraft. The Pima of Arizona believe that a coyote's strength can cause several diseases that must be treated by a shaman. Eating a melon into which a coyote has previously bitten, or killing a coyote, can trigger one of these illnesses. The cure often consists of waving a coyote tail over the ailing person and singing appropriate songs.

The bear (*Ursus* spp.) possesses a number of qualities that have led most Native Americans to regard it with great reverence. Although recognized as an animal and a supernatural being, it also shares many traits with humans. Perhaps most important is that it sometimes walks upright and flat-footed. Its front paws are much like human hands in the way they rotate and grasp things. The bear is omnivorous, consuming roots, berries, corn, and also many kinds of animal prey; it is thus both a hunter and a gatherer. While many animals are predictable in their behavior patterns, bears seem to have a repertoire of moods similar to people, ranging from playful to violent. Because of this similarity, some tribes have taboos against eating bear meat or killing a bear except in self-defense. According to the Pueblos, a person who kills a bear must join a scalp society, just like one who has killed a person. The combination of its humanlike appearance and its tremendous strength undoubtedly contributed to the selection of the bear as an important totem among the Tlingit, Haida, and other Northwest Coast tribes, the establishment of the Bear clan and Bear *katsina* among the Hopi, and Bear Dances among the Utes and various Plains tribes. Its habit

Bear mask

The lower jaw on this forehead mask can move like a growling bear. It was probably used by a dancer who claimed the bear as a clan or family crest.

TSIMSHIAN?,
COLLECTED 1904
CMNH 3178-27

of hibernating and fasting through the winter months caused the bear to be held in great awe by many Native American observers. Upon its emergence in spring, the Blackfeet, Kutenai, and Crow tribes celebrated a spring solstice ritual. The Micmac killed the bear while it was hibernating, apologizing to the bear for taking its life and treating its body with great reverence to avoid offending its spirit. The powerful bear paw, with its formidable claws, serves as a clan or ceremonial symbol for many tribes, and is also used in medical treatments and for magic. In prehistoric times, the strong canine teeth and the claws of bears were worn as amulets and ornaments and bear cubs were sometimes given ceremonial burials.

Ungulates

Members of the family Cervidae, including white-tailed deer, mule deer, caribou, moose, and wapiti (American elk),

Robe

Painted rows of horses, elk, and buffalo adorn this robe. The depiction of the urinating male elk following the female elk (middle row) gives a clue about this robe's function. Bull elk spray urine, wallow, and bugle during the courting cycle.

A Crow suitor may have worn this powerful robe while courting a young woman. It signified that the suitor was an elk man with special powers for captivating women.

CROW, COLLECTED 1904
CMNH 2418-124

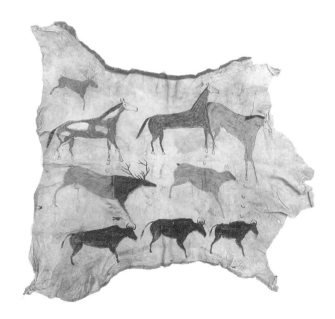

constituted some of the most important components of the Native American diet. Deer were hunted with bows and arrows or spears and generally by stalking rather than through communal drives. Historic accounts in Virginia tell of local people donning deerskin disguises in order to approach the animals without frightening them. The cloak of deer hide included the skin of the face, which was worn over the hunter's head. The antlers were hollowed out to make them lighter, and the hunter peered through the eye holes in the face. The legs of the hide were stuffed with grass and stitched up to add to the realism.

Cervid antlers were important for making a variety of tools, especially those used to knap flint into arrow points. The skins were sewn into clothing, bags, and blankets, while awls, needles, rings, hide scrapers and other objects were manufactured from the bones. Sinew from back and foot tendons provided a strong thread for sewing or hafting stone points and tools onto shafts and handles. Deer brains were used to soften hides during the tanning process.

Because deer were important game all across North America, they were revered and respected by nearly all tribes. As an example, the Zuni and Hopi painted the cranium and other deer bones with red ochre and placed them in a pile as a small shrine so that the deer would continue to let the tribe hunt them. Great ceremony was associated with the deer hunt; among the Pueblo, there was a song to locate the trail of a deer, a song to be sung while tracking a deer, one to accompany the first physical contact with a fallen deer, and separate songs for skinning, butchering, and carrying the meat of the deer home.

Bison (*Bison bison*) are the only other large mammal that could contend with cervids in terms of their importance to Native Americans. Their geographic range was smaller, being concentrated primarily on the Plains, but where they were plentiful they were usually the central focus of the cultures. Before their mass slaughter by European settlers with firearms, it is estimated that there were between 50 and 75 million head of bison in North America. In the year 1889, their numbers had been reduced to only 256 individuals in the United States and fewer than 600 in Canada.

Volumes have been written on the Plains Indian and the bison, so its economic, social, and religious importance can barely be touched upon in this brief summary. (The history of the bison is discussed more fully in chapter 8.) Bison served as the major source of meat and animal by-products for people living between the Mississippi Valley and the Rocky Mountains. Their large hides were used in making tipis, blankets, clothing, and other objects. Their broad shoulder blades made fine hoes for breaking up the soil and weeding the fields. For sedentary farmers like the Omaha, Wichita, Hidatsa, Mandan, Pawnee, and Arikara, bison were hunted primarily through limited seasonal forays when the family groups moved around with their tipis. For other more nomadic tribes like the Flathead, Blackfeet, Comanche, Gros Ventre, Kiowa, and Sarsi, who were primarily hunters, the movements of the bison were followed closely by migrations of the people year round. The Assiniboine, Cheyenne, Crow, Lakota, and Arapaho, faced with pressure from European settlers in the East, migrated into the Plains to become full-time bison hunters.

Hunting strategies were dependent on two key factors, regional terrain and bison social ethology. Bison groups shift in age and sex composition and population size at different times of the year. Normally, a herd consists of a few hundred cows and juveniles. The adult males form smaller satellite bands maintaining a short distance from the central herd. During the summer rutting season, the males join the herd and breeding takes place. Although the herds are the largest and least alert to predators during rut, the presence of fierce males greatly increases the danger of hunts at this time. Just after the spring calving, the females are more skittish than usual and hence flee more rapidly at the first scent of a predator. This makes them easier to drive. During the winter, bison often break up into smaller groups to take shelter in river valleys or forests. The choice of hunt thus depended on the size and composition of the bison herd. Large herds of females and calves could be successfully driven off cliffs, into box canyons, arroyos, parabolic dunes, or into specially constructed corrals. An event of this nature required much cooperation and often involved the participation of several communities. When small groups of bison were encountered, stalking by just a few hunters with bow and arrow was preferred. The cooperative nature of the hunt stimulated contact within and between tribes through trade, ceremonies, marriages, and other social exchanges. Black Elk of the Oglala Lakota summarized the importance of the bison to Native Americans in the Plains when he said that it was the chief of all animals, representing the earth and the totality of all that is.

Conclusions

It is impossible to present a complete picture of the interrelationships between Native Americans and the animal world in North America. This essay is but a patchwork quilt of examples from various tribes gathered to show the diversity of roles animals played, without claiming to be comprehensive for even one tribe. It is perhaps unfair to pull individual examples from the whole ecological or cosmological realm of a tribe for the sake of illustration. The reader should recognize that the belief systems of American Indian tribes were extremely complex. Animals were linked to one another and to other elements of their environment through overlapping or shared powers, folktales, ceremonies, taboos, and a whole host of symbols. If one reads any book on the roles animals play in a tribe's universe, it is immediately apparent how far those roles exceed beyond just the nutritive aspect of animals. The supernatural, the medicinal, the ancestral, and the social aspects of animals as symbols must weigh heavily in any assessment of their importance to the Native American.

This essay provides a somewhat protohistoric view of Native American beliefs and practices. Today, things have obviously changed tremendously. Europeans introduced two very important concepts: that wild animals could be exploited to the point of extinction with no regard for their welfare, and that humans could survive completely on domestic plants and animals.

When European explorers came into North America, they were primarily concerned with exploiting the economic resources of the continent. Early reports to their own governments in Europe would sound familiar to any modern stockbroker as they determined the potential value of various assets, including the American flora, fauna, and minerals.

Where animals were concerned, this is most poignantly observed in the bison and its tragic decline to near extinction. However, numerous species suffered because of the fur trade and overhunting, including beaver, muskrat, caribou, moose, swans, geese, ducks, the Passenger Pigeon, and various fish like the salmon. The establishment of a trade link between Native Americans and such European businesses as the Hudson Bay Company—exchanging animal pelts for European-manufactured goods—led to a disintegration of the spiritual connection between living animals and the people. At first there was resistance to killing animals for trade, but eventually the desire for prestigious European items like beads and knives prevailed.

The early Spanish explorers and English colonists brought domestic horses, cattle, sheep, goats, and chickens to America. Of these, the horse and sheep made the biggest impact. The horse changed societies in the Plains, not just by facilitating hunting, travel, and communication. As in the Old World, when humans first began to ride horses, those cultures that took to life in the saddle were often victorious over sedentary farmers who lacked equestrian skills. In North America, warfare ensued on a level not seen previously. Coupled with population pressure from the European invasion, the horse increased skirmishes for territory. Enemy tribes were able to sweep into a region with disastrous results.

Sheep and goats changed the economy of tribes like the Navajo by allowing them to have a more reliable subsistence base compared to hunting, but these animals rapidly caused irreparable damage to the environment in the West. Areas like Utah and northern Arizona, which were already arid, were stripped of most of their native vegetation. The inconsistencies of U.S. government policy, which first encouraged an increase in the size of Indian herds and then seriously curtailed it, has caused great suffering to many tribes in the West.

In prehistoric and protohistoric times, animal populations were generally able to bear the impact of human exploitation. Numbers of people rarely exceeded the carrying capacity of the land, and native economies were balanced so as not to destroy any one resource. The conservative use of fauna was insured by strong religious beliefs and taboos that instilled a sense of respect for wildlife. Sadly, that balance has suffered greatly in the last 200 years. Many lessons could be learned from the relationships between Native American cultures and wildlife.

Recommended Readings

Beaglehole, E. *Hopi Hunting and Hunting Ritual.* Yale University Publications in Anthropology 4. 1936.

Brown, J. E. *Animals of the Soul: Sacred Animals of the Oglala Sioux.* Rockport, MA: Element, 1992.

Fradkin, A. *Cherokee Folk Zoology: The Animal World of a Native American People, 1700–1838.* New York: Garland Publishing, 1990.

Goodchild, P. *Survival Skills of the North American Indians.* Chicago: Chicago Review Press, 1984.

Hargrave, L. L. *Mexican Macaws: Comparative Osteology and Survey of Remains from the Southwest.* Anthropological Papers of the University of Arizona 20. 1970.

Hallowell, A. I. "Bear Cult Ceremonialism in the Northern Hemisphere." *American Anthropologist* 25 (1926): 1–175.

Leydet, F. *The Coyote, Defiant Songdog of the West.* Norman: University of Oklahoma Press, 1979.

Martin, C. *Keepers of the Game: Indian-Animal Relationships and the Fur Trade.* Berkeley and Los Angeles: University of California Press, 1978.

Orchard, W. C. *The Technique of Porcupine Quill Decoration Among the Indians of North America.* 1916. Reprint, Ogden, UT: Eagles View Publishing, 1984.

Rockwell, D. *Giving Voice to Bear: North American Indian Rituals, Myths, and Images of the Bear.* Niwot, CO: Roberts Rinehart, 1991.

Schorger, A. W. *The Passenger Pigeon, Its Natural History and Extinction.* Norman: University of Oklahoma Press, 1955.

Stewart, H. Indian *Fishing: Early Methods on the Northwest Coast.* Seattle: University of Washington Press, 1977.

Tanner, A. *Bringing Home Animals: Religious Ideology and Mode of Production of the Mistassini Cree Hunters.* New York: St. Martin's Press, 1979.

Tyler, H. A. *Pueblo Animals and Myths.* Norman: University of Oklahoma Press, 1975.

———. *Pueblo Birds and Myths.* Flagstaff, AZ: Northland Publishing, 1991.

Ubelaker, D. H., and W. R. Wedel. "Bird Bones, Burials, and Bundles in Plains Archaeology." *American Antiquity* 40 (1975): 444–52.

Wilson, G. L. "Hidatsa Eagle Trapping." *Anthropological Papers of the American Museum of Natural History 30* (1928).

———. "The Horse and the Dog in Hidatsa Culture." 1924. *Reprints in Anthropology,* vol. 10. Lincoln, NE: J & L Reprint Company, 1978.

7

Ethno-Ornithology of the Zuni

EDMUND JAMES LADD

THE A:SHIWI (the Zunis) have lived in present-day southwestern New Mexico along the banks of the Zuni River, a small intermittent stream, for well over a thousand years. Geographically, the Zuni region was, in prehistoric times, and is, in modern times, a cultural crossroad. Culturally, the A:shiwi were influenced by the people known to archaeologists as the Anasazi, Mogollon, Sinagua, Mimbres, and Hohokam.[1] We do not know, for example, what language the producers of the Anasazi or the Mimbres cultures spoke, but we do know that the Zuni language (*Shiwi/m ja:tiya:wa*) today is unique, unrelated to any other language north of Mexico—not to Tanoan, Keresan, Athabascan, or Utoaztecan.

Prior to the establishment of modern political boundaries, the Pueblo cultures covered an area that extended on a north-south line approximately from Durango, Colorado, to Durango, Mexico, and on an east-west line from Las Vegas, New Mexico, to Las Vegas, Nevada. The Zuni area is in the north-central portion of a huge geographical region containing different linguistic groups but similar cultures. These boundaries fluctuated over time as climatic changes forced people to move. As people moved from one area to another, either being absorbed or absorbing other groups, new cultural groupings were created. This may be the basis for Zuni traditions of "migrations, in search of the Center Place."

It is generally agreed that the predecessors of the A:shiwi moved into the Zuni River valley between A.D. 700 and A.D. 1000 and in time settled in six small villages along the riverbanks where they were encountered by Friar Marcos de Niza and Estevenico in 1539. From east to west the villages are Kya/ki:ma, Ma tsa:kya, Halona:wa, Pin na:wa, Kechipa:wa, and Hawhiku. All are now in ruins except the main village of Halona:itiwann/a, present-day Zuni.

The Zuni River was and is of major importance to the A:shiwi. In precontact times it provided life-giving water for the people as well as for the animals, birds, and plants on which their lives depended. It also watered the plants growing in the "waffle gardens" along the banks of the river—so-called because the women constructed small clay enclosures, or "pans," to conserve water, in which they grew various garden plants; the pattern looked like a waffle. This muddy little stream is not only of economic importance, it is also significant in the religious belief system, tying together the present, living world and the afterworld. The most sacred place in Zuni belief lies at the end of this stream, at the junction of the Little

Zuni women working in their "waffle" garden, 1911

The clay walls helped to retain water to nourish a variety of plants grown within them.

PHOTO BY JESSE L. NUSBAUM, MUSEUM OF NEW MEXICO, 43170

Colorado and Zuni Rivers, north of St. Johns, Arizona. It is called *ko-lhu-wa:la:wa*, or *kokko* village (*kokko* meaning "masked god" or "spirit being"). It has also been called "Zuni heaven" and "dance hall of the gods." It is the sacred lake where, four days after death, the spirits of the dead go to live. The A:shiwi believe that humans occupy the present world together with spirit beings, the *k/apin a:ho/i*, which includes the spirits of all living things.

Nearly every aspect of the Zuni religious system is tied to the river in some way. Along its banks and in the stream, food offerings are made to the gods and the ancestral spirits for continued protection, spiritual guidance, and long life. The ancestors are said to return to *itiwannia* (Zuni land) by making their way back up the river in the form of ducks whenever the masked dances are performed. They also return in the form of rain during the summer and snow during the winter to replenish the stream and thus ensure an abundant harvest. In this way the stream links the living world with the spirit world of the afterlife.

Another key element in Zuni culture is the close observation of the growing season, that is, the time for planting, the time required for germination and growth, and the timely arrival of the rains. At the latitude of Zuni, the rains originating in the Gulf of Mexico occur during the months of July, August, and September. Rainfall is variable but is generally eleven to sixteen inches per annum at an elevation of 6,000–7,000 feet, with about 150 (or less) frost-free days. It takes about 120 days of optimum temperatures (above 40° F) to grow a corn crop. To survive in this semiarid climate on the edge of the Colorado Plateau, the inhabitants had to be able to read and interpret all the seasonal, cyclical variables. The A:shiwi developed their awareness of the climate by observation of the movements of the Sun and the Moon and the timely supplication of the gods. Time for Planting, Time for Harvest, and Time for Thanksgiving were the critical elements.

Before contact with Europeans, the A:shiwi had developed a very complex religious system that is still observed through elaborate ceremonial cycles. All of Zuni life, from birth until death, revolves around rituals, ceremonies, special observations, and crises of transition from one age or status to another—all for the good of the individual, the tribe, and the world. The A:shiwi believe that all people carry within them their own personal life-road (/onnane). The life-way, also known as the breath-way, is "kept" by the spirit beings who watch over our life-roads (ho/ne a:wona:williap/ona). Personal conduct in this life assures a smooth and long road, that is, a long and healthy life. Elders say, "There is but one joyous life; love each other." That enjoyment of life is achieved through active participation in various rituals and ceremonies provided by the Zuni socioreligious system. By making appropriate offerings at the appointed times, humans appease and supplicate the spirit beings who keep our roads.

The socioreligious system is composed of four separate but interrelated and interlocking systems; each operates independently and synchronically to provide for the physical and psychological needs of the users. Superimposed one upon the other are fourteen matrilineal clans, six men's groups (kivas), ten curing societies, and the Rain Priest and Bow Priest. Around these four interlocking systems moves the annual religious and ceremonial calendar that holds the entire socioreligious system together. The coordination of the annual calendar was the responsibility of the *pequinne*, the Sun Priest. The position has been vacant for over fifty years, because it is exceedingly time-consuming and the physical demands are very strenuous. It is now the responsibility of the House Chief, the Rain Priest of the north. As in most agricultural societies, the winter and summer solstices are the most ritually significant. During these two periods everyone in the community participates in some way in the numerous religious activities.

The preceding are highlights of the A:shiwi *a:wan tewusu* (the Zuni religion) and ritual systems that are active today. Paralleling the ceremonial and religious calendar are individual actions that assure the person a long life. The A:shiwi believe that if they participate in these group events they are being good Zunis and are adding to their life-road. Zuni religion is not limited to special times or places. It encompasses life everyday, everywhere, not only on Sunday. The basic offering to the spirit beings includes food, tobacco, and prayer meal, a coarsely ground white corn meal with crushed sea shells and turquoise. Prayer sticks or prayer feathers are offered on special occasions.

Patterns of Bird and Feather Usage

The Zuni reservation, established by executive order in 1877, lies along the Arizona-New Mexico border in McKinley and Valencia Counties. In general this area embraces the region drained by the Zuni River and lesser tributaries of the Little Colorado River. The vegetation of the region follows the main topographical features and is representative of the Upper Sonoran and Transitional ecological life zones.

The southwestern portion of the Zuni basin, about 5,000 feet above sea level, sustains only meager stands of sagebrush, rabbit brush, yucca, small cacti, and occasionally, along underground watercourses, cottonwoods and willows. The mesa country and foothills of the plateau, at about 6,000 feet, harbor large stands of juniper, piñon, and a variety of woody shrubs; along the north-facing canyon walls, a mixture of piñon, juniper, oak, and western yellow pine form the cover. In the upper elevations, above 6,000 feet, at the northeast end of the reservation and along the western slopes of the Zuni mountains, can be found large stands of western yellow pine, spruce, oak, and occasionally aspen. Throughout this whole range occurs a variety of bird life, both resident and migratory, typical of the Upper Sonoran and Transitional life zones.

Zuni men (because women do not hunt) at a very early age must learn to recognize all the various species of birds that are reserved for specific usage so that they may "gift" the appropriate species to the right elders when taken; they must also know which are taboo for other reasons.

There are seventy-three bird species that migrate through or are residents of the Upper Sonoran life zone in the Zuni reservation. Of these, sixty-six are used by the Zuni; three are taboo and sixteen are reserved for special usage by specific religious elders (see appendix). Birds were never a major part of Zuni diet although in the past 100 years certain small birds were eaten, not as a main course but as a delicacy. The Horned Lark at one time was taken in large numbers in the fall and roasted over hot coals. Other birds that were eaten include robin, sparrow, and jay. Only in the past fifty years have turkey and ducks became a part of the regular diet.

The general patterns of bird and feather usage among the Zuni extend throughout a wide range of rituals and ceremonies.[2] The feathers of exotic or introduced birds such as macaw, peacock, pheasant, guinea hen, and domestic chickens may decorate masks or other paraphernalia but are not

Feather case

A feather case was the personal property of a Pueblo man, who stored his feathers in it until he needed them to make prayer sticks.

HOPI, ARIZONA, COLLECTED 1904
CMNH 3165-233

used in ritual offerings (prayer sticks) only because they are not native species and thus were not traditionally used. Native species such as raven, crow, owl, and Turkey Vulture are not used because they are carrion eaters and associated with winter, but, like the exotic species, their feathers may appear as mask decorations. Birds such as the Horned Lark, dove, quail, Pinyon Jay, Rock Wren, House Sparrow, House Finch, junco, and gnatcatcher are not used ritually because they are winter birds and have other, associated taboos. Many of the dance masks, however, are decorated with large ruffs made from raven, crow, and vulture feathers. It takes fifteen to twenty birds to make one ruff. A mask decorated with owl feathers requires two or three birds. Bones from these three species are the most commonly found bones in archaeological sites in the Pueblo region, in addition to the turkey, which was domesticated by the Pueblos in prehistoric times.

Depending on the individual's religious position in the community, he or she must "plant" ritual offerings (prayer sticks) from four to twenty times a year, using from sixteen to eighty prayer sticks. Everyone participates during the summer and winter solstices, when offerings are made to the Sun (male) and the Moon (female). Others must plant prayer sticks monthly: all members of the curing societies, the Rain Priest, Sun Priest, Bow Priest, and *sha/lak/o:kwe* (council of the gods). Throughout the series of monthly, biannual, and annual offerings, the prayer sticks for the ancestors *(/a:lhashina:we)* and the masked gods *(kokko:que)* predominate.

The initiated male members of each household construct all prayer sticks. The summer and winter solstices are the two principal occasions on which the "poor," those individuals who have no religious position, participate. At these times the elder of the household, with the assistance of the younger initiated males, make the prayer sticks for the family, including any children who may be living elsewhere and those who have been ceremonially adopted. The prayer sticks are generally constructed the day before the offerings are to be made, but never at night because the night is for the night people, the dead.

To start the construction process the appropriate number and kind of feathers for each member of the household for whom the prayer sticks are being made are laid out in their proper order. The first must be a turkey feather, the second an eagle feather, the third position must be a duck feather; these three positions on the stick are fixed by tradition.

CLOCKWISE FROM UPPER LEFT:

Figure 1. Prayer stick for *kokko* with pendant series. Feathers are from the following birds: (from top right) turkey, eagle, duck, jay, nighthawk, Yellow Warbler, duck contour feather in reverse position; (pendant series) same feathers in reverse order.

Figure 2. Prayer stick for *kokko* without pendant series. Feathers are from the following birds: (from right) turkey, eagle, duck, jay, Red-shafted Flicker, robin, duck contour feather in reverse position.

Figure 3. Prayer stick for ancestors with pendant series. Feathers are from the following birds: (from top right) turkey, eagle, duck, jay, American

Kestrel, Red-shafted Flicker, bluebird; (pendant series) same feathers in reverse order.

Figure 4. Prayer stick for ancestors without pendant series. Feathers are from the following birds: (from right) turkey, eagle, duck, jay, robin, sparrow, bluebird.

Figure 5. Prayer stick for Sun. Feathers are from the following birds: (from right) eagle, duck, jay, American Kestrel, tanager, Yellow Warbler.

Figure 6. Prayer stick for the Moon. Feathers are from the following birds: (from right) eagle, duck, jay, nighthawk, Red-shafted Flicker, bluebird.

After the duck feather come any number of the summer birds: Red-shafted Flicker, jay, nighthawk, warbler, and/or bluebird. The usual number is four or six of the summer birds, depending on what is available in the feather box.

For each adult female there are two turkey feathers for the ancestors, one downy feather from a turkey for the pendant series (the feathers attached by a cord to the main prayer stick, called a *la/sho wan ne*, with the same number and kind of feathers as on the main portion of the prayer stick), and a downy feather from an eagle for the Moon. For the initiated males there are generally four turkey feathers: two for the ancestors, one with the pendant series and two for the *kokko*, one with pendant series. Regardless of the number of feathers in the erect and pendant series, the prayer stick for the *kokko* is identified by the last feather in each series—a contour duck feather (body feather) facing backward. A downy feather from an eagle in the first position for the Sun completes the set. For all other members of the family, male and female, there are two turkey feathers with or without pendant series for the ancestors. (See figures 1–6 on page 125.) A man with wife, one daughter, a son, and a ceremonially adopted child must provide seventeen prayer sticks for the summer solstice and seventeen for the winter solstice. These thirty-four prayer sticks require a maximum of 350 or a minimum of 250 feathers annually, not counting the monthly offerings for members of the esoteric societies, the winter dance series, or those offerings made when a family member dies.

When all the feathers have been tied, the sticks are painted. Those for the *kokko* and the ancestors are painted black with *ja/k/wi-na*, or pyrolurite, a hydrate oxide of manganese; those for the Sun are painted yellow with *je:lhup z/iqua* or limonite, hydrated oxide of iron, sometimes called yellow ocher; and those for the Moon are painted blue, using two pigments, */aqualhi* (malachite) and *ma:lhaya:luk/o* (azurite). The number and kinds of feather, after the turkey, eagle, and duck, are not fixed. It depends entirely on the individual and the feathers available. Only the first two (downy eagle and duck) for the Sun and the Moon, and the first three (turkey, eagle, and duck) for the *kokko* and ancestors are required.

The prayer sticks are gifts to the ancestors, the *kokko*, the Sun, and the Moon. They are deposited in the cornfield, with prayers, and are allowed to disintegrate into the earth, thereby being received into the afterworld to honor the ancestors and the spirit beings.

Hunting Methods

In prehistoric times, the Zuni probably hunted birds with many different kinds of snares and traps made from local materials. Although many of these techniques have been forgotten, some are still remembered and occasionally used. With the introduction of small firearms and the use of the slingshot, all the older snaring methods will soon be completely abandoned, especially since the younger boys who kept the feather boxes supplied in the past think them old-fashioned and degrading. At present, young boys use the slingshot, especially during the summer months, for hunting small birds; the older men use a .22 caliber rifle, although they may also use one or another of the snares discussed below. Large birds such as owls, hawks, ravens, crows, and eagles are sometimes hunted with steel traps or rifles or by collecting road kills. Macaws, once traded from Mexico, and eagles, once captured and kept for their feathers, have now been abandoned. The last captive macaw was given to the Sun Priest in the 1920s. It spoke Zuni and knew the names of a dozen or so individuals.

Zuni eagle cage, 1879

Zunis captured young eagles and raised them to maturity for their feathers.

The methods of snaring all involved an intimate knowledge of the habitat and feeding behavior of each bird, for which specific snares were designed. These fall into the four general types described below. All, however, utilized the same basic principle and differed only in method of construction and materials used.

Snare for Field Birds: sho/shu/wanne (notched reed type)

This is the most complex of the four types of snares (see figure 7). The base is made from a dry sunflower stalk, one to one-and-a-half inches in diameter, ten to eighteen inches long, cut square at both ends. One end is prepared by slicing the tip off at a $45°$ angle, leaving about a half inch of the square-cut surface. A hole one-half to one inch in diameter is made two to three inches below the square-cut surface (front). All the pith is removed to just below the hole in the front. The snare is ready to be assembled.

The snare is made of several strands of twisted horsehair. An anchor stone, one-half to one pound in weight, is attached

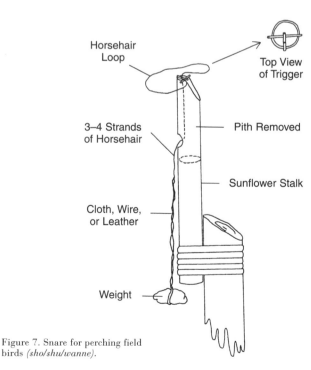

Figure 7. Snare for perching field birds *(sho/shu/wanne)*.

to one end of the twisted horsehair with a strip of cloth, wire, or leather. A slender stick, about three-quarters of an inch long, which will serve as the trigger, is wrapped or tied, about eight inches from the free end of the horsehair strands, which are then fashioned into a sliding noose. The trap is ready to be set.

To set the snare, the base is securely strapped to a post near an open field. The snare extends above the pole. Once the base is secured, the horsehair noose is threaded through the small hole in the front and pulled through the top. To trigger the snare a small stick is balanced on the square-cut edges of the open end; the noose end of the snare, with the stone weight, is gently lowered so that the small stick tied to the horsehair is balanced on the small cross stick and the square-cut surface of the base. The noose is arranged directly over the hole and the snare is set. When a bird lands on the snare, the small stick springs the trap, the weight at the bottom pulls the sliding noose around the bird's feet, and the bird is captured.

Snare for Bush-feeding Birds: ja/tepowanne (bundle of weeds)

This snare is constructed in a stand of sunflowers or willows along the banks of a stream or near a spring (see figure 8). The stems of several plants are tied together or bundled. Two bundles are then looped over at the top forming an arch. Starting from the top and about eight inches apart, four or six sticks are placed across the opening formed by

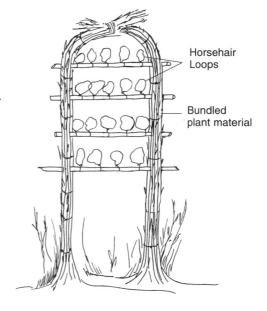

Horsehair Loops

Bundled plant material

Figure 8. Snare for brush-feeding birds (ja/tepowanne).

the arch. Horsehair strands, two to three inches apart, are tied to the crossbars and formed into sliding loops. In this method the bird is snared in two ways; as it perches on the bar, or as it tries to fly through the crossbars.

Snare for Water-feeding Birds: pi/tonne (snare or trap)

This snare is specifically designed for use at ponds or water holes (see figure 9). Brush is placed along one or both sides of the pond to force the birds to take a defined path. Long strands of horsehair are placed across the path at various intervals, like landing cables on an aircraft carrier, anchored securely at each end with a daub of mud and bundle of rush. As the bird flies in to feed or drink, it becomes entangled in the horsehair, and the rush bundles, like the South American *bolas* used by gauchos to capture cows, prevent the bird from flying away. This method was used primarily for the Common Nighthawk, Violet-green Swallow, Cliff Swallow, Purple Martin, and White-throated Swift. It is suspected that larger birds like ducks and geese were also captured in this manner.

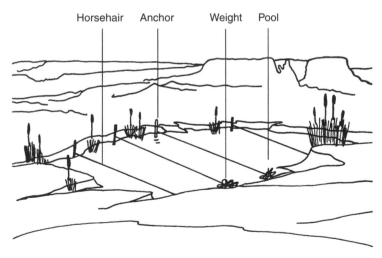

Figure 9. Snare for water-feeding birds *(pi/tonne)*.

Snare for Ground-feeding Birds: pi/tonne (snare or trap)

There are several variations of the snares made for hunting ground-feeding birds. These all employ an anchor of some sort to which is tied a sliding horsehair loop. It is buried in an area where birds feed, and seeds, chili, amaranth, or wheat is scattered on the ground to attract the birds. One type (figure 10) features horsehair loops tied to a hoop made from willow or juniper; in a variation of this type, the loops are tied to stones (/apalonne) (figure 11). A snare for birds that come to drink at springs or along stream banks consists of horsehair loops tied to a small stick which is placed at the edge of

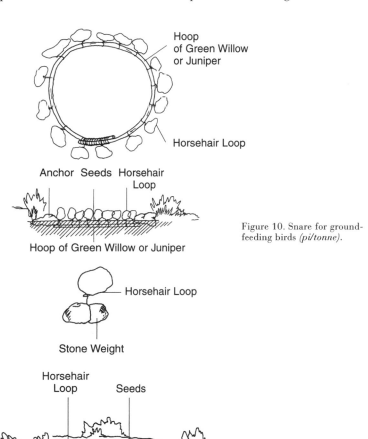

Figure 10. Snare for ground-feeding birds *(pi/tonne)*.

Figure 11. Snare for ground-feeding birds *(/apalonne)*.

the stream or spring, weighted down at both ends. When the bird perches on the stick to drink it gets entangled in the sliding loops (figure 12).

Figure 12. Snare used at ponds and springs *(pi/tonne)*.

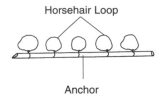

Special Snares

A snare designed specifically to capture the Violet-green Swallow, Purple Martin and White-throated Swift features a small bundle of cotton to which are tied horsehair loops. It may be anchored with a strand of cloth to a small stone, to a pole near a cliff, or even thrown over the cliff. The bird is attracted by the cotton, tries to snag it, and gets tangled in the horsehair loops. (See figures 13–15.)

Figure 13. Snare for swallows and martins *(pi/tonne)*.

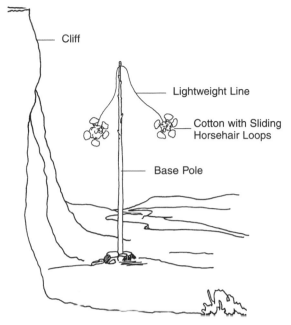

Cliff

Lightweight Line

Cotton with Sliding Horsehair Loops

Base Pole

Figure 14. Snare specific for swallows *(pi/tonne)*.

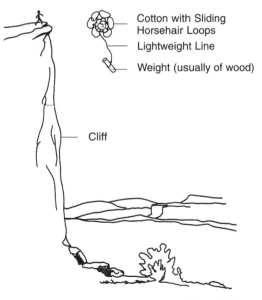

Cotton with Sliding Horsehair Loops

Lightweight Line

Weight (usually of wood)

Cliff

Figure 15. Snare specific for cliff swallows *(pi/tonne)*.

Another species-specific snare is the one used to capture hummingbirds (figure 16). Selecting a good stand of rocky mountain beeplant, the hunter ties horsehair loops to the blossoms. The birds become entangled and are captured.

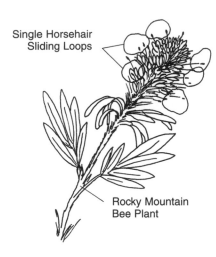

Single Horsehair
Sliding Loops

Rocky Mountain
Bee Plant

Figure 16. Snare specific for hummingbirds *(pi/tonne)*.

Conclusion

Objects made for ritual and ceremonial use by the A:shiwi were never meant to be preserved, replicated for exhibition, or collected for other uses. These offerings are made to the spirit beings, the ancestors, in the belief that they will be received in the afterworld only by disintegrating into the earth and air. In this way they benefit the individual and the world and provide spiritual protection, abundant rain, snow, good harvest, and, most especially, "a long and healthy road." To preserve these objects in museum collections is very insensitive to A:shiwi spiritual beliefs.

Appendix: Scientific and Zuni Names of Birds

Abert's Towhee, *Pipilo aberti*, k/ewiya
American Coot, *Fulica americana*, ji:lu/k/i
American Crow, *Corvus brachyrhynchos*, q/alashi
American Kestrel, *Falco sparverius*, zililik/o
American Robin, *Turdus migratorius* (Mearns),
    qi:sha/japak/o
Ash-throated Flycatcher, *Myiarchus cinerascens*,
    /iz/u:wakka k/at/ajjon/ona
Bald Eagle, *Haliaeetus leucocephalus*, pa/k/oja
Black-billed Magpie, *Pica pica*, k/ate tasha
Black-headed Grosbeak, *Pheucticus melanocephalus*, /onoj
    lhi/ka shi ga:nan
Blue-gray Gnatcatcher, *Polioptila caerulea*, pa:cha/le

Brewer's Blackbird, *Euphagus cyanocephalus*, k/echcho

Broad-tailed Hummingbird, *Selasphorus platycercus*, z/uyya

Brown-headed Cowbird, *Molothrus ater*, /oto:lhana

Bullock's Oriole, *Icterus bullockii*, /onoj lhi/ka

Burrowing Owl, *Athene cunicularia*, ju:z/uk/i

Canada Goose, *Branta canadensis*, /owa

Canyon Towhee (Brown Towhee), *Pipilo fusus*, k/ewiya

Canyon Wren, *Catharpes mexicanus*, jala: wisho/

Cassin's Kingbird, *Tyrannus vociferans*, /iz/u:wakka
    lhan/ona

Cliff Swallow, *Petrochelidon pyrrhonota*, k/apchik/o

Common Nighthawk, *Chordeiles minor*, /awati:lhana

Common Raven, *Corvus corax*, k/otolo//a

Cooper's Hawk, *Accipiter cooperii*, /ane lha:wa

Dark-eyed Junco, *Junco hyemalis*, zu/piya

Downy Woodpecker, *Picoides pubescens*, tamtununu

Golden Eagle, *Aquila chrysaetos*, poshqa

Grasshopper Sparrow, *Ammodramus savannarum*, z/uz/u/a

Greater Roadrunner, *Geococcyx californianus*, poyyi

Great Horned Owl, *Bubo virginianus*, mujuqui

Green-tailed Towhee, *Pipilo chlorurus*, k/ewiya

Hairy Woodpecker, *Picoides villosus*, tamtununu

Horned Lark, *Eremophila alpestris*, silo

House Finch, *Carpodacus mexicanus*, tanaya:wiwish ka

House Sparrow, *Passer domesticus*, wi/wish ka

Killdeer, *Charadrius vociferus*, tolo:wa

Lark Sparrow, *Chondestes grammacus strigatus*
    (Swainson), k/ata:k/oja/qa

Lazuli Bunting, *Passerina amoena*, /onoj lhi/ka lhi/anna

Lesser Goldfinch, *Carduelis psaltria* (Say), piz/iz/i

Lewis' Woodpecker, *Melanerpes lewis*, joquisho q/inna

Loggerhead Shrike, *Lanius ludovicianus*, su:lulu/ka

Macaw, *Ara* sp., mula

Mallard, *Anas platyrhynchos*, /eya

Mountain Bluebird, *Sialia currucoides*, ma:lhya/luk/o

Mourning Dove, *Zenaida macroura*, ni:shapak/o

Northern Harrier, *Circus cyaneus*, shok/apiso

Northern Mockingbird, *Mimus polyglottos*, k/ay cho/wa

Northern Rough-winged Swallow, *Stelgidopteryx serripen-
    nis*, jeyalo:seto

Pinyon Jay, *Gymnorhinus cyanocephalus*, /a/akka
Purple Martin, *Progne subis*, k/awulok/i
Red-shafted Flicker, *Colaptes auratus*, joquisho
Red-tailed Hawk, *Buteo borealis*, pippe
Red-winged Blackbird, *Agelaius phoeniceus*,
    k/echocho/chuti:shilowa
Rock Wren, *Salpinctes obsoletus*, z/ili:sho
Sage Thrasher, *Oreoscoptes montanus*, tashisho
Sandhill Crane, *Grus canadensis*, k/o:lokta
Say's Phoebe, *Sayornis saya*, /iz/u:wakka z/an/ona
Scaled Quail, *Callipepla squamata*, /ush a
Sharp-shinned Hawk, *Accipiter striatus*, jachuz/ana
Spotted Towhee, *Pipilo maculatus*, k/ewiya
Steller's Jay, *Cyanocitta stelleri*, maya
Townsend's Solitaire, *Myadestes townsendi*, su:pa
Turkey Vulture, *Cathartes aura*, shu/zina
Violet-green Swallow, *Tachycineta thalassina*,
    /awi/sho:seto
Western Bluebird, *Sialia mexicana*, lhayaluk/o
Western Meadowlark, *Sturnella neglecta*, ta/chilhchi
Western Scrub Jay (Woodhouse's Scrub-Jay), *Aphelocoma
    californica*, chaya//a
Western Tanager, *Piranga ludoviciana*, /onoj lhi/ka
White-breasted Nuthatch, *Sitta carolinensis*, no/tek to lha/
    paniyle:n /ona
White-crowned Sparrow, *Zonotrichia leucophrys*, z/uz/u/a
White-throated Swift, *Aeronautes saxatalis*, /aqasukta
Wild Turkey, *Meleagris gallopavo*, tona
Yellow-headed Blackbird, *Xanthocephalus xanthocephalus*,
    pala/tu
Yellow Warbler, *Dendroica aestiva*, z/appa

Notes

This outline of the modern ethno-ornithology of the A:shiwi (Zuni), with brief descriptions of ceremonial and ritual usage of avifaunal material, is based in part on my master's thesis, "Zuni Ethno-Ornithology," from the University of New Mexico, 1963. Except for the few minor references to other sources, this material is based entirely on my own personal knowledge as a member of the A:shiwi (a kiva and clan member). The information presented is common knowledge and is not secret. I take full responsibility for the contents herein.

1. These are not to be confused with living tribal people. They are names given by archaeologists to the ancestors of the Pueblo people; it is not known what they called themselves or what languages they spoke.

2. I use the term *ceremonial* to mean those group events that are public in nature, such as the "plaza dances," and the term *ritual* to mean those community events in which individual members prepare and give offerings to the spirit beings, such as the community prayer stick "planting" at the winter and summer solstices.

Recommended Readings

Ferguson, T. J., and E. Richard Hart. *The Zuni Atlas.* Norman: University of Oklahoma Press, 1985.

Crampton, C. Gregory. *The Zunis of Cibola.* Salt Lake City: University of Utah Press, 1977.

Ortiz, Alfonso, ed. *Handbook of North American Indians, Southwest,* vol. 9. Washington D.C.: Smithsonian Institution, 1979.

Stevenson, Matilda Coxe. *The Zuni Indians.* Twenty-third Annual Report of the Bureau of American Ethnology. Washington D.C.: Smithsonian Institution, 1904.

Tyler, Hamilton A. *Pueblo Birds and Myths.* Norman: University of Oklahoma Press, 1991.

8

Ecology, Conservation, and the Buffalo Jump

SHEPARD KRECH III

FOR THOUSANDS OF YEARS, the Piegans and their predecessors used a particular cliff in southern Alberta for a buffalo jump.1 Today the cliff falls away abruptly for thirty-five or forty feet to the top of a thirty-foot thick deposit of bone and soil that attests to past successes. Called Head-Smashed-In Buffalo Jump—a boy's, not a buffalo's, head was crushed here—Unesco selected it in 1981 as a World Heritage Site. An interpretive center was built with the stated aim of presenting a Native rather than anthropological or archaeological perspective. As reported by the New York Times, it offers "much to ponder," including "the skills" of Native people who cooperated to drive buffalo toward a precipice and death and "the wastefulness" of White hunters who caused the extermination of 60 million bison. Others agree. In *American History Illustrated*, one can read that Head-Smashed-In Buffalo Jump is "representative of the North Americans' ingenuity, of their understanding of ecological balances, and of their economical use of the land and its bounty." This is the rhetoric of buffalo hunting on the Plains: White men wasted and exterminated the buffalo whereas Indians were skillful, ecologically aware

Head-Smashed-In Buffalo Jump in Alberta, Canada

The practice of driving buffalo over this cliff was continued intermittently at this site until the introduction of the horse and gun.

conservationists. Hundreds of thousands of people have heard this message at Head-Smashed-In Buffalo Jump alone. But this story about conservation and waste is more complicated, as stories often are.[2]

No one really knows how many buffalo there once were. Asked in the late nineteenth century how many there had been, one Plains Indian signed, "The country was one robe."[3] But it was too late—the buffalo hunt was over—and the magnitude even then too difficult to grasp, although that Native American framed his attempt revealingly in the metaphor of economy not natural history. In the sixteenth century, the buffalo was spread virtually across the continent; but by the nineteenth century, eradicated in many parts of its range, it was confined to the western plains and prairies. Eighteenth-century traders and surveyors spoke of "millions" in sight, and as late as 1871, "an immense herd" stretching for twenty-five miles was observed.[4] For over 200 years, the language of buffalo herds was cast in phrases like "countless thousands" and "dense masses." When Europeans arrived there may have been from 30 to 100 million buffalo in North America, but greater precision seems elusive.[5]

Today, all agree that the near-extinction of the buffalo is one of the grimmest narratives in the history of wildlife. The causes have been debated, with both Native Americans and White men implicated. It is a complicated business to estimate the numbers of Indians and buffalo at any single moment, or of the kill itself. The Indian impact was affected by a preference for cows for meat and hides for domestic use, and by horse herds that increased greatly through time to compete with buffalo for grasses.[6]

But no matter how sharp the Native demand, new markets and means of transportation doomed the animal: the rapidly expanding population of European-Americans with boundless appetite for meat; expansive new commodities markets for tongues, skins, and robes; and, finally, railroads that pushed into the heart of buffalo territory to transport buffalo meat and hides to markets elsewhere. In the eighteenth century, the exploitation of the buffalo was fueled by developing European-American demand for meat, tongues, and hides. By 1800 all Plains Indians had been affected by European presence. By that year, smallpox and other epidemic diseases had assaulted all. By then, most Plains people had acquired the two major European goods, the horse and the gun, and were participating in an exchange of buffalo products for European goods and horses, often through middlemen who were other Indians. Some had a large stake in maintaining the relations and level of exchange that guaranteed a constant flow of horses and renewal of Europeanized technology. In the nineteenth century, almost all were caught up intensely in the exchange of furs or buffalo products for European-manufactured goods. Jockeying for power against each other; deciding what course of action to take against greater numbers of White people as well as Eastern Indians pouring into and through their lands to trade, trap, and live; reacting to governmental demands for economic and political concessions: the nineteenth-century political and military scene was fluid, opportunistic, and violent.

Buffalo tongues and meat were universally commodified during this century, and the increased intensity of the hunt took a toll on many herds. The final stage, from 1867 to 1884, was remarkable for its fury. In 1867, the first of five railroads punched into and through the heart of buffalo range to split the population forever into northern and southern herds, and to splinter these herds again and again. Demand increased both for buffalo meat during construction and for buffalo-hunting sport afterward. Pressure of a different kind came from cattle claiming buffalo range in Kansas, Texas, and elsewhere, and from farmers craving tall-grass prairie. But these pressures paled beside those generated by the railroads which made buffalo hides a cheap alternative to cowhides, and by the subsequent international demand for skins to tan for leather products, including belting for machinery. Hunters flooded in; unskilled, they wasted three to five times the numbers they killed. The carnage defied description. Native American complaints about White hunters fell on deaf ears; their guardians in the Department of the Interior linked the disappearance of the buffalo to civilizing and eventual assimilation of the Indian. From 1871 to 1883, four million hides may have been taken, with each hide representing at first five dead. From 1871 to 1878 the southern herd was hunted to extinction, and by 1883 the northern herd was exterminated. The commercial hunt was finished. Indians, confined to reservations and distressed from hunger, took part until the bitter end. If Red Cloud actually said what has been attributed to him, he may not have been far off the mark: "Where the Indian killed one buffalo, the hide and tongue hunters killed fifty."[7]

In the end, their bones were left. Buffalo bones littered the prairies so thickly that in places it was impossible to walk without rattling against their skeletons. Over the course of several years, hundreds of entrepreneurial "bone pickers" took them all away. They vacuumed the prairies. The bones, it was discovered, were a useful carbon filtering agent in sugar refining and, crushed, valuable as phosphate fertilizer. Enormous rectangular mounds of bones lined the tracks, and mountainous piles stretched to the sky at carbon works where they were processed. From 1872 to 1874, 11 million pounds of bones went east on the railroads, and the departure by boxcar from Saskatoon in 1890 of bones of 200,000 buffalo marked the end of most traces of the wild buffalo. From then on, remnant herds sought refuge in Yellowstone National Park, were nurtured for travel with Buffalo Bill Cody, or

Rope, brush, pail, bladder bags, and horn ladle

Every part of the buffalo was used. Plains people made ropes from twisted strands of hair taken from the buffalo's forehead and braided tightly together. They made ladles and other implements from the horns and sweat-house brushes from strips of rawhide taken from the buffalo's shoulder, where the hair is longest. Quillworkers stored their dyed porcupine quills in the bladder because the sharp points of the quills could not penetrate its walls. Even the scrotum was turned into a pail used to carry liquids. After the buffalo disappeared, parts of cattle were substituted whenever possible, as was the case with the pail shown here.

ROPE AND BRUSH: CROW, CA. 1880
CMNH 2418-104, 2418-146

PAIL: ARAPAHO, COLLECTED 1903
CMNH 3179-233

BLADDER BAGS: PLAINS, CA. 1880
CMNH 35752-99 a & b, GIFT OF BENJAMIN D.
BERNSTEIN IN MEMORY OF EVELYN GLAUSER BERNSTEIN

LADLE: LAKOTA, COLLECTED CA. 1890
CMNH 1171-106

were privatized and crossed with cattle for a domestic meat market. The Buffalo Era had come to an end.[8]

In this story, the role of market hunters is undisputed. They exploited the commons—a resource owned by no one powerful enough to stop them from taking too many. There was neither will on the part of government nor might on the part of Indians or Whites appalled at the slaughter to halt it. These hunters, who were responding to market forces international in scope, occupy a special place in lists of agents of destruction. But neither they nor market forces are at issue here. What is, in part, is the role and antiquity of conservation in Plains Indian communal hunting.

The buffalo, as many have remarked, was the mainstay of Plains Indians, who killed them in large numbers both for domestic use and to exchange for corn produced by village-dwelling Indians. It was of paramount importance in economy and subsistence. "Principal" or "real" food, the buffalo was lauded while other foods, especially fish, were denigrated and scorned (one exception being the corn that was grown and valued by agricultural people). People ate with considerable relish an incredible variety of buffalo parts: meat, fat, most organs, testicles, nose gristle, nipples, blood, milk, marrow, and fetus. They dried, roasted, and boiled the meat, and ate it raw; they pounded bones to make bone grease; and they mixed dry, pounded meat with fat to make pemmican. For people like the Blackfeet, the buffalo provided over 100 specific items of material culture, many related to the possession of horses and thus to the coming of Europeans. Exclude them and the list remains impressive and must be quite ancient: robes (hair on) for bedding, gloves, winter clothing, ceremonial and decoy costumes; hides (hair off) for tipi covers and linings, cups, parfleches, moccasins, leggings and other clothing, kettles, shields, and maul covers; hair for stuffing and ropes; sinew for thread, bowstrings, and snowshoe webbing; ribs to straighten arrows; the paunch and large intestine to make containers; gall stones for yellow pigment; hoofs for rattles or glue; tibia and other bones for fleshers, brushes, awls, and other tools; horns for arrow points, bow parts, ladles, cups, spoons, or tobacco and medicine containers; brains to soften skins; fat as a paint base or to polish stone; the penis for glue; dung as fuel; and teeth as ornaments. From a purely material standpoint, it would have been virtually impossible to be out of sight, touch, or smell of a buffalo product at any time of day or night. The buffalo was "a tribal department store," as Tom McHugh has said, a "builder's emporium, furniture mart, drugstore, and supermarket rolled into one."[9]

Given the buffalo's importance, it is no surprise that Plains Indians developed highly efficient hunting techniques. Some were solitary and others communal. All people, it seems, knew some form of solitary hunting.[10] Getting close to buffalo may not have been as difficult as in the days when the press of constant hunting made herds skittish. Many men of European extraction thought buffalo "stupid," but they might have said that they relied on the herd for security and that bulls often seemed fearless and stolid in their strength relative to all save man. At times buffalo were virtually unmovable. On his voyage across the continent in 1804–1806, Meriwether Lewis remarked that they were "extremely gentle the bull buffaloe particularly will scarcely give way to you." On one stretch, Lewis reported, "the men frequently throw sticks and stones at them in order to drive them out of the way." Buffalo possess an acute sense of smell and sharp hearing (their sight has been depicted as both weak and keen), and spooked easily if dangerous scent were upwind. But Indians and Whites alike discovered that so long as wind direction was taken into account, buffalo were rather easily killed.[11]

Opportunistic communal techniques, like running the animals onto soft ice, into deep snow, off a ledge, or into a ravine or box canyon, were widespread. Some people surrounded a herd on foot by waving robes. Others used fire to encircle herds. Still others lured or drove buffalo to their doom over the edges of cliffs or into enclosures called pounds—two especially common techniques on the central and northern plains in fall and winter. Crow Indians called guiding and urging buffalo to a tumbling and jumping death over precipices, "driving buffalo over embankments." These techniques resulted in resources shared throughout the community, and when not completely opportunistic they were preceded by pragmatic policing, which was necessary to prevent individual hunters from premature action spoiling chances of communal success, and by ritual.

Ritual was often important for the success of the planned hunt, marking the entire effort from beginning to end. Powerful medicine bundles, sweetgrass offerings, tobacco pipes, stones with the power to charm in zoomorphic or other shapes, esoteric knowledge, and songs sung to buffalo: each people had their own way, but collectively brought all to bear to ensure success. Smoking tobacco and offering the pipe to propitiate whomever had power to ensure success were common. Failure in the hunt, if not due to an impetuous hunter spoiling it for others, was easily ascribed to improperly performed ritual.[12] For Assiniboines and others, the center of the circular enclosure was ritual space where a sacrificial pole was erected. From it offerings like scarlet cloth or utensils were suspended, and red painted buffalo skulls might be placed nearby.[13] According to John McDonnell, a North West Company trader, Assiniboines in the 1790s offered a pipe to an old bull in a pen and said something like, "My Grandfather, we are glad to see you, and happy to find that you are not come to us in a shameful manner, for you have brought plenty of your young men with you. Be not angry at us; we are obliged to destroy you to make ourselves live."[14]

Certain men were imbued with special power or knowledge, perhaps because they knew how to lure buffalo into the trap by imitating the actions and call of a calf or adult buffalo, relying on the animals' curiosity and poor sight, as well as on their own camouflage under the skin and head of a buffalo. The elder Alexander Henry said of Assiniboines dressed in buffalo robes with horns attached that "their gestures so closely resembled" the animals that "had I not been in the secret I should have been as much deceived" as the buffalo.[15] The "chaser" or "runner"—"He-Who-Brings-Them-In," Assiniboines called him—trolled buffalo toward their demise, funneling them into a narrowing V-shaped lane whose lines were defined by stacked buffalo chips, stone piles, or implanted trees. Men and women crouched behind these brakes, ready to jump up, wave robes, and yell and startle the animals into a panicked run toward the trap or cliff edge.

The runner's task was demanding and dangerous, and he might have to jump into a cliff-edge hole at the last moment to avoid being swept over. No wonder he enjoyed respect.[16]

White men who witnessed the final stages after the buffalo had tumbled off a precipice or were trapped in a surround reacted strongly. Some culture-bound observers were affronted because the animals were not hunted and killed in the "proper" or "sporting" way.[17] Europeans who came to America for sport were a varied lot, some bemoaning the decline of the "noble" buffalo and others shooting hundreds merely for the killing. Yet it is not uncommon to read complaints against the "indiscriminate slaughter of cows" and suggestions that the only "legitimate" way to hunt buffalo was "by running them down and killing them at close quarters by a rifle or revolver-shot."[18] In a pound, many discovered their sensibilities assaulted by "maimed" and "mangled" animals—by their first experience of a slaughter house. Audubon spoke of "murdered" buffalo; George Catlin of sensitivities rudely shocked in a surround where the "noble" buffalo was "doomed"; the artist Paul Kane of killings "more painful than pleasing."[19]

Winter Meat

W. H. D. KOERNER, 1932
CMNH 35063-1, GIFT OF
MR. AND MRS. WILLIAM H.
D. KOERNER

It is true that buffalo which tumbled over a precipice were likely to break their legs or backs, if they were not killed outright by the fall. They and others driven into enclosures were shot with bows and arrows (later, with guns), stabbed with lances, or smacked on the heads with stone mauls. Peter Fidler, a Hudson's Bay Company surveyor, described the scene in a Piegan enclosure in 1792, after a chief killed the first animal: "The young Men kill the rest with arrows, Bayonets tyed upon the end of a Pole, &c. The hatchet is frequently used & it is shocking to see the poor animals thus pent up without any way of escaping, butchered in this shocking manner, some with the stroke of an axe will open nearly the whole side of a Buffalo & the poor animal runs some times a considerable while all thro' the Pound with all its internals dragging on the ground & trod out by the others, before they dye."[20]

By design or not, communal hunts sometimes produced fantastic quantities of meat. The Blackfeet called the enclosure at the base of a cliff *piskun*, which has been translated as "deep blood kettle."[21] Hunts surrounded or drove not merely dozens but sometimes hundreds of animals: 600, 800, 1,000, and 1,400 are estimates for particular hunts.[22] The average mature cow yielded from 225 to 400 pounds of meat, a bull at least 550 pounds. Even small numbers of animals produced prodigious weights—taking 600 animals, the smallest number, which seems the cautious tack, the yield was potentially 180,000 pounds of meat, and even just fifty cows would produce more than 15,000 pounds of usable meat. Perhaps knowledge that great quantities of meat were possible led Indians to gourmandize rather than to store or dry meat against future want, and to behavior that elicited from European observers disapproving remarks on "profligacy," "improvidence," and "indolence"; yet much was still dried or pounded into pemmican.[23]

Except for tongues, which were often given to the leader responsible for the pound or hunt, or to the "caller" who lured the animals on, meat was generally shared widely. The decision on how heavily to butcher animals depended on how much meat one had or expected, distance to camp, means of transportation, and so on. But given the quantities and weight sometimes involved, it may not be surprising that light butchering, or very light butchering like taking tongues and humps only, or tongues alone, was reported. Sometimes, meat was cached under skins or snow or left on ice, to be consumed days or weeks later.[24]

When buffalo were still numerous, Native Americans indulged their taste for cows and for the parts considered to be delicacies. Marrow, hump, and ribs were often mentioned as especially desirable. The tongue was greatly sought. In 1804, Charles MacKenzie, a trader for the North West Company, wrote that "large parties" of Gros Ventres were daily killing "whole herds" only for the tongues. The following year they took only "the best parts" home, leaving the rest "to rot in the field." In the month of February, according to Peter Fidler, the Piegan hunted buffalo for the fetus, of which they were "remarkably fond." He concluded that "The Greater part of the Cows the Indians now kill is merely for nothing else but for the calf."[25]

Many also noticed animals left untouched. The meat was wasted. The hides were wasted. Animals putrefied. The statements, which extend from the 1790s to the 1850s, are unequivocal. When he left one Piegan pound in 1792–1793, Peter Fidler remarked that it was "quite full laying 5 or 6 feet one on the other, all thro which in the whole was above 250 Buffalo." From it came "an intollerable stench of the great number of putrified carcasses."[26] One decade later, Meriwether Lewis saw "the remains of a vast many mangled carcases of Buffalow which had been driven over a precipice of 120 feet by the Indians and perished." The river currents, Lewis thought, had washed some animals away but "the fragments of at least a hundred carcases" remained.[27] Other reports could be cited—in 1805, Mandans killing "whole droves" of buffalo but taking only "the best parts of the meat" and leaving the rest "to rot in the field"; four years later, "mangled carcasses strewn about" a Blackfeet pound, with the "bulls . . . mostly entire" and "none but good cows having been cut up"; in 1840, "half-devoured carcasses" of buffalo in a Cree pound, "the spoils of previous captures"; and in 1857, a pound filled with buffalo and abandoned because of "the stench . . . from the putrefying bodies" of over 200 dead animals.[28]

These descriptions confirm a radical selection of favored parts, or outright waste of meat, hides, and sometimes the entire animal. One should not, however, assume that Native Americans always wasted buffalo. Nothing could be further from the truth. At times, some carried "every eatable part of the animal . . . to the camp" where all was "preserved."[29] Moreover, one should not too hastily conclude that animals left to putrefy were not eaten. As Audubon commented (and others confirmed), Indians ate drowned buffalo "no matter how putrid their flesh may be."[30] In winter, Charles MacKenzie wrote, Mandans drove "large herds" onto the weakest sections of ice on the Missouri, where they fell through and drowned but were recovered downstream and left to "take flavor." The Mandan preferred drowned buffalo over all other types of food, thought bottle-green soup made from the ripe meat of such animals "delicious," and were so fond of "putrid meat" that they buried animals all winter and ate them in spring.[31]

Since wasting is antithetical to conservation, Native Americans who forever abandoned entire animals or left whole parts untouched were not by definition conservation-ists—unless the definition is altered. But might their behavior have been produced by the European presence? Perhaps Indians who wasted at a pound or jump were themselves trapped by the insatiable demand of European-American markets for hides and tongues. Perhaps their behavior was not typical of Indians prior to the arrival of those markets. Indeed, all historical descriptions of communal hunting post-date the onset of the trade, and by the time they were written, Native Americans had changed their behavior in many ways. To obtain trade goods, many Plains people participated in the new markets for beaver pelts and buffalo hides, and observers like Audubon remarked that buffalo were impounded in fall months "when the hides are good and sal-able." Indians who wasted clearly also had in their possession goods of European manufacture. But the linkage between waste at communal hunting sites and the trade of buffalo for European commodities is far from explicit.[32]

Moreover, the archaeological record provides abundant evidence for the antiquity of communal hunting techniques—hunting, fortunately, has greater visibility than other forms of behavior—and helps determine how ancient waste might be. Archaeological sites throughout the Plains show that luring or driving buffalo into shifting sand dunes or bogs, against arroyo cutbanks, into rivers, or over cliffs are techniques that have been used to kill buffalo for over 11,000 years.[33] Sites were used repeatedly at different seasons (but especially in winter) over periods of time measuring in the hundreds and thousands of years.[34] Jump sites have particular interpretive problems stemming both from the intermingling of bones deposited in repeated incidents and from the commercial exploitation of bones; conclusions about any single episode are often problematic.[35]

One site that does not have these problems is Olsen-Chubbuck, located in southern Colorado. Olsen-Chubbuck records a single episode that took place eight millennia ago, its excavation has been well controlled, and it offers compelling evidence of the antiquity of butchering techniques. One day 8,500 years ago, it seems, hunters drove a herd of buffalo (of a species one-third larger than today's) over the bank of a dry gulch where almost 200, a mixed group of adults and juveniles, cows and bulls, perished. It probably happened in a flash and represented a purely opportunistic event. The buffalo in advance plunged head-first into the bottom of the arroyo, and others behind crashed into and over them. At Olsen-Chubbuck, skeletons are massed on twisted skeletons, wedged in massive piles against piles and against the steep banks of the narrow gulch. The butchering began, and piles of articulated segments grew: forelegs, pelvic girdles, spinal columns, skulls missing jawbones. Animals at the bottom of the arroyo were touched either not at all or barely. From the tongue bones scattered throughout the site, it seems that tongues were eaten as the butchering progressed. When it was over, three of every four buffalo had been completely butchered, and the others partly or not at all. Those on top were completely cut up, the ones beneath them were cut less thoroughly, and the ones on the bottom especially in the deepest parts of the arroyo, were left as they died. At least forty, or one of every four, were whole or nearly whole, essentially not used at all. Inaccessible because of the narrowness of the arroyo and violent nature of their deaths below others on top of them, and perhaps not needed, they were left as they died, where they rotted unused. The kill produced over

50,000 pounds of meat, enough to sustain 100 people with 100 dogs for a month and to dry half for future use.[36]

From Olsen-Chubbuck we discern the antiquity of waste in communal hunting. Indians who hunted buffalo at Olsen-Chubbuck evidently had as little interest in conservation as Indians in the eighteenth and nineteenth centuries. This conclusion may sit uncomfortably with many convinced by the contemporary rhetoric of the buffalo hunt. It presents a very different picture from late nineteenth- and twentieth-century Native accounts—memories of the communal hunt, or accounts of others' memories of it—that omit mention of waste while simultaneously stressing the sacrality of the hunt. Blackfeet Indians, for example, told George Bird Grinnell at the end of the nineteenth century that after butchering, an enclosure "was cleaned out, the heads, feet, and least perishable offal being removed," leaving only scraps for small scavenging animals and birds. In 1948, an Assiniboine remarked that enclosures were "sacred" and cleaned up. In the 1950s, a Blood Indian remarked that his mother and others told him that "everything was taken and the surplus meat was either dried or made into pemmican." And Joseph Epes Brown, whose work with Black Elk is well known, wrote recently that "considering how efficiently the Indians used the total animal [buffalo] in their diet and daily needs, it is understandable that they were so repulsed by the wasteful non-Indian hide hunters who often took no more than the tongue and hide."[37]

These accounts might not be "wrong," only ungeneralizable. The most recent ones lack direct knowledge of the days when buffalo were driven. Most important, perhaps, is that in their blanket denials of indigenous waste and quickness to contrast presumed Native with non-Native behavior, they all reflect genuine horror at the excesses of the final stages of the demise of the buffalo. But as historical evidence they must be used with caution, for embedded in them may well be understandings of conservation and ecology co-opted by a discourse in which native people are seen predominantly as existing in harmony with nature.

In days when buffalo were driven into enclosures and

over jumps, the most pressing daily practical problem to solve was to obtain and preserve meat within culturally defined canons of edibility, not to avoid wasting what one killed. A first priority of Plains people was to ensure that they had an adequate supply of the animal on which they were totally dependent. With tens (or hundreds) of thousands of buffalo within sight each year, there may have been no compelling reason to curb waste. Moreover, the communal hunt in general, and the jump in particular, could not easily be controlled; it could not, as others have said, be turned off and on like a switch. Even if one wished to control the number of animals killed, it might often have been impossible; Alexander Henry said of Blackfeet drives that "no effort of man suffices to arrest a herd in full career after the cow that leads them."[38]

But to suggest that there were no compelling reasons to conserve is to assume that Plains Indians somehow acted purely from more widely shared practical or rational premises. One might argue that it is mere common sense to kill without regard to conservation because there were so many buffalo, because they were the mainstay of the economy, or because a herd once moving was difficult to stop. Yet to focus only on practical or utilitarian premises runs the risk of ignoring cultural considerations which stem from Plains Indian belief systems, embedded in reason and common sense. Indigenous religious and ethnoecological or ethnoconservationist thought appropriate to specific historical moments have traditionally been excluded from the discourse on conservation and ecology for cases like the buffalo hunt, perhaps because it seems so inaccessible. But if revealed it can clearly inform our understanding of such cases. We must, therefore, try to "see" with the "Native eyes" of those who drove buffalo over jumps and into enclosures.[39]

Important as the buffalo was to daily existence, it is not surprising that it figured significantly in mythology and religious expression. Typically, however, religious and economic activities were not compartmentalized but interpenetrated one another. The degree to which religious belief was embedded in the hunt has already been mentioned, from the extensive ritual considered necessary to "call" the buffalo successfully, and the decorated pole and skulls at the center of the enclosure, to the prayer to the buffalo before the final killing, when they were addressed as sentient beings. It is also clear that attention was lavished on buffalo souls. In 1810, John Bradbury came upon fourteen buffalo skulls with artemisia in the eye sockets and nostril vents, that Arikaras had placed in a row on bluffs. He interpreted this as an "honour" to "the buffaloes which they had killed, in order to appease their spirits, and prevent them from apprising the living buffaloes of the danger they run in approaching the neighbourhood."[40]

Among the most widespread beliefs for Plains Indians were, first, that a force or power pervaded the universe and that when it came to reside in certain geophysical features, meteorological phenomena, spiritual essences, natural beings, and artifacts (or when it was considered in its totality), it made them what might be called sacred or holy; and second, that relations with other-than-human beings like buffalo, bear, plants, and so on, were regulated by the expectations and obligations of kinship. Diffuse power, whose existence was more important than its source, received different labels. The Sioux called it, in its totality, *wakan tanka*, which has been translated as "great spirits" or "great incomprehensibility."[41]

Drum

Because the buffalo was once the central provider for nearly all the needs of the Plains people, it has been philosophically connected with the creation of life. Lakota artists depicted buffalo on their objects in homage to it.

ARAPAHO, COLLECTED 1903
CMNH 3179-231

Plains Indians animated the buffalo in ways that were fundamentally unfamiliar to the White men who observed their communal hunting. Buffalo figured prominently in myth and history and were among the most important of all the beings in which power was distributed. For some, the buffalo had ascendancy over man in the distant past, a state reversed by a culture hero (man or woman) who taught men how to use bows and arrows, or how to lure buffalo over cliffs. Particular culture heroes, or figures who have received names like creators, transformers, and tricksters because of their abilities, entered into relationships with various nonhuman animals; they also transformed themselves into—or were themselves—animals. But so did ordinary men and women. For them also there was a time when men and women conversed with, fought, killed, had sexual intercourse with, shared food with, and were kin to buffalo and other animals; as with other humans, those relations varied from beneficent to harmful. The buffalo figured in both public and private ceremonies. Formal societies used buffalo imagery or parts of the buffalo to call the buffalo or to cure the sick. The Sun Dance, the annual world-renewal ceremony held in early summer at the same time as important communal buffalo hunting, was one of the most public ceremonies. For many people, buffalo tongues, meat, skulls, and myths were important sources of food, ritual paraphernalia, and metaphor and imagery during the Sun Dance, and the relationship between man and buffalo, and between buffalo and the sources of power however diffuse or particular were evoked as a central focus.[42]

Understanding that buffalo were animated, other-than-human persons may help make sense of two beliefs linked intimately to conservation and ecology. The first is that buffalo who escaped from an enclosure or jump would warn others away. In 1792, Peter Fidler remarked that the same Piegans who wasted meat were also "always very anxious never to let a single buffalo escape that has been in a Pound" and quick to hunt down those that wandered off, legs broken, from a jump.[43] It may seem contradictory to kill even more when all is not used to start with but, according to Fidler, Piegans said that "should these that escape be at any future time be in the Band of Buffalo that they might be bringing to the Pond, by their once being caught in the Trap they would evade going into it again."[44] John McDougall, a missionary, reporting from his experiences with Crees in the 1860s, was even more explicit about this attitude: "Not one buffalo is

Oglala Sioux ceremony, 1907

A sacred buffalo skull, resting on a bed of sage, occupies the place of honor.

PHOTO BY EDWARD S. CURTIS. SMITHSONIAN INSTITUTION NATIONAL ANTHROPOLOGICAL ARCHIVES, 55-940

allowed to escape. The young and the poor must die with the strong and fat, for it is believed that if these were spared they would tell the rest, and so make it impossible to bring any more bufalo into a pound."[45]

The "telling" (McDougall's word) opens a window on Plains Indian ethology. No doubt people who depended so utterly on the buffalo studied and discussed thoroughly its behavior and life cycle as well as its anatomy. But ethology is cultural and, for Plains people, it encoded beliefs about buffalo as other-than-human persons. Buffalo, it was believed, not only profited from experience and avoided similar dangers in future, but warned other buffalo away just as human beings might do. It is clear that many animals did in fact manage to escape, but this may not have been as important as the belief that one that did get away would jeopardize future efforts. The consequences of the belief are clear: kill all regardless of whether they are used. Waste of meat is irrelevant given this belief. How many other Native Americans were like the Algonquian Piegans and Crees in holding to this belief, or how long this belief persisted, is uncertain. According to Dodge, whose information is secondhand, when buffalo escaped from surrounds in the 1870s, mounted Indians let them go if pursuit risked alarming other herds.[46]

The second belief, which seemed widespread, is that when buffalo disappeared for the season, they went to lake-bottom prairies and that when they reappeared they came from those lands through certain cave mouths, springs, or other egresses. Again according to Dodge, Cheyennes, Arapahoes, and others "firmly believed that the buffalo were produced in countless numbers in a country under the ground; that every spring the surplus swarmed, like bees from a hive, out of great cave-like openings to this country." Some had seen buffalo coming "in countless throngs" from certain caves, or knew of others who had witnessed this. One Southern Cheyenne told Dodge (before, apparently, losing faith) that "the Good God had provided this means for the constant supply of food for the Indian, and that however recklessly the white men might slaughter, they could never exterminate them."[47] Others thought that buffalo went to and came from a certain lake in Canada "whose waters never rested: 'See, it is from under our lake that our buffalo comes. You say they are all gone; but look, they come again and again to us. We cannot kill them all—they are there under that lake. Do you hear the noise which never ceases? It is the buffalo fighting with each other far down under the ground, and striving to get out on the prairie—where else can they come from?'"[48]

Such a belief would have fundamental consequences for how an ecological "system" is conceptualized. Neither the relational nor spatial aspects of Plains Indian ecology would coincide with the western ecologist's ecology. It is easy to see how beliefs like these would impede conservation or management of a declining resource. If buffalo did not return when they were expected or in the numbers anticipated, it was not because too many were being killed but because they had not yet left their lake-bottom prairies. If buffalo returned each year from underneath the surface of the earth because this is where they had gone, how could they possibly go extinct? How could one possibly kill too many?[49]

One might argue that these beliefs somehow arose recently as rationalizations of waste and killings, after buffalo had become a market commodity, or when they were in sharp decline. But historical evidence does not support such a claim—and the days of jumps and enclosures were largely over by the 1860s. This again raises the possibility that the terms of the discourse are faulty: to insist that Native Americans thought about ecology as do modern western ecologists is to do injustice to their thought, just as to insist that Native Americans conserved as might modern western conservationists is to do injustice to what or how they conserved.

Perhaps conservation and waste should be construed in other than narrowly utilitarian terms. It may be that wasting one's relationship with buffalo—a relationship expressed in religious and kinship idiom—was far more risky than wasting a hide or an entire herd. But there is also danger in going too far in this direction, especially given the incomplete and fragmentary nature of historical evidence. Indians surely did not always react to the buffalo only in sacred idiom just because it figured significantly in myth and ritual and, when filled with power or force, became, like other essences, sacred.

Nor did they all show "respect" to the animated world in exactly the same way.

If there was one constant it was that Native Americans needed buffalo for domestic use. When they had more than they needed, they unhesitatingly focused on the choice parts and "wasted" what they did not need or want. There is no doubt that buffalo existed in prodigious quantities or that Native Americans were keen observers of buffalo behavior and efficient predators. But were they ecologists or conservationists? To call them ecologists one must allow for the presence in their ecological systems of lakes under which buffalo disappeared, as well as an ethology in which buffalo comprehended past experiences and could communicate dangers of impoundment to others. And to brand them conservationists is to accept that what was most important to conserve was not buffalo parts, or an entire buffalo, or even a herd, but one's culturally defined and ritually expressed relationship with the buffalo.

Notes

1. This essay is an adaptation of "Ecology and the American Indian," *Ideas* 3 (Summer 1994), 4–22; a revised version will appear in *The Ecological Indian* (New York: Norton, forthcoming).

2. John F. Burns, "Head-Smashed-In Journal: In the Bison's Land, Pride Lives On," *The New York Times*, August 10, 1990 A4; Nicole Bernshaw, "Head-Smashed-In Buffalo Jump," *American History Illustrated* 20 (March 1985): 38–41, p. 41. See also Ian Darragh, "The Killing Cliffs," *Canadian Geographic* 107 (1957): 55–61; B.O.K. Reeves, "Six Millenniums of Buffalo Kills," *Scientific American* 249 (October 1983): 120–35; John E. Foster, Dick Harrison, I. S. MacLaren, eds., *Buffalo* (Alberta, Canada: University of Alberta Press, 1992), 19–59.

3. George Bird Grinnell, "The Last of the Buffalo," *Scribner's Magazine* 12 (1892): 267–86, p. 268.

4. Colonel Richard Irving Dodge, *Our Wild Indians: Thirty-three Years' Personal Experience Among the Red Men*

of the Great West (1882; reprint, Freeport, NY: Books for Libraries Press, 1970), 283–84. See also David A. Dary, *The Buffalo Book: The Full Saga of the American Animal* (Chicago: Swallow Press, [1974]), 22–29.

5. On buffalo population history, numbers, and distribution, see Joel Asaph Allen, *The American Bisons, Living and Extinct* (1876; reprint, New York: Arno Press, 1974); William T. Hornaday, *The Extermination of the American Bison, with a Sketch of Its Discovery and Life History*, 1887 Annual Report, part 2 (Washington, D.C.: U.S. National Museum, 1889), 367–548; Ernest Thompson Seton, *Life-histories of Northern Animals: An Account of the Mammals of Manitoba*, vol. 1, *Grass-Eaters* (New York: Scribner's, 1909), 247–303; Ernest Thompson Seton, *Lives of Game Animals* (1909; reprint, Garden City: Doubleday, 1927), 639–703; Frank Gilbert Roe, *The North American Buffalo: A Critical Study of the Species in its Wild State* (Toronto: University of Toronto Press, 1970); Francis Haines, *The Buffalo* (New York: Thomas Y. Crowell, 1970); Tom McHugh, *The Time of the Buffalo* (New York: Knopf, 1972); Dary, *The Buffalo Book*.

6. The lines were drawn clearly by Hornaday, *The Extermination of the American Bison*, 527, and Roe, *The North American Buffalo*. On pressure from horse herds, see Dan Flores, "Bison Ecology and Bison Diplomacy: The Southern Plains from 1800 to 1850," *Journal of American History* 78 (1991): 465–85.

7. The quotation is in Dary, *The Buffalo Book*, 68. The analysis in the preceding several paragraphs is drawn largely from Hornaday, *The Extermination of the American Bison*; Seton, *Lives of Game Animals*, 662–69; Roe, *The North American Buffalo*; Allen, *The American Bisons*; William Swagerty, "Indian Trade in the Trans-Mississippi West," *Handbook of North American Indians*, vol. 4, *Indian-White Relations*, ed. Wilcomb Washburn (Washington, D.C.: Smithsonian Institution Press, 1988), 351–74. See also Francis Haines, *The Plains Indians* (New York: Thomas Y. Crowell, 1976), 16–69; Mark Judy, "Powder Keg on the Upper Missouri: Sources of Blackfeet Hostility, 1730–1810," *American Indian Quarterly* 11 (1987): 127–44; Thomas F. Schilz and Jodye L. D. Schilz, "Beads, Bangles, and Buffalo

Robes: The Rise and Fall of the Indian Fur Trade Along the Missouri and Des Moines Rivers, 1700–1820," *The Annals of Iowa* 49 (Summer–Fall 1987): 5–25; Dodge, *Our Wild Indians*, 293–96; Richard Irving Dodge, *The Plains of the Great West and Their Inhabitants* (New York: G. P. Putnam's Sons, 1877), 133–44; E. Douglas Branch, *The Hunting of the Buffalo* (Lincoln: University of Nebraska Press, 1962), 127–222; James L. Haley, "Prelude to War: The Slaughter of the Buffalo," *American Heritage* 27 (February 1976): 36–41, 82–87.

8. Seton, *Lives of Game Animals*, passim; Branch, *The Hunting of the Buffalo*, 221–22; Dary, *The Buffalo Book*, 121–43; Michael C. Wilson, "Bison in Alberta: Paleontology, Evolution, and Relationships with Humans," in *Buffalo*, ed. John E. Foster et al., 1–17.

9. John C. Ewers, *The Blackfeet: Raiders of the Northwestern Plains* (Norman: University of Oklahoma Press, 1958), 72–87; McHugh, *The Time of the Buffalo*, 109; Eleanor Verbicky-Todd, *Communal Buffalo Hunting Among the Plains Indians: An Ethnographic and Historic Review* (Alberta: Archaeological Survey of Alberta, 1984), 168–96.

10. Verbicky-Todd, *Communal Buffalo Hunting*. This is an invaluable synthesis and contains numerous quotations from unpublished and published primary sources.

11. Frank Bergon, ed., *The Journals of Lewis and Clark* (New York: Penguin Books, 1989), 115, 120; Dodge, *Our Wild Indians*, 291–92; Dodge, *Plains of the Great West*, 119–20. See also Dary, *The Buffalo Book*, 12, 34–35.

12. On organized drives and jumps, ritual, etc. see Carling Malouf and Stuart Conner, eds., *Symposium on Buffalo Jumps*, Montana Archaeological Society, Memoir 1 (1962); Donald J. Lehmer, "The Plains Bison Hunt—Prehistoric and Historic," *Plains Anthropologist* 8 (1963): 211–17; George W. Arthur, *An Introduction to the Ecology of Early Historic Communal Bison Hunting Among the Northern Plains Indians* (Ottawa: National Museums of Canada, 1975); Leslie B. Davis and Michael C. Wilson, eds., *Bison Procurement and Utilization*, Memoir 14, *Plains Anthropologist* 23 (1978); Joseph Medicine Crow, *From the Heart of the Crow Country: The Crow Indians' Own Stories* (New York: Orion Books,

1992); Edwin James, *Account of an Expedition from Pittsburgh to the Rocky Mountains Performed in the Years 1819, 1820*, vol. 14 of *Early Western Travels, 1748–1846*, ed. Reuben G. Thwaites (Cleveland: Arthur H. Clark, 1905–1906), 288–301; George Bird Grinnell, *The Cheyenne Indians: Their History and Ways of Life*, 2 vols. (1923; reprint, New York: Cooper Square, 1962), 1:262–73.

13. Edwin Thompson Denig, *Indian Tribes of the Upper Missouri*, ed. J.N.B. Hewitt, Forty-sixth Annual Report of the Bureau of American Ethnology (Washington, D.C.: Smithsonian Institution, 1930), 532–33.

14. John McDonnell, "Some Account of the Red Deer River (About 1797) with Extracts from His Journal, 1793–1795," in *Les Bourgeois de la Compagnie du Nord-Ouest*, vol. 1, ed. Louis Masson (Québec: L'Imprimerie Générale A Coté et Cie, 1889), 280; also Verbicky-Todd, *Communal Buffalo Hunting*, 73.

15. Quoted in Verbicky-Todd, *Communal Buffalo Hunting*, 71.

16. On Blackfeet drives, see Claude E. Schaeffer, "The Bison Drive of the Blackfeet Indians," in *Symposium on Buffalo Jumps*, ed. Malouf and Conner, 33; James Willard Schultz, *Apauk: Caller of Buffalo* (Boston: Houghton Mifflin, 1916). See also Verbicky-Todd, *Communal Buffalo Hunting*, 47.

17. Dodge, *Plains of the Great West*, 103; Verbicky-Todd, *Communal Buffalo Hunting*, 100.

18. H.A.L. [Henry Astbury Levenson], *Sport in Many Lands: Europe, Asia, Africa and America, Etc., Etc.* (London: Frederick Warne and Co., 1890), 513–15; John I. Merritt, *Baronets and Buffalo: The British Sportsman in the American West, 1833–1881* (Missoula, MT: Mountain Press, 1985).

19. J. Russell Harper, *Paul Kane's Frontier* (Toronto: University of Toronto Press, 1971), 79; George Catlin, *Letters and Notes on the Manners, Customs, and Conditions of the North American Indians*, 2 vols. (New York: Dover Publications, 1973), 1:199–201. See also Henry Youle Hind, *Narrative of the Canadian Red River Exploring Expedition of 1857 and of the Assiniboine and Saskatchewan Exploring Expedition of 1858*, 2 vols. (Edmonton: Hurtig, 1971), 1:355–59, 2:142–43; Rev. Pierre-Jean De Smet, *Western*

Missions and Missionaries: A Series of Letters (New York: T. W. Strong, Late Edward Dunigan & Bro., Catholic Publishing House, 1859), 146–55; Verbicky-Todd, *Communal Buffalo Hunting*, 83, 88, 91, 139.

20. J. G. MacGregor, *Peter Fidler: Canada's Forgotten Surveyor, 1769–1822* (Toronto: McClelland and Stewart, 1966), 69.

21. George Bird Grinnell, *Blackfoot Lodge Tales: The Story of a Prairie People* (1893; reprint, Lincoln: University of Nebraska Press, 1962), 228–29.

22. De Smet, *Western Missions and Missionaries*, 146–55; Branch, *The Hunting of the Buffalo*, 35; Verbicky-Todd, *Communal Buffalo Hunting*, 81–83.

23. Estimates of weight, consumption etc. from George C. Frison, *Prehistoric Hunters of the High Plains* (New York: Academic Press, 1978), 315–28; Joe Ben Wheat, "The Olsen-Chubbuck Site: A Paleo-Indian Bison Kill," *Memoirs of the Society for American Archaeology* 26 (1972): 85–86, 107–13; Joe Ben Wheat, "A Paleo-Indian Bison Kill," *Scientific American* 216 (January 1967): 52; Arthur J. Ray, "The Northern Great Plains: Pantry of the Northwestern Fur Trade, 1774–1885," *Prairie Forum* 9 (1984):272; Seton, *Life-histories*, 249; Branch, *The Hunting of the Buffalo*, 89–90; Verbicky-Todd, *Communal Buffalo Hunting*, 174; John C. Ewers, *The Horse in Blackfoot Indian Culture*, Bureau of American Ethnology Bulletin 159 (Washington, D.C.: Smithsonian Institution, 1955), 160.

24. On heavy versus light butchering see Clark Wissler, *Material Culture of the Blackfoot Indians*, Anthropological Papers of the American Museum of Natural History 5, part 1 (New York, 1910), 42; Verbicky-Todd, *Communal Buffalo Hunting*, 168–84.

25. Wheat, "The Olsen-Chubbuck Site," 100; Charles MacKenzie, "*The Mississouri Indians: A Narrative of Four Trading Expeditions to the Missisouri*, 1804–1805–1806, for the North-West Company," in *Les Bourgeois de la Compagnie du Nord-Ouest*, vol. 1, ed. Louis Masson (Québec: L'Imprimerie Générale a Coté et Cie, 1889), 331, 366; Bergon, *Journals of Lewis and Clark*, 82–83; MacGregor, *Peter Fidler*, 81.

26. MacGregor, *Peter Fidler*, 69–70.

27. Bergon, *Journals of Lewis and Clark*, 141. See also John Bradbury, *Travels in the Interior of America in the Years 1809, 1810, and 1811*, vol. 5 of *Early Western Travels 1748–1846*, ed. Reuben Gold Thwaites (Cleveland: Arthur H. Clark, 1904), 174.

28. MacKenzie, "The Mississouri Indians," 366; Elliot Coues, ed., *New Light on the Early History of the Greater Northwest: The Manuscript Journals of Alexander Henry, Fur Trader, and David Thompson, Official Geographer and Explorer of the North West Company*, 3 vols. (New York: Francis P. Harper, 1897), 2:576–77; Hind, *Narrative of the Canadian Red River Exploring Expedition*, 1:355–58; Verbicky-Todd, *Communal Buffalo Hunting*, 62, 87–90.

29. James, *Account of an Expedition*, 301.

30. Maria R. Audubon, *Audubon and His Journals*, vols. 1–2, ed. Elliott Coues (1897: reprint, Freeport, NY: Books for Libraries Press, 1972), 1:496–97.

31. MacKenzie, "The Mississouri Indians," 337, 366.

32. Audubon, *Audubon and His Journals*, 2:145.

33. For the archaeology of communal hunting, see Malouf and Conner, eds., *Symposium on Buffalo Jumps*; Davis and Wilson, eds. *Bison Procurement and Utilization*; Frison, *Prehistoric Hunters of the High Plains*; Liz Bryan, *The Buffalo People: Prehistoric Archaeology on the Canadian Plains* (Edmonton: University of Alberta Press, 1991).

34. George C. Frison, "Animal Population Studies and Cultural Inference," in *Bison Procurement and Utilization*, ed. Davis and Wilson, 44–52; George C. Frison, *The Wardell Buffalo Trap 48 SU 301: Communal Procurement in the Upper Green River Basin, Wyoming* (Ann Arbor: University of Michigan, 1973); Richard G. Forbis, *The Old Women's Buffalo Jump, Alberta*, National Museum of Canada Bulletin 180 (Contributions to Anthropology, 1960), part 1 (Ottawa: Department of Northern Affairs and National Resources, 1962); Thomas F. Kehoe, *The Gull Lake Site: A Prehistoric Bison Drive in Southwestern Saskatchewan*, Milwaukee Public Museum Publications in Anthropology and History 1 (1973); J. Michael Quigg, "Winter Bison Procurement in Southwestern Alberta," in *Bison Procurement and Utilization*,

ed. Davis and Wilson, 53–57; Dennis J. Stanford, "The Jones-Miller Site: An Example of Hell Gap Bison Procurement Strategy," in *Bison Procurement and Utilization*, ed. Davis and Wilson, 90–97.

35. Leslie B. Davis, ed., "Panel Discussion: Symposium on Bison Procurement and Utilization," in *Bison Procurement and Utilization*, ed. Davis and Wilson, 287–311.

36. Wheat, "The Olsen-Chubbuck Site"; Wheat, "A Paleo-Indian Bison Kill"; Joe Ben Wheat, "Olsen-Chubbuck and Jurgens Sites: Four Aspects of Paleo-Indian Economy," in *Bison Procurement and Utilization*, ed. Davis and Wilson, 84–89.

37. Grinnell, *Blackfoot Lodge Tales*, 231; Mary Weekes, "An Indian's Description of the Making of a Buffalo Pound," *Saskatchewan History* 1 (1948): 14–17; Verbicky-Todd, *Communal Buffalo Hunting*, 68 (for the Blood Indian); Joseph Epes Brown, *Animals of the Soul: Sacred Animals of the Oglala Sioux* (Rockport, MA: Element, 1992), 15.

38. Quoted in Wissler, *Material Culture of the Blackfoot Indians*, 34.

39. Barre Toelken, "Seeing with a Native Eye," in *Seeing with a Native Eye: Essays on Native American Religion*, ed. Walter Holden Capps (New York: Harper, 1976), 9–24.

40. Bradbury, *Travels in the Interior*, 141.

41. See Raymond J. DeMallie, "Lakota Belief and Ritual in the Nineteenth Century," in *Sioux Indian Religion: Tradition and Innovation*, ed. Raymond J. DeMallie and Douglas R. Parks (Norman: University of Oklahoma Press, 1987), 25–43; Raymond J. DeMallie, "Kinship and Biology in Sioux Culture," in *North American Indian Anthropology: Essays on Society and Culture*, ed. Raymond J. DeMallie and Alfonso Ortiz (Norman: University of Oklahoma Press, 1995), 125–46; Howard L. Harrod, *Renewing the World: Plains Indian Religion and Morality* (Tucson: University of Arizona Press, 1987).

42. Verbicky-Todd, *Communal Buffalo Hunting*, 197–245.

43. MacGregor, *Peter Fidler*, 68–69.

44. Quoted in Verbicky-Todd, *Communal Buffalo Hunting*, 125.

45. John McDougall, *Saddle, Sled and Snowshoe* (Toronto: William Briggs, 1896), 282; see also John McDougall, *Parsons on the Plains*, ed. Thomas Bredin (Ontario: Longman, Don Mills, 1971), 183.

46. Dodge, *Our Wild Indians*, 289.

47. Ibid., 286–87, 580–81; Flores, "Bison Ecology and Bison Diplomacy," 485.

48. Branch, *The Hunting of the Buffalo*, 2–3; see also Roe, *The North American Buffalo*, 643–44; Dary, *The Buffalo Book*, 54–55; Verbicky-Todd, *Communal Buffalo Hunting*, 198.

49. DeMallie, "Lakota Belief and Ritual," 32.

Botany

Korosta Katsina Song

Yellow butterflies,
Over the blossoming virgin corn,
With pollen-painted faces
Chase one another in brilliant
throng.

Blue butterflies,
Over the blossoming virgin beans,
With pollen-painted faces
Chase one another in brilliant
streams.

Over the blossoming corn,
Over the virgin corn
Wild bees hum.

Over the blossoming beans,
Over the virgin beans,
Wild bees hum.

Over your field of growing corn
All day shall hang the thunder-
cloud;
Over your field of growing corn
All day shall come the rushing rain.

—HOPI, SOUTHWEST

9

American Indian Plant Use: An Overview

FRANCES B. KING

AMERICAN INDIANS DEPENDED ON PLANTS in virtually every aspect of their lives, including not only food and medicine, but also clothing, shelter, and transportation. Because they relied so heavily on plants and have lived so intimately with them, they know much more about native plants than do most Americans of European descent, who are more familiar with the botanical "camp-followers" that accompanied the colonists from the Old World over three hundred years ago.

Melvin Gilmore, an ethnobotanist working in the early 1900s, found that American Indians knew more than Whites about the habits and requirements of plants, as well as their potential uses. He also found that Indians were very sensitive to the annual growth cycle, timing their own activities to correlate with the natural calendar.[1]

Among the Chippewa Indians of the Upper Great Lakes, for example, the best time to remove bark from paper birch trees without injuring the trees coincided with the ripening of wild raspberries. The Iroquois planted corn when the first leaves on the oak in spring were as big as a red squirrel's foot or when blossoms appeared on the juneberry trees.[2] Because such events are tied to length of day and weather conditions, they are probably at least as "scientific" as the widespread and popular custom of planting by the signs of the Moon or by astrological calendars such as those annually published in the *Farmer's Almanac.*

Spiritual Beliefs and the Environment

Native Americans have a long heritage of respecting plants as living beings, and their spiritual beliefs reflect in many ways their interrelationship with nature. Although they gather the plants as needed, Indians customarily acknowledge their gratitude to the plant and to the source that gave it life. This recognition might include a spoken prayer or a token sacrifice left at the place where the plant was growing. Such offerings, like those made by many unrelated groups around the world, might include cornmeal, tobacco, a few seeds, or a portion of a root or tuber just harvested and now returned to the earth.

Although beliefs vary among different tribes, all Native Americans share a common reverence for nature. For example, the Hopi believe that all life is one and that each living thing also has another home where it exists in human form. Thus, when a Hopi goes out to collect a certain kind of plant, the first plant is spared and offered a sacrifice so that it may convey the message of need to other plant people.[3] Obviously, while this is a spiritual belief, it is also sound ecology, ensuring that at least a few plants are left to repopulate an area.

Despite their reverence for nature, the activities of Native Americans, as well as European Americans and others, have drastically altered the environment. The adoption of sheep by the Hopi, for example, led to the displacement of antelope and other wild game, the abandonment of hunting in favor of domestically raised animals for meat, and to the substitution of wool for cotton fiber. Sheep grazing has also increased soil erosion and eliminated many native plants formerly used by the Hopi.

The greatest environmental changes, however, were those associated with prehistoric agriculture. At the time of Columbus, Native peoples across much of North America were cultivating corn and other crops and, although there were no potential herd animals, the turkey had been domesticated in Mexico. Throughout the New World, increased dependence on crops was both a cause and a result of population growth because, although agriculture supports more people in a given area, it also requires more labor. The need for a larger labor force creates continual pressure toward larger populations; children cease to be just "another mouth to feed" and become economic assets.[4] Even prior to European settlement, new areas were being continually disturbed as Native Americans struggled to feed growing populations by increasing crop production. This struggle may have caused increased warfare during late prehistoric times when good agricultural land was at a premium and the role of men as hunters was diminished by growing dependence on women's agricultural activities.

Varied Environments

The use of plants varied greatly in different regions of North America according to human life-ways and environmental constraints. Across the continent, plants supplied many basic needs, in part or totally: food, medicine, shelter, clothing, as well as the tools necessary for procurement, processing, or construction. Humans also used plants to create a myriad other, less utilitarian objects that might be viewed as "wealth" but that promoted physical and psychological well-being.

Southwest

Most parts of the southwestern desert are hot and arid with limited standing water or rainfall. In this harsh environment, many plants are dormant for most of the year, completing their life cycles within a few days or weeks following seasonal rainfall. Even slight differences in topography may mean significant differences in available moisture or shade during the heat of the day; this difference is reflected in the vegetation "zones" encountered as one climbs in elevation or descends into sheltered valleys.

Hopi farmer in his cornfield

Clumping corn plants by dropping a handful of seeds into a single deep hole is a distinctly Hopi technique. This farmer has a healthy stand of corn that will withstand wind, drought, and pests.

PHOTO BY GORELON L'ALLEWARD, SOUTHWEST MUSEUM, LOS ANGELES, N.24788

Perhaps more than in any other region, successfully living in the Southwest depends on a deep understanding of the environment and the behavior and adaptations of many plants and animals. A successful gatherer should know where to dig for edible roots even when the plants are dormant for the season and the tops have disappeared, or that seeds are gathered and stored by mice whose nests could be robbed if necessary.[5]

Cultivated plants were introduced to the American Southwest from Mexico long before Spanish contact, and many groups in that region had elaborately irrigated fields even in prehistoric times. Crops included corn, beans, squash, cotton, and tobacco, with other plants, such as devil's claw, grown more casually.[6]

California and the Great Basin

This is a region with a varied, but generally mild, climate and environments ranging from deserts and mountains to rivers and seashore. The diversity and abundance of wild resources was great, and the area was unique in that it supported a relatively large human population based on hunting and gathering, rather than on agriculture. Although raising food crops may have been unnecessary, the supply of wild tobacco was inadequate to meet social and ceremonial needs and tobacco was cultivated.

Of the many wild plant foods, the most important were the acorns of several species of oak. These were gathered (sometimes from managed groves), stored, ground, leached if necessary to remove poisonous tannins, and ultimately cooked into acorn mush. Many kinds of wild seeds were also eaten, including those of numerous grasses. In the Great Basin and other areas where oaks seldom grew, the seeds of piñon and other species of pine were especially important sources of food.[7] Although their pottery was poorly developed, the inhabitants of this region produced exquisite baskets; some were loosely woven for winnowing seeds, and others served as watertight containers for water storage or as cooking pots (by adding heated rocks).

Northwest

The Northwest Coast area, often called the "temperate rain forest," is mild in temperature and rainy, supporting magnificent stands of conifers with a lush understory of ferns and other species. The economy of its inhabitants, shared by the Tlingit and others ranging from northern California to southern Alaska, was based on marine fishing and the extensive use of the western red cedar for dugout canoes, plank houses, boxes, and other wooden objects.

Harpoon head and sheath

The folded red cedar bark sheath (left) was made to house the barbed whaling harpoon (right). The cord attached to the harpoon is also constructed from cedar bark.

NUUCHAHNULTH, VANCOUVER ISLAND, BRITISH COLUMBIA, COLLECTED PRE-1914 CMNH 23102-15926a & b, GIFT OF JOHN A. BECK

Although these coastal peoples relied heavily on the ocean for food, they also gathered animals available in the forests and the many plants growing in meadows or along lakes and streams. Because of the climate, topography, and the abundance of wild food, coastal groups grew no crops except tobacco until after European contact. Potatoes, one of the earliest plants to be introduced, rapidly became an important addition to the diet.[8]

Plains and Prairies

In the rain shadow east of the Rocky Mountains, inhabitants of the plains and prairies must endure hot dry summers and cold winters. Trees are limited to sheltered river valleys, and prairie plants consist primarily of grasses and herbs that tolerate frequent prairie fires and grazing by animals such as the bison that were so important to Plains Indian cultures. Although the diversity of plant species is high, most are of the type that dies back to the ground each winter; woody plants, and the products they provide, are rare.

Prairie villages tended to be located in valleys where they would be protected from wind and fire and near sources of wood, water, and the more abundant food resources available in the floodplains. Unlike the prairie sod, the ground in the valleys could be easily worked with sharpened digging sticks or hoes that might be made from the shoulder bones of bison or deer. Crops included corn, beans, squash, tobacco, and sunflowers.[9]

One of the most important foods gathered in the prairie itself was the prairie turnip, a member of the pea family with an enlarged root resembling a turnip. The roots were collected during the early summer when their growth was complete but before the tops had broken off and blown away; they were eaten fresh or strung and dried for winter use. In western Washington, Idaho, and Montana, the edible bulbs of the blue camas, a member of the lily family, were similarly collected in large numbers. Both of these plants were traded far beyond the areas where they were harvested.[10]

Bandolier bag, vest, and quilled birch-bark box

The numerous images of indigenous plants that Native artists have used in their work reflect the importance of plants in their lives.

BAG: ANISHINABE, WESTERN GREAT LAKES, PRE-1900 CMNH 23102-16921, GIFT OF JOHN A. BECK

VEST: ANISHINABE, WESTERN GREAT LAKES, CA. 1885–1890 CMNH Z-9-523

BOX: OTTAWA?, WESTERN GREAT LAKES, CA. 1990 CMNH 35409-5 a & b

Eastern North America

The Great Lakes and Northeast regions also have hot summers and cold winters, but plentiful summer moisture promotes the growth of many kinds of deciduous and coniferous trees. There are many sources of water and an abundance of wild plants and animals that were often supplemented in earlier times by the cultivation of corn, beans, squash, tobacco, and sometimes other crops as well. Wild plant foods included many species of nuts, greens or "potherbs," fruit, seeds, and roots and tubers. The collection of maple sap to make syrup or sugar leaves little direct evidence and its antiquity has been questioned. Experiments suggest that syrup could be made in bark or pottery vessels by boiling with heated stones, but that sugar requires too hot a temperature to be made without an iron kettle.[11] Birch-bark containers apparently release chemicals that prevent the spoilage or fermentation of syrup or other foods stored in them.[12]

The Southeast has a milder climate than the Northeast but is also forested, and Native American plant use in the two regions was similar. The diverse and abundant natural resources in the Southeast supported cultures that were both complex and varied, although many groups depended on corn and other crops for most of their food after about A.D. 1150.

Plant Foods

Plant foods dominate the diets of most people; even those who claim to follow a strictly meat diet may eat many plants in the form of snacks, teas, and medicines. The sole source of carbohydrate in the diet, plants also supply some protein and fat as well as various vitamins and other nutrients. As many vegetarians have proved, people can live healthy lives on a well-chosen diet of vegetable foods.

Plant foods include sap, leaves and "greens," flowers and flower buds, stems, seeds and fruit, nuts, and roots and tubers. Each food varies in nutritional value, season of availability, abundance, and ease of collection, preparation, and storage. Taste, also, is not to be discounted in the selection of foods to be gathered or grown. Although fruit and greens, for example, are low in calories, they are high in vitamins, minerals, amino acids, and so on, and form

Julia Scrogg, a Seneca woman on New York's Tonawanda Reservation, pounding kernels into cornmeal, 1903

PHOTOGRAPHER UNKNOWN, 1903. ROCHESTER MUSEUM AND SCIENCE CENTER, ROCHESTER, NY, 1621

an essential part of the diet; fruits also offer one of the few sources of natural sweetness. Nuts and seeds are abundant in some places, high in calories, and easily stored. Roots and tubers tend to be starchy, like the cultivated potato, but can be dried and stored or even collected throughout the winter if one knows where to search for them.

When Europeans first arrived in North America, most Native American groups already cultivated a variety of plant foods or traded for them, the most important crops being the famous triad of corn, beans, and squash. However, even before the introduction of corn from Mexico about 1,700 years ago (and its subsequent acceptance and spread), several groups in the West cultivated tobacco, and native plants such as bottle gourds, sunflowers, and Jerusalem artichokes were grown in eastern North America.[13]

Corn, or maize, has a high yield of food per plant or per acre; its kernels contain about 72 percent carbohydrate, nine percent protein, and four percent fat (the low fat content can be remedied by eating sunflower or squash seeds, which contain nearly 50 percent fat). The problem with corn is that it has an unbalanced ratio of amino acids such that only a fraction of the protein can be used by the human body; the resulting protein deficiency may cause the disease pellagra. The food value of corn can be much improved either by adding complementary proteins, such as those in beans, or by alkali processing to improve the ratios of the amino acids. Most agricultural groups in North America used both methods, growing beans along with corn and treating the corn with lye made from wood ashes (hominy) or lime (the familiar Mexican corn tortillas). Paper-thin Hopi *piki* bread, made from blue cornmeal, is normally a blue-gray color, but it becomes a festive and highly desired deep blue green when the ashes of saltbush,[14] or other form of alkali, are added. Similarly, Buffalobird Woman, an elderly Hidatsa woman interviewed about 1910, describes how her people much preferred seasoning their staple corn and bean stew with ashes rather than with mineral salt collected from salt springs.[15]

Because of its productivity, corn was raised throughout most of North America, even in northern Minnesota and parts of Canada, where varieties

Piki *making, ca. 1975*

A Hopi woman quickly spreads blue cornmeal batter on a hot griddle stone. In a moment the paper-thin bread will be cooked, and she will roll it into a cylinder.

PHOTO BY OWEN
SEUMPTEWA

were developed that needed growing seasons of only 90–100 days compared to the 120–160 days of other varieties.[16] Uses were found for every part of the plant. The mature, hollow stalks, which are full of sweet sap when green, furnished containers for medicine, like those made of bamboo in Asia. Shredded cornhusks provided filling for pillows and mattresses and could be made into floor mats, dolls, baskets, and other objects, usage that was intensified by the tourist trade. The silk was sometimes used for medicine, although not smoked, and for the hair of cornhusk dolls; cobs provided fuel for smoking meat and hides and served as pipe bowls.

Native American Medicine

Native Americans suffered from ailments that would be expected among people living a rigorous outdoor life on a coarse and unpredictable diet. Some of the most common maladies included gastrointestinal problems; smoke-induced eye irritations, coughs, colds, and fevers; burns, insect bites, and other skin problems; and bone fractures and sprains.[17] Other problems such as those surrounding childbirth occur in every society, as do the aches and pains of arthritis and "rheumatism," although these were undoubtedly exacerbated by harsh conditions.

Nearly 2,000 plants were used medicinally by Native Americans.[18] Some of these plants continue to be used today, and numerous species have found places in orthodox medicine. Certainly, many "Indian medicines" would be familiar to anyone interested in herbal medicine, including the ten plants most commonly used by Native Americans in historic times: sweetflag, yarrow, sagebrush, mint, black cherry, bloodroot, chokecherry, cow parsnip, wild parsley, and white pine.[19]

Herbal medicines were carefully collected, dried, and stored in bags or bundles. A single medicine might contain a dozen or more different ingredients, some were included, perhaps, because they produced a synergistic effect in combination with others. Fragrant herbs were added to improve the flavor or to prevent identification of the essential ingredients by competing healers.

Although healers treated common ailments, shamans, or

medicine men or women, dealt with those aspects of illness that involved the spirit world. When the cause of the illness was not apparent, prepared medicine might be only a minor part of the treatment. Deemed equally important were ceremonial activities such as ritual purification, chanting, dancing, and smoking of tobacco mixtures or ingestion of mind-altering compounds on the part of the shaman to induce visions during diagnosis or to communicate with the spirits responsible for the illness.[20]

Tobacco

Tobacco was the most important ceremonial plant and one of the few with psychoactive properties; a number of wild and cultivated species were used medicinally, socially, and ritually.[21] Early observations in eastern North America that tobacco was hallucinogenic may have reflected the widespread use of *Nicotiana rustica*, a species with a very high nicotine level which is used today primarily in the production of nicotine-based pesticides.

Other plant material was frequently mixed with tobacco to provide flavoring, to extend a limited amount of tobacco, to increase its medicinal value, or to produce specific effects. For the Hopi, for example, tobacco smoke symbolizes clouds, and they will add a certain herb for use in ceremonies designed to bring rain but a different herb for medicinal mixtures.

Other Psychoactive Plants

Despite the certainty that stored foods must sometimes have fermented, there is little evidence that beer or other alcoholic beverages were produced outside Mexico or the American Southwest. Datura, or jimson weed, was used by some southern and western tribes as a hallucinogen during important ceremonies although they knew that it was very dangerous and could easily kill the user.[22]

Charms

Charms served a number of purposes: to attract a lover

or worldly goods; to ensure safety or success in hunting and fishing; to repel snakes and the "bad medicine" carried by another person; or even to work evil. Charms were ceremonially prepared from the appropriate materials, which might be parts of plants, feathers, hair, magic stones, or other items. Some, such as hunting charms, were meant to be chewed or smoked while hunting to attract game. A medicine bag or bundle might contain a number of individual charms and medicines to be used as needed, or it might have a single purpose such as bringing success in war or providing birth control.[23]

Musical Instruments

Native Americans often manufactured the rattles, drums, flutes, whistles, and other musical instruments that were used on social and ceremonial occasions from plant materials alone or in combination with animal materials. Rattles might be made from gourds filled with hard seeds or small stones, and drums from hollowed sections of tree trunks covered with tautly stretched hides.

Gourd musical instrument and gourd rattle

Hopi farmers have cultivated gourds for centuries. When dried and boiled to harden the shell, gourds are incredibly useful for a variety of purposes— canteens, dippers, masks, rattles, and other musical instruments.
HOPI, CA. 1904

RIGHT TO LEFT:
CMNH 3165-30,
3165-278, 3165-278c,
3165-278a

Plant Symbolism

All societies seem to recognize plants as symbols. In earlier European society, for example, there was literally a "language of flowers" such that a carefully chosen bouquet could convey a complex message. Likewise in North America, certain plants (as well as animals) came to symbolize clans or other groups, or to represent water, air, earth, the cardinal directions, and so on. These plants might be depicted on ceremonial or other objects.

Domestic Crafts and Technology

Native Americans spent a large amount of time crafting

the articles they needed for daily living. For their dwellings, they had to cut and fasten wooden structural elements and bark, hide, or woven thatching material. Food procurement required hunting weapons; tools for digging, grinding, and scraping; pots for cooking; containers for collection, transportation, and storage. Additional objects were required for treating the sick, for rituals and ceremonies, and other purposes, and all were made laboriously by hand.

Hopi basketweaver Bessy Monongya collecting *si'wi (Parryella filifolia)* stems to be used in wicker baskets made by women of Third Mesa, 1991

PHOTO BY HELGA TEIWES. ARIZONA STATE MUSEUM, THE UNIVERSITY OF ARIZONA, 85839

Containers are significant domestic and ceremonial objects, and their manufacture reveals much about the environment and activity of a group. The simplest containers are hollowed-out, dried gourds—either yellow-flowered or white-flowered—or squash. These were often made from small, wild species with thin rinds, similar to the orna-

Spruce root hat, small trinket basket, and large basket

Tlingit women achieved fame for their finely twined spruce root hats and baskets decorated with dyed grass applied in a technique termed "false embroidery." Harvesting and preparing the spruce root took 75 percent of the time spent making a spruce root object.

HAT: TLINGIT, COLLECTED 1904 CMNH 3178-123a

TRINKET BASKET: TLINGIT, PRE-1923 CMNH 8946-11a & b, GIFT OF H. J. HEINZ

BASKET: TLINGIT, COLLECTED 1904 CMNH 3167-57

mental gourds we buy in the fall; also used were the larger and thicker shelled bottle gourds. After several thousand years of cultivation, bottle gourds were being grown in a larger variety of shapes and sizes and with a thicker and more durable rind than their ancestors, whereas squash were selected for greater edibility. Gourds could be fashioned not only into containers, but also into utensils, rattles, fishnet floats, or birdhouses. Among the Hopi and many other groups, the larger ones were used for storage while the smaller served as dippers, canteens, spoons, cups, water jars, and so on. The use of gourds predates the invention of pottery in most places by several hundred to a thousand years.

American Indians wove their baskets from many types of pliable plant materials, including the fragrant sweet grass that is widely distributed in North America; young, flexible, tree branches (such as willow) or the slender new growth of certain shrubs; wood or roots split into fine strips; or bark.

The methods may vary from region to region, as do the shape and the decoration, but every basket reflects the relationship between its maker and the local environment. Spruce and other conifers have strong roots that can be peeled and split and woven into the fine flexible baskets of the Tlingit and other Northwest Indians. The Tlingit work their patterns with the shiny black stems of maidenhair fern, horsetail roots, or the stems of certain grasses. The Hopi make baskets from split yucca leaves and the colored stems of rabbit brush or other shrubs; some of the basketry materials might also be dyed with one of several native dyes. In the Northeast, baskets are made of bark or woven from grass, slender branches, or thin strips of wood.

Bowls and plates might be fashioned from wood, bark, gourds, stone, or ceramics, while accompanying utensils might be made from wood, gourds, bone, or antler. The Iroquois made bowls by folding and sewing elm or pine bark, or they carved them from fine-grained woods like maple, basswood, or beech.

Elm bark trays

In the spring and early summer, when the sap was up, bark was peeled from elm trees and bent to make serving trays and bowls.

LEFT: GEORGE KEY, CANADA, WOLF CLAN, SENECA, PRE-1910 CMNH 8220-120, GIFT OF MRS. JOEL W. BURDICK

RIGHT: SENECA, PRE-1910 CMNH 8220-117, GIFT OF MRS. JOEL W. BURDICK

Plaited basket

The yucca sifter basket, made by women on all three Hopi mesas, is the basic utility basket. It is used for a variety of tasks—as a colander, a sifter, a winnowing tray, and a catch basin for shelling corn.

HOPI, CA. 1900 CMNH 2128-5

The Chippewa made containers from the bark of paper birch, folding the ends and sewing them with strips of basswood bark. Not only was birch bark easy to work, but it also supposedly protected from decay whatever was stored in it. The most common "plates" were sheets of bark or large leaves.

Instead of bags or baskets, inhabitants of the Northwest Coast region used wooden boxes. These are made of sheets of cedar that have been split with wedges and mauls, softened by steaming, and then molded and bent into shape. The wood is then polished by rubbing with sharkskin or with the siliceous stems of horsetails.[24] Boxes and other wooden objects were often decorated with precise, symmetrical, painted designs or relief carvings, often of stylized marine animals.

Mats are constructed from long, slender leaves or stems. Most commonly used are cattail leaves, reeds and rushes, grasses, or fibrous bark. In the past, these were either woven or sewn together with twine and a needle made of bone or a spine from a cactus or honey locust. Mats were traditionally made during the summer, when the plant materials were available, and stored for later use as floor or ground covers, sleeping mats, wall or door coverings, or thatching over house frames.

Painted storage box, painter's pattern, paintbrush, and elbow adze

Northwest Coast men are renowned for their tradition of wood carving and painting. Northern Coastal artists share a set of design principles even though no two pieces are exactly alike. They draw freehand or use cedar bark templates to trace symmetrical patterns before painting the objects in the preferred colors of red, black, and blue-green.

BOX: HAIDA, COLLECTED 1904
CMNH 3178-118

PATTERN: TLINGIT,
PURCHASED 1894
CMNH 638-8

PAINTBRUSH: CHILKAT TLINGIT,
PURCHASED 1888
CMNH 638-7

ADZE: TLINGIT, YAKUTAT,
ALASKA, PRE-1970
CMNH 24386-2, GIFT OF
DR. OSHIN AGATHON

Fibers, Cordage, and Weaving

Natural fibers add strength to the stems or leaves of many plants and protect the seeds of others such as cotton. Leaf fibers, like those found in yucca or agave leaves, are rather stiff and coarse; they are mostly used for rope or heavy twine. The inner wood of some trees, such as basswood, or the stems of herbaceous plants like nettles and milkweed, produce softer and finer fibers. Indian hemp, which was widely distributed in eastern and northern North America, was considered to have the finest fiber.[25]

Although the "fluff" found in milkweed pods or cattails is not long enough or strong enough for cordage or weaving, it was used as padding for mattresses, as an absorbent lining for diapers and cradleboards, and for other similar purposes. The Saanich of British Columbia sometimes spun cattail-seed fluff with dog hair to make blankets.[26]

Cultivated cotton was introduced into the southwestern United States about A.D. 300 from Mexico, where it had been earlier grown by the Aztecs. Among the Hopi it was raised and woven by the men (women produced baskets). After sheep were introduced by the Spanish in the sixteenth century, wool became an increasingly important source of fiber for the Hopi and other tribes, and cotton was largely forgotten, except for wedding clothes.[27]

Stem fibers were obtained either by retting the stems (decaying in water as is done with flax) or by pounding and twisting the dried stems to remove the pith material. In British Columbia, for example, Native Americans harvested Indian hemp stems in September or October, searching out plants with tall, thick stems. After the branches and leaves were removed, the stem was flattened, split, and the outer skin removed. The stems were then dried and the brittle pithy tissue was removed by pounding and twisting, leaving the soft, flexible fibers. Fiber from stinging nettle (related to ramie) was collected and prepared

Brocaded sash

This cotton sash is embroidered with wool threads. Interpretations of the standardized decoration on the sash vary among villages and even among individuals. The following description by H. R. Voth resulted from his conversation with a resident at Oraibi on Third Mesa in 1904: "This beautiful sash forms a part of nearly every Katcina costume. It is used, however, in other ceremonies, also. . . . The red [triangles] in the border represent blossoms of melons, squashes, herbs and flowers. The white crook-shaped lines, sprouting beans" (CMNH Accession Notes, 3165-23).

HOPI, TWENTIETH CENTURY CMNH 35752-121, GIFT OF BENJAMIN D. BERNSTEIN IN MEMORY OF EVELYN GLAUSER BERNSTEIN

similarly and was considered nearly as good. Fibers from milkweed and dogbane stems, however, were regarded as inferior and only used when other kinds were unavailable.

Once cleaned, the fibers were spun into thread by rubbing against the thigh or, like wool, by using a spindle. Individual strands could be twisted together to form multiple-strand twine or rope. In this way, plant fibers were transformed into cordage with thicknesses ranging from fine thread to coarse rope. From these various weights of cordage Native Americans produced finely woven fabrics, knotted bags or fishnets, rope, twine, fishlines, and bowstrings.

Chilkat blanket

A Chilkat Tlingit woman used yellow cedar bark as the core of this blanket's warp threads. Thin strands of the bark were spun with mountain goat wool.

TLINGIT, KLUKWAN, ALASKA, LATE 1800s CMNH 34939-4

The way in which a bundle of fibers is rolled against the thigh produces one of two otherwise identical twists that are mirror images of one another and that are termed *s-twist* and *z-twist*. Because the process is taught, the twist tends to be consistent within families or groups of related workers. Other forms of cultural information at archaeological sites in eastern North America is often sparse compared to pottery, which was often decorated by impressing it with a cord or cord-wrapped sticks. At such sites, a change in the relative proportion of these two types of twist has sometimes been interpreted as reflecting a change in the population to include weavers from the opposite school who might represent a different family or tribe.

Among the Tlingit and other groups of the Northwest Coast, fiber from the shaggy bark of both red-cedar and yellow cedar was commonly used for making clothing, rope, blankets, and mats. It was pulled off the trees in long strips, sometimes thirty feet long. The brittle outer bark was removed, leaving the leathery inner bark that could be split and woven into baskets or shredded and pounded to make it soft. Yellow cedar was softer and was therefore preferred for weaving clothing and blankets; often it was interwoven with duck down or mountain goat wool.[28]

Other plants also served as rope or line. Vines, such as grape, were used for coarse tying, as were, of course, strips of animal hide and sinew. The Tlingit and other coastal Indian groups used the long, ropelike stalks of brown algae to make fishing lines, nets, and ropes, sometimes joining together many stalks to make lines hundreds of feet long that could reach deep water fish such as halibut. (See the halibut hook on page 101.) The brown algae have bulblike floats at the top to hold the leaves near the surface. These floats were cured and used to hold water, fish oil, or in more recent times, molasses.[29]

Natural Dyeing

Natural dyes and tanning materials were usually prepared by boiling a water-soluble coloring material in water, often with the addition of *mordants*, chemicals that help a fiber accept a dye that it would otherwise reject. Mordants not

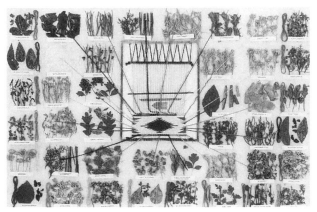

Navajo dye chart

Although both the colors and captions are lost in this photograph of a Navajo dye chart, the great variety of plants used in dyeing is obvious.

ELLA MYEN, 1992
CMNH 35480-1

only make many colors last longer, but each alters the final result so that one dye plant might produce a broad spectrum of colors when used with different chemicals. The simplest "natural" mordants, including raw alum, cedar ashes, salt, urine, and coal or charcoal, act by making the dye bath more acidic or alkaline, but the result may not be colorfast. Pretreatment with metallic salts, or the use of copper, iron, or aluminum pans, produces a more complex chemical bond and often increases both the intensity and fastness of dyes.[30]

Natural colors tend to be earth-toned (yellows, greens, browns, oranges) and many fade relatively rapidly. Bright red and blue are difficult to obtain except as rather transient colors produced by the colored juice of fruit such as grapes and pokeberries. The Aztecs of Mexico had both colors, producing bright red from the bodies of the cochineal insect and blue from a native indigo. In the Southwest, yellows and greens were produced by rabbit brush or sagebrush; the orange-ochre-brown colors came from mountain mahogany or canaigre; and purple could be produced with either sunflower seeds or purple corn.[31]

In the Great Lakes region, natural dye colors were limited by the use of the acidic juice of crab apples and other fruits as mordants. After European contact, however, Native Americans quickly learned to boil their dyes in copper vessels and to add alum or copperas to fix the colors. Reddish dyes were produced by plants like alder, bloodroot, bedstraw, pokeweed, and sumac; yellow by goldthread and goldenseal; black by walnut; bright orange by bittersweet; green from ash; blue from grapes and larkspur. These and other natural dyes have been largely replaced by brighter, more convenient, and more durable aniline dyes developed from coal tar products in the nineteenth century.

Conclusion

I have barely touched upon the uses of plants by Native Americans and have neglected some of the most important. For example, they made most of their weapons primarily from plants, even though interest usually focuses on the chipped stone point rather than on the wooden shaft to which it was attached. They preferred hardwoods for spears, bows and arrows, and war clubs—those with straight, fine grains that would not shatter under rough usage. Canoes and boats were made either by sewing bark over a wooden framework and sealing it with resin, or by hollowing out a large tree trunk, usually by a combination of burning and scraping. Hollowed sections of tree trunks also served as mortars in which to pound corn.

In an age when most objects are made of some form of plastic, it is difficult to visualize the importance of natural materials in the past. It is equally hard not to marvel at the tremendous knowledge and skill of the people who collected, processed, and transformed those materials into what have literally become museum pieces. Fortunately many of the crafts—and the crops—are being kept alive by American Indians concerned about preserving their own heritage, as well as by interested hobbyists who revere the older and simpler ways of life.

Notes

1. Melvin R. Gilmore, *Indian Lore and Indian Gardens* (Slinger-Comstock, 1930).

2. F. W. Waugh, *Iroquois Foods and Food Preparation*, Canada Department of Mines Memoir 86 (1916; facsimile edition, Ottawa: Government Printing Office, 1973).

3. Alfred F. Whiting, *Ethnobotany of the Hopi*, Museum of Northern Arizona Bulletin 15 (Flagstaff, 1939).

4. Jack R. Harlan, *Crops and Man* (Madison, WI: American Society of Agronomy, 1975).

5. Mice and packrats collect and store large amounts of piñon nut seeds, especially during years when there is a bumper crop. Following such a bumper crop in 1992, the time-honored tradition of raiding nests by Navajo piñon nut collectors brought the collectors into close contact with mouse excrement and may have been partly responsible for the outbreak of *Hantavirus* in the Four Corners area. Interestingly, the Indians historically believed that a good nut crop would

be followed by an epidemic of smallpox. H. D. Harrington, in *Edible Native Plants of the Rocky Mountains* (Albuquerque: University of New Mexico Press, 1967), attributes this to the intermingling of various groups of people and the spread of a highly contagious disease, but it seems possible that it may actually have been misdiagnosed *Hantavirus*.

6. Paul A. Minnis, "Earliest Plant Cultivation in the Desert Borderlands of North America," in C. Wesley Cowan and Patty Jo Watson, eds., *The Origins of Agriculture: An International Perspective*, 121–43 (Washington, D.C.: Smithsonian Institution Press, 1992).

7. According to Catherine Fowler, "Historical Perspectives on Timbisha Shoshone Land Management Practices, Death Valley, California," *Journal of Ethnobiology* 14 (1994): 246–47, both honey mesquite (*Prosopis glandulosa*) and single-leaf piñon (*Pinus monophylla*) stands were also carefully pruned and managed.

8. Nancy J. Turner, *Food Plants of British Columbia Indians*, 3 vols., Handbooks 34, 36, 38 (Victoria: British Columbia Provincial Museum, 1975, 1978, 1979).

9. Mary J. Adair, *Prehistoric Agriculture in the Central Plains*, Publications in Anthropology 16 (Lawrence: University of Kansas, 1988).

10. Kelly Kindscher, *Edible Wild Plants of the Prairie: An Ethnobotanical Guide* (Lawrence: University of Kansas Press, 1987); *Medicinal Wild Plants of the Prairie: An Ethnobotanical Guide* (Lawrence: University of Kansas Press, 1992).

11. Patrick J. Munson, "Still More on the Antiquity of Maple Sugar and Syrup in Aboriginal Eastern North America," *Journal of Ethnobiology* 9 (1989): 159–70. This article is the most recent article on maple sugaring; it summarizes earlier work and presents some pretty firm conclusions.

12. Frances Densmore, *Uses of Plants by the Chippewa Indians*, Forty-fourth Annual Report of the Bureau of American Ethnology (Washington, D.C.: Smithsonian Institution, 1928); reprinted as *How Indians Use Wild Plants for Food, Medicine, and Crafts* (New York: Dover, 1974).

13. C. Margaret Scarry, ed., *Foraging and Farming in the Eastern Woodlands* (Gainesville: University Press of Florida, 1993). This is only one of many recent books on the

development of Native American agriculture. Native domesticates included squash (*Cucurbita pepo*), bottle gourd (*Lagenaria siceraria*), sunflower (*Helianthus annuus*), chenopod (*Chenopodium berlandieri*); cultigens also included Jerusalem artichoke (*Helianthus tuberosus*), erect knotweed (*Polygonum erectum*), little barley (*Hordeum pusillum*), maygrass (*Phalaris caroliniana*), and possibly others.

14. Whiting, *Ethnobotany of the Hopi.*

15. G. L. Wilson, *Agriculture of the Hidatsa Indians: An Indian Interpretation* (1917; reprint, Lincoln, NB: J. & L. Reprint Company, 1977).

16. George F. Will and George E. Hyde, *Corn Among the Indians of the Upper Missouri* (1917; reprint, Lincoln: University of Nebraska Press, 1964).

17. D. E. Moerman, *Medicinal Plants of Native America,* Technical Reports 19 (Ann Arbor: University of Michigan Museum of Anthropology, 1986). A two-volume compilation of medicinal plant use by Native Americans.

18. Ibid.

19. Ibid., xiv. Scientific names for plants listed are *Acorus calamus, Achillea millefolium, Artemisia tridentata, Mentha arvensis, Prunus serotina, Sanguinaria canadensis, Prunus virginiana, Heracleum maximum, Lomatium dissectum,* and *Pinus strobus.*

20. V. J. Vogel, *American Indian Medicine* (Norman: University of Oklahoma Press, 1970).

21. Several species of tobacco grow in western North America, and these were variously collected in the wild and/or cultivated. No native species occur in eastern North America, and the first tobacco in this region was *Nicotiana rustica,* which was introduced about A.D. 1000 from Mexico or the West Indies. The tobacco commonly grown today, *N. tabacum,* probably originated in South America but was first encountered by the Spanish in Yucatan early in the 1600s.

22. *Datura stramonium.*

23. Because charms are an integral part of Native American religion and medicine, they are described in many books on ethnobotany, for example: Gladys Tantaquidegeon, *Folk Medicine of the Delaware and Related Algonkian Indians,* Anthropological Series 3 (Harrisburg: Pennsylvania

Historical and Museum Commission, 1977).

24. *Equisetum* spp., also known as "scouring rushes" or "Indian sandpaper."

25. Nettles (*Laportea canadensis, Urtica gracilis, Boehmeria cylindrica*), milkweed (*Asclepias*, especially *A. incarnata*, and *A. syriaca*), Indian hemp (*Apocynum cannabinum*), dogbane (*A. androsaemifolium*).

26. Turner, *Food Plants of British Columbia Indians,* vol. 3, *Plants in British Columbia Indian Technology* (1979), 152.

27. Ibid., 68–71, 74–90.

28. Ibid., 68–71.

29. Ibid., 44–45.

30. Two inexpensive publications on natural plant dyeing are handbooks reprinted from the Brooklyn Botanic Garden Record, *Plants and Gardens: Dye Plants* and *Dyeing and Natural Plant Dyeing* 20:3 (1964). They are sometimes available at botanical gardens or garden centers. There are many other publications.

31. L. S. M. Curtin, *By the Prophet of the Earth: Ethnobotany of the Pima* (Tucson: University of Arizona Press, 1984). Also see Whiting, *Ethnobotany of the Hopi.*

10

The Sacred Cedar Tree of the Kʷakʷaka'wakʷ People

DAISY SEWID-SMITH (MAYANILTH)
AND
CHIEF ADAM DICK (KʷAXSISTALA)

INTERVIEWED BY NANCY J. TURNER

IN THIS INTERVIEW, Daisy Sewid-Smith and Chief Adam Dick explain the profound and long-standing importance of *wilkʷ*, the western red-cedar (*Thuja plicata*), to their people, the Kʷakʷaka'wakʷ (formerly known as Southern Kwakiutl) of

Daisy Sewid-Smith, Mayanilth (left), and Chief Adam Dick, Kʷaxsistala (center), talking with their friend and relative Kim Recalma-Clutesi (right), 1994

PHOTO BY NANCY J. TURNER

northeastern Vancouver Island and the adjacent strait, islands, and mainland of British Columbia. Western red-cedar is a tree in the cypress family (*Cupressaceae*), whose distribution extends along the northwest coast of North America from California to British Columbia and Alaska, and eastward to the Rocky Mountains. It grows in rich, moist sites, and is shade-tolerant. Its wood is soft and even-grained, easily split, and rot-resistant. Its bark is gray and vertically fissured on the outside; the inner bark is tough and fibrous and the bark can be pulled off the tree in long strips. The leaves are small, overlapping scales, and the cones are small and ellipsoid, often produced in large numbers on the scaly green boughs.[1]

Background

Nancy Turner: Daisy, who were your most important teachers in preparing you for your role as historian, writer, and language and culture specialist?

Daisy Sewid-Smith: There were several people who were very influential in my life, but the most important teachers were my father, Chief James Sewid, my grandmother Daisy Roberts, and my other grandmother Agnes Alfred, whom everybody knew as 7Axuw.

When I could barely remember, my grandmother Agnes used to take me home weekends, and I'd sleep with her, and my aunt, who's only a couple years older than myself, and all night she would be teaching us history, the legends, customs, traditions, taboos. Then, my grandmother Daisy was known for her knowledge of the potlatch system, and everything was done by memory. She knew every seat. She knew who occupied those seats, who had rights to the potlatch standing as we called them. . . . In fact, she was like the way my granny Agnes was. People came from the whole Kʷakʷaka'wakʷ Nation to get advice from her.[2]

And my father was the same. . . . [He] was very knowledgeable. He was raised traditionally and . . . his training was based on his future as a hereditary

Western red-cedar,
wilkʷ (Thuja plicata)

PHOTO BY NANCY J. TURNER

chief. . . . He lived in both cultures, where my two grand-mothers were strictly traditionalists, but my father lived in two worlds . . . he taught me that education was the best way to handle the prejudices and bigotry in the world. And instead of keeping things from Europeans, he said it was bet-ter to teach them . . . because, he said, bigotry came out of ignorance.[3]

Traditional
Use of Plants

Nancy Turner: Could you describe some of the ways in which wild plants were important to your people, and maybe give some examples of plants that were culturally important, and how they were important?

Daisy Sewid-Smith: Plants were used as foods, a lot of the roots were used as foods, and a lot of the roots were used to make baskets, and some of the other utensils. But the most impor-tant, I think, is that plants were used as medicine. And this was very, very important to the Native people. And many of the herbs were harvested, put away. This is what a lot of the medicine men and women used to cure people with. And many people themselves would gather these plants and use them, on themselves. I, myself—the doctors gave up on me and I was saved through plants. My grandmother used three plants to cure me. So, I know [the medicine] works. I had tuberculosis and I know it works.

Nancy Turner: How old were you when you were so sick?

Daisy Sewid-Smith: Twice, I had tuberculosis. When I was nine, and then it recurred in my kidney when I was twenty-three. And, they used red alder (*X̱ax̱ʷm̓əs, Alnus rubra*) bark, and . . . *məmt'aneẏ* [grand fir, *Abies grandis*] . . . and, I can't remember the name of the third medicine they used on me. But, there's the yew tree (*Taxus brevifolia*), they used a lot of the yew tree.[4] And there were certain leaves that they used for swellings, and there's a variety of things that they used for certain illnesses, certain ailments.

Nancy Turner: I've heard from various of the elders I've worked with that when they were harvesting the bark for medicine, for example, they'd just take one strip from the sunrise side of the tree. Have you heard of that?

Daisy Sewid-Smith: Yes . . . if you remove too much of the bark you will kill that tree. And that was something that they were really careful of, that you do not remove too much to harm that plant. And even when they used to cut boards from [red-cedar] trees, they were very careful not to cut more than that tree could bear. It might be one or two boards from a tree, and then leave that tree standing to continue growing.

The Cedar Tree

Nancy Turner: Could you tell more about the cedar tree—its Kʷakʷʼwala name, and how it is important to the Kʷakʷaka'wakʷ people?

Daisy Sewid-Smith: We call the cedar *wilkʷ* and . . . the bark was used and, in fact, every part of that tree was used. Our houses, the beams, they were all made out of the cedar tree. The boards that were on the houses, they were from this tree. The utensils we have, the canoes, there was just so much that came from this tree. And the bark, of course, was stripped during the spring when it was easily removed and then the outer part was stripped off and then they worked on [the inner bark] until it became soft. And this was our clothing, and our blankets, and our mats, and our towels. And so, every part of that tree was very important for us.

Nancy Turner: Did they use the branches as well?

Daisy Sewid-Smith: They used that [the boughs] for . . . preparing food, sometimes using it as mats, and sometimes decorating the big house, so, it was used as well.

Nancy Turner: And the wooden part of the branches, have you ever heard of making rope from the branches themselves, or using those for baskets?

Daisy Sewid-Smith: They used it for baskets. For rope [and fishing line], they used kelp [*Nereocystis luetkeana*].

Nancy Turner: Cedar is described as a sacred tree for the Kᵂakᵂaka'wakᵂ people and other Northwest Coast First Nations. Why is it special? And how is its sacredness expressed?

Origin of the Cedar Bark Ceremony
from Daisy's Ancestor

Daisy Sewid-Smith: I guess I have to tell the story about *c'e-qameý—c'eqameý* was my ancestor. At the beginning I said I'm a *mamaliliqəla* actually I'm a *mamaliliqəla-qᵂiqᵂasut'in-uxᵂ*. Every tribe has their origin, what they call their sacred origin, and they talk about how they originated, and how their ancestors came down. And that's exactly what they call it, *gelgalis* —how they originated, and how they survived after the flood. Every tribe has their own flood stories. And my ancestor *c'e-qameý* was told that this flood was coming, and he was told how to prepare for it. And he was told to go to look for a large cedar tree, and to hollow it out. And when I talk about a cedar tree today, people cannot even visualize what the great trees were like. When I talk about

Basket

The KᵂakᵂakaⱯwakᵂ and other Northwest Coast peoples made baskets and many other objects from red-cedar bark, wood, and roots.

UNKNOWN TRIBE, NORTHWEST COAST, COLLECTED PRE-1916 CMNH 7851-63, GIFT OF MATHILDE AND DOROTHEA W. HOLLIEDT

a cedar tree, they think about a little cedar tree that you see [today] in comparison to the trees we had before. But the cedar trees were enormous. They were like big huge buildings, if you hollowed them out, they were so enormous. I'm talking about first growth forest cedar trees.

And so *c'eqameý* was told to go and look for one of these [giant cedar trees] and hollow it out. And then he was told to put pitch on all the different holes in the tree so that the water wouldn't come in.[5] And he was told that out of his whole tribe, there was only himself, his wife, his daughter, and his four sons that were to enter this cedar tree. And it was to be sealed with pitch when he went inside the hollow tree, and he was not to open it until he was again told when [to do so], even though people would be begging to go into the tree. And so that's what he did. He prepared the tree and he put all the food and all the things he would need in the tree, and then he sealed himself and his family in this tree.

And then bumblebees were ordered to guard the tree and to sting anyone who tried to swim toward the tree and get into it. . . . While he was inside the cedar tree, *c'eqamey* was told to weave the first cedar headdress, the first cedar neck ring, wrist rings, and ankle rings. And he was told to put the faces of men all around his cedar head ring and his cedar neck ring, and this was to signify two things . . . that he was saved, from out of all his tribe, and also that from that day on, he was to honor and respect the cedar that saved his life, and that he was going to be the first one ever to perform what we now call the cedar bark ceremony. And he was told how it was going to be performed.

When he entered the cedar tree, his name was *hawilk^w- alal*, which means, "cedar tree," but when he came out, he was told, "You will no longer be *hawilk^{w}alal*; your name will be *c'eqamey*, which means that you will be the first person ever to perform the cedar bark ceremony. And, from there, it'll spread among your nation." And so, when he came out [when the flood waters receded], this is what happened. Through him, the cedar bark ceremony spread among all the K^{w}ak^{w}aka'wak^w people.

Nancy Turner: And that name *c'eqamey*—did you say once that that means "pomp and ceremony"? Is that how it would translate?

Daisy Sewid-Smith: *c'eqa*, we call the red-cedar bark ceremony *c'eqa*. If we refer to someone as being *c'eqa*, it means a person that is doing whatever chore they're doing very slowly and very pompously—regally, yes, very regally. And you could call a person *c'eqa*, like if you're in a hurry to go somewhere and you're taking your sweet time, they will say that you're *c'eqa*, meaning that you're taking it slow and regally, not in a hurry for anything. So that word is used everyday in that [meaning].

Use of Spruce Pitch, Spruce Branches, and Yew Wood

Nancy Turner to Adam Dick: Would you describe the spruce pitch [used, for example, to seal the cedar tree by *c'eqamey̓*] and how they would prepare it?

Adam Dick: My grandfather goes in the woods and looks for this good-sized spruce tree [ʔalúwas, *Picea sitchensis*], and puts a notch in it. So they put a [piece of] bark in it. That pitch will drip onto the bark, [or] on a leaf; in the summer they use the skunk-cabbage leaves [*k'aoq'ʔw̓*, *Lysichiton americanus*]. And that's the "waxed paper" the old people use. It doesn't stick on there, 'cause there's some kind of wax in it, I guess, whatever it is, I don't know. [**Daisy Sewid-Smith:** Yes, it's got a waxy surface.] And when they think they got enough [pitch], they roll it in a ball . . . if this is [to be] put in a crack on a canoe, they roll it until it softens up, and that wood has to be dry. And they fill up the [crack]. [**Nancy Turner:** Push it right down into the crack?] Yes, they push it right down with something, a stick. And after that they go get the ends of the spruce branches, *dəwix* [branches of the young spruce tree], and they twist it. And they drill a hole and put it through there and tie a knot. And they put a yew wood [*xemqiy̓*, *Taxus brevifolia*] wedge there, to close it up when that pitch is in there, to tighten it up.

They use lots of that [yew wood] for a wedge. . . . It's like oak, I guess, it's hard, really hard, tough wood. And my grandfather used lots of those [yew] branches for a wedge, to build a canoe with. [The wedges] are all different shapes, and all got names. . . . I just remember one . . . *wixtoləxs*. It's bent like this [curved] . . . that's what we dig in the [wood], wedging the wood when you hollow the canoe. They used lots of that [kind of wedge]. And the *dəwix* [spruce branches]. . . . They take all those little branches out of there, the needles, and then you twist it, 'til it gets really soft, and that's what they use for tying up [as a rope]. . . . They use lots of that.

Cedar Bark and Its Preparation
for the Cedar Bark Ceremony

Nancy Turner: What is the Kʷak̓ʷala name for cedar bark?

Adam Dick, Daisy Sewid-Smith: It's *xagʷigey* when . . . it's still on the tree. . . . When you've fallen it, then it's *xudzigeŷ*.

Daisy Sewid-Smith: And then you turn it into *dənas* [when it's stripped].

Adam Dick (explaining the different words used for different states of the cedar bark): It's just like . . . those clouds out there. When that [cloud] comes down to the water, we call it *p̓əlxala* [fog], but when it's up there [higher up], it's *ʔənweŷ* [cloud].

Nancy Turner: Would you say more about the cedar bark guardian?[6]

Daisy Sewid-Smith: In the early days, every family was designated a certain [type of work], it was kind of like employment. . . . Like if your family was a fisherman, your sons would probably be fishermen, and if they were hunters, they were probably going to be hunters, [or] canoe makers [and so on]. . . . The cedar bark [for ceremonial use] was not just gathered by anyone. This . . . is different from those that might be making baskets—they would gather their own. I am talking about the sacred cedar bark . . . for the cedar bark ceremony, that *c̓eqameŷ* started. . . .

This particular position [harvesting cedar bark for sacred ceremonies] was handed down since the flood. Right after the flood, apparently, every tribe picked a certain family that would be responsible for the gathering of the cedar bark for the cedar bark ceremonies for the winter. And that family was responsible for gathering it, stripping it from the tree, and stripping the bark, and then softening the bark with what they called *kadzayuŵ*; it reminds me of a large fillet knife, except it's made out of wood. You lay the cedar bark on [a piece of wood] that looks like the table [edge], and it's rounded, and you tap this large wooden instrument on the cedar . . . after you wet it. This is how you soften it.

And then they work it. . . . They work it, and work it into cedar strips. There's a large ring that is made, that the eldest daughter of that particular family will stand inside. That is how the cedar is presented in the big house. It's quite a regal presentation. No one's allowed to speak when the cedar

bark is brought in. The cedar is referred to as ʔada—that means "something that is revered, very highly respected." And usually the person standing inside the cedar is called ʔAda [or] ʔAdagilaxʷ—they get a name referring to this cedar ring. And the family dyes it, like when they're preparing it, they dye it, and get it ready. And then they weave hamac'a head rings.

Only the hamac'a and the nulcistalal and q'uminəwaGas—

those hamac'a societies—they were the only ones with woven headdresses. That [headdress] was kept by the cedar bark guardian and then given to them at this ceremony. The hamac'a had pure red-cedar bark ring headgear, and the others had what we call mixed; it was mixed white and red. And so, anyway, they would bring this large cedar bark ring in. And again, from the time of the flood, the person that cuts the cedar ring at the ceremony— they cut it, and then they cut it into pieces later— that's also hereditary, it's handed from father to son since the flood. And this particular person that does the cutting would have a name like ʔAdagilakʷ [or] ʔAʔadaGəmey, referring to the cedar. And now, the grandmothers and mothers are given the name ʔAda to reflect the reverence, the importance, the respect [for which] . . . society

TOP: *The late Herbert Martin*, Mica, *friend and relative of Daisy Sewid-Smith, beside the big dance house at Alert Bay, British Columbia 1969*

He is dressed in his ceremonial regalia, including headgear and cedar bark neck rings. Two young dancers sit nearby.

PHOTO BY ROBERT D. TURNER

BOTTOM: *Red alder*, X̌əx̌ʷmes (Alnus rubra)

Its bark was used for medicine and also to dye the cedar bark for ceremonial regalia.

PHOTO BY NANCY J. TURNER

197

considers that position. And, fathers and male figures that are considered very important would have the name ʔAdagilakʷ, ʔAʔadaGəmey.

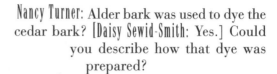

Nancy Turner: Alder bark was used to dye the cedar bark? [Daisy Sewid-Smith: Yes.] Could you describe how that dye was prepared?

Daisy Sewid-Smith: You would just put the alder [X̌əx̌ʷm̓əs, *Alnus rubra*] in water, you pour hot water [over it], and that dye will come out . . . the water will turn red. And that's when you would take the cedar bark—it's not white, it's kind of a yellowish—and you would dip it in there and soak it . . . and then it would pick up the dye.

Bentwood cedar box, with cedar bark canoe bailer and woven basket, items belonging to Kim Recalma-Clutesi

PHOTO BY NANCY J. TURNER

Nancy Turner: Did the bark that was used for the dye come from a tree of a certain age? Did it have to be collected at a certain time of year?

Daisy Sewid-Smith: Usually in the spring; in the spring they collect it. Yes, and it had to be an adult tree [with thicker bark], not a young tree.

Nancy Turner: And, I guess it would be made in a big pot? [Daisy Sewid-Smith: Yes.] About how much bark would you need?

Daisy Sewid-Smith: I don't know, I guess it depends on how much cedar bark you'd be soaking. I drink alder bark tea . . . you know immediately the color when you pour water on it [bright reddish-orange]? Well they used to leave it soaking for a couple of days, and the longer you have it soaking, the stronger and darker the color it gets.

Bentwood Cedar Box

Nancy Turner: Chief Dick, could you describe for us how the bentwood cedar box was made?

Adam Dick: Well . . . that's that *wilkʷ* again, the cedar. . . . You split it in half [the trunk], then you slice it after that [into wide boards]. They used that tool called *lat'ayuw* to slice that wood. And when it's sliced, and you start working on the box, and when you got it something like this [board of the right size], how big a box you want . . . you measure it with your hands. There's no rulers. They don't use those rulers or anything like that. My grandfather used to just go like this [measure length with his hands]—then you put a mark on it. Then you cut in where you're going to bend [it]. But it's gotta be straight 'cause it has to be squared off. They made a wooden square [called] *ńińamanuuʔ*, that's the square that they use to measure something. That come out of the wood [cedar] too. They use that, to square it off.

And [then] they put water on it [the board], or a lot of times they take it down to the river and soak it. They put heavy rocks on it to keep it under for two or three days, 'cause [when] it's all soaked, the water's soaked in it, then you bend it. But nowadays, they use steam. They steam it now, but they don't do that in them days. They just soak it in the river, they soften it up . . . before they bend it. But if it's dry, it'll break. It has to be soaked.

[To bend it] . . . they use a pole, a pole about this big [about six inches long] where they're going to bend [at the transverse kerf, or groove]. And they put weight on it so that it will never move when you lift this [end] up, that's after it's soaked, with water.

Nancy Turner: So they have the sides of the box, and they come together, the ends come together at the corner? [Adam Dick: Yes.] Then how do they fix the ends together at the last corner?

Adam Dick: When you got it together, you *yəlcəm* [tie] with *dəwix*, those [spruce] branches, you twist it. Then you drill it. Then you put wooden pegs in it to hold it together. And that's yew wood pegs.

Daisy Sewid-Smith: That was our nails, 'cause it was hard.

Adam Dick: It was hard. And they had it shaped like that, real sharp at the end. Pointed. And then you hammer it in. Well, my grandfather used the hammers you got now, but in the early days, they used a *peqpelq* [stone mallet], Dad had one. . . .

Nancy Turner: And then they would put another piece of board, fix it for the bottom of the box? And peg it the same way?

Adam Dick: Yes, everything is pegged. Just the lid, is just fit right on the top.

Nancy Turner: The boxes, then I guess they would often paint them?

Adam Dick: No, no, they don't, there's no paint. All the bent-wood boxes that my grandmother left, there's no paint on them. And it just turned black, darker than this oak here [dark brown], after a while. You know, that's where you put all your smoked fish, for the winter supply, when it's all dried up, they put it in, especially that *t'əqa* [dried cakes of berries or seaweed], you know the dried salmonberries [*q'əmdzək*ʷ, *Rubus spectabilis*] . . . dried salalberries [*nək'*ʷ*əl, Gaultheria shallon*], dried seaweed [*ləq'stən, Porphyra abbottae*]. . . . They're all piled in there. [Daisy Sewid-Smith: They're flat . . . cakes.] Yes, they're all piled [in].

And there's all different sizes, you know. There's big ones, there, for *cəlx*ʷ *sta*, wild crabapples *[Malus fusca;* preserved-in-water], and they fill it up, they boil it first and they pour it into the thing, and they seal it with the *xina*, with the eulachon oil, about that thick [two to three inches], and when it gets hard, like that, it's something like a wax, to seal it . . . in those boxes. I guess that's why they [the boxes] turn black, 'cause that oil gets right into that wood, sinks right into that wood.

Nancy Turner: The highbush cranberries *[Viburnum edule],* they did do that with those as well?

Adam Dick: Oh, yes, oh yes . . . *qiqəlis,* yes [highbush cran-berries]. You know, just the cranberries and the *cəlx*ʷ— wild crabapples, but the salmonberries, you dry them

[Daisy Sewid-Smith: In cakes.], same with huckleberries and blueberries [*Vaccinium parvifolium, V. membranaceum, V. ovalifolium*, and other species] and so on.

Daisy Sewid-Smith: And then when you're ready to use it [dried berry cake], you put it in water and then it comes back.

Adam Dick: Yes, you soak it overnight. That's your dessert, your dessert in the winter months, when there's no more berries.

Nancy Turner: Is there any more you would like to say about the bentwood box?

Bentwood chest with lid

Bentwood boxes made for everyday use often were not decorated. Ornately carved and painted chests like this one held the family heirlooms and regalia. On special occasions the house-master sat on a chest, and on his death it sometimes became his coffin.

HAIDA, MID 1800s
CMNH 3178-109a & b

Daisy Sewid-Smith: Adam's already mentioned they store food in it. We also had large bentwood boxes to store clothing. We also had bentwood boxes that were kept at the clan chief's house—a lot of people don't like me using "clan," but it's the only way to explain it—and they would store mountain goat fur, which is equivalent to [money], it was our cash.[7] We would use it to buy things from other tribal groups or within our own Nation. . . . And eventually, Hudson's Bay [Company] changed the mountain goat fur into Hudson's Bay blankets. . . . They would give a certain amount of Hudson's Bay blankets to our people for one of the mountain goat furs. And they could use Hudson's Bay blankets to purchase things at the [Hudson's Bay] store. So it was really equivalent to cash.

Nancy Turner: I see, yes. When you say mountain goat fur, is that with the wool still attached to the hide?

Daisy Sewid-Smith: To the hide, right.[8]

Nancy Turner: Did the boxes have special places in the house where they were stored? Did they put them on the floor?

Daisy Sewid-Smith: In the bedroom, what they called the bedroom. . . . The bedrooms were partitioned off. See, the big houses, when you go to the big houses—we just use it for ceremonial houses now—but in the early days, you had about thirty-five or more people living in them; you had several families living in those big houses. They would have four fires, one on each corner. And then the big houses would be partitioned off into bedrooms. Your chief was always in the back portion of the house, and the [people] of lesser importance were in the front. And that was because of raids. They had to protect the chief and his family, and give them a chance to get out if they were raided. That's the reason why they had that, the way that big house was laid out.

Explanation of the Difference
Between Prayer and Words of Praise

Nancy Turner: We were talking another time about the work of [the anthropologist] Dr. Franz Boas. He spent a lot of time with your people. He worked with people to try and record your cultural traditions. But sometimes he might not translate things the way they really should be translated. . . . For example, in *The Religion of the Kwakiutl Indians,* he uses the word prayer when he's talking about how people would address the things that they used in the woods, the plants and other things.[9] Could you elaborate on that word and why it's not really appropriate?

Daisy Sewid-Smith: Well, we have three words we use in worshiping, in sacred things we do. *hawaxʔela* means "to pray," *c'əlwaqa* means "to praise," and *ʔəmẏaxa* means "to worship." And the word that's constantly in Boas's book is *c'əlwaqa.* A person would *c'əlwaqa* a tree for giving its life for whatever project that person had. They would *c'əlwaqa* a salmon for giving its life for them; *c'əlwaqa* means "praise." So, the way it's written [in Boas's book] looks like we're worshiping everything in nature, that we're nature-worshipers, but we're not. We are stewards of nature. Yes, we did acknowledge a plant, a tree, a salmon, an animal for giving its life so that we may live. There's a big difference between *c'əlwaqa* [and *ʔəmẏaxa*]—I could *c'əlwaqa* a person; I can *c'əlwaqa* you. To do that, I would gather a group of people, and I would praise you for the things you've done. I'm not worshiping you. I am praising you for the things you've done. And that's a big difference for the two words, of worshiping and praying. If we had been praying to that tree, the person that recorded it would have used the word *ʔəmẏaxa*, not *c'əlwaqa*.

Comparing Traditional Kʷakʷaka'wakʷ and "Western" Attitudes Toward Nature

Nancy Turner: How would you characterize or describe the traditional attitude of the Kʷakʷaka'wakʷ people to the natural world, and how would you say that attitude differs from the prevailing European attitude?

Daisy Sewid-Smith: When we're talking about Kʷakʷaka'wakʷ people, there are two types—the traditionalists, and the people who I guess you would call "Euro-Kwagulhs" because they are . . . not different from Europeans. But traditionalists are very close to their environment, and they know that to survive in this world, you have to have respect for your environment, because without the environment you cannot live. If you destroy your environment, you are destroying yourself. And this is something that the Europeans don't seem to understand, or they don't want to think about it. . . . They seem to think that they are immortals, that they will live on forever, not realizing that when they do destroy all the trees, all the plant life, that oxygen will cease to exist and we will die. And, this is something that our people were very aware of. . . .

Nancy Turner: So, not only did you use resources from nature, but you respect those resources. Is that what you're saying?

Daisy Sewid-Smith: Yes. When we took something from the environment . . . we were careful just to take what we needed. And that is something that . . . is a difference between traditionalist Kwagulhs and Europeans today. We only took what we personally needed, and no more, whereas the Europeans are reaping our resources to supply the rest of the world, not thinking of its effects, how it's going to affect us in the future.

Nancy Turner: In the traditional lifestyle, were there people who were always monitoring, watching carefully what changes might be occurring, so they would know when they were harvesting too much, for example?

Daisy Sewid-Smith: It was not the idea of harvesting too much; sometimes something would happen where a certain plant won't grow as much as it did last year. And they said it's a cycle that happens—fish will disappear and there won't be very much fish—and yes, they did have people monitoring this. And when they could see that there was going to be scarcity, then they were not allowed to go to that particular area. They were told to go to another area, and let that area build up. And yes, they did have people within the clan or tribal groups that monitored these changes.

Nancy Turner: You were telling me once about how they would notice the deer, and if the deer had twins it meant that the populations were healthy. If they just had single fawns that year, they would be more careful because they knew they wouldn't be as plentiful?

Daisy Sewid-Smith: Yes. Well, there were certain signs that they looked at. Like, I remember my grandmother telling me that if there is snow in the late spring on top of the mountains then there'll be a lot of fish, and if there isn't then there is a danger that there'll be scarcity. There were certain things that they looked at. The Moon, how the Moon would appear in the sky—there were certain things that they always looked at to tell them how things were going to work out for the season.

Impacts of Industrial Forestry
on the Kʷakʷaka'wakʷ People

Nancy Turner: What have been some of the impacts that you have observed or experienced of industrial forestry on your people and on the traditional life-ways of your people?

Daisy Sewid-Smith: Well, clearcut logging . . . is the most devastating of all the practices. The reason for that is that they clear large areas of forest with no concern of any of the other plants. . . . When they fall a tree, all they're looking at is a tree. And when we try and fight for a particular area, they're just thinking, "the tree." But we are not just thinking of the tree. We are thinking holistically of the whole environmental damage. The plants, the tree that was used for medicine. . . . It's medicine that's our greatest concern. The area where my grandmother used to go to get my medicine, it's not there anymore. The plants have disappeared because of clearcut logging. . . .

I sympathize for loggers, because it is their job, their employment, and they have families. But, on the other hand, we had to change our lifestyle . . . because of the changes that came. . . . And yet, if they continue the practices that are going on now there'll be *nothing* left. They're saying now that they've started to change the practices. I don't know.

That has just been recent. I'm hoping that they have, that they are more aware of what is the damage that has been happening. And also, by the removal of the trees, many hillsides are sliding. They're sliding down, damaging more plants. Some of them are sliding into the river, and blocking the rivers, [so] that the salmon can't go up, or destroying spawning grounds. There are so many little things that are happening. And many of them claim, "No, it's not happening," but those that grew up there, those that are more aware of their surroundings than many of the people, can see the changes. We see the changes. It's really not very good.

And another thing, too, is that [in] the forest, there's boundaries. Our people used the mountains, the rivers, as their boundaries, and the edge of the forest as their boundaries.

It is now obvious to me that we were not the only ones that recognized these boundaries, that there were certain boundaries that you didn't cross over. The animals of the forest also recognized these boundaries, and would not cross it. And now, with the clearcut logging, I have never seen so many animals crossing those boundaries, going right into cities. And now they are attacking people. . . . The cougars, the bears, the wolves, there's no more boundaries, because there's no more forest. So that is what we see.

Nancy Turner: If you had anything that you thought it was very important to teach the people from our mainstream society, say, with cedar, what would be your message?

Daisy Sewid-Smith: Concerning cedar? Well, it's not only cedar, it's the rest of the plants that are out there. Many of the same people that see nothing wrong with the forest companies removing trees, on the other hand, might be very offended if you kill an animal, because they are animal activists, and they're worried about the extinction of the animals. Well, it applies to the forest and the plants as well . . . they balance each other. And if you continue to reap the things, it's going to become extinct. And many of the plants have become extinct. They've disappeared. . . . I know that many plants are now used in floral decoration, in making flower arrangements and things like this. I know salalberry leaves are very important to the florist industry now and things like that. And so, I just feel that many of the plants and trees will become extinct.

Notes
___

Daisy Sewid-Smith is historian of the Mamaliliqela Tribe of Village Island, presently with the Campbell River School District, Campbell River, British Columbia. Her name, *Mayanilth* was given to her by Chief Henry Bell. She is author of *Prosecution or Persecution?* (Cape Mudge Village, Quathiaski Cove, British Columbia: Nu-yum-balees Society, Kwagulh Museum, 1979), on the outlawing of the potlatch and the arrest and imprisonment of her people who were charged with participation in a potlatch. The laws banning the potlatch were not lifted until 1952.

Adam Dick is hereditary chief and elder of the Kᵂakᵂaka'wakᵂ Nation, presently of Qualicum and Victoria, British Columbia. His name, *Kᵂaxsistala*, was given to him by his late father.

Nancy J. Turner is professor, School of Environmental Studies, University of Victoria, Victoria British, Columbia. The interview was taped on October 30, 1994. Our friend and colleague Kim Recalma-Clutesi is acknowledged for her help and support in hosting us and for providing the cedar articles shown in the photographs.

1. For further information on this tree and its uses, see V. J. Krajina, K. Klinka, and J. Worrall, *Distribution and Ecological Characteristics of Trees and Shrubs of British Columbia* (Vancouver, British Columbia: Faculty of Forestry, University of British Columbia, 1982); Franz Boas, *Ethnology of the Kwakiutl*, Thirty-fifth Annual Report of the Bureau of American Ethnology, parts 1 and 2 (Washington D.C.: Smithsonian Institution, 1921); Nancy J. Turner, *Plant Materials of British Columbia First Peoples.* (Victoria: Royal British Columbia Museum and Vancouver: University of British Columbia Press, 1998); Hilary Stewart, *Cedar: Tree of Life to the Northwest Coast Indians* (Seattle: University of Washington Press, 1984); Nancy J. Turner and Marcus A. M. Bell, "The Ethnobotany of the Southern Kwakiutl Indians of British Columbia," *Economic Botany* 27 (1973): 257–310. In addition, a film, *Gathering the Cedar Bark*, featuring Chief Adam Dick and Kim Recalma-Clutesi, which demonstrates the gathering, preparation, and use of cedar bark in the cedar bark ceremonial dances, is available from Wadzid Productions (c/o Kim Recalma-Clutesi, Qualicum, British Columbia.

In general, the orthography used to transcribe Kᵂak'ᵂala [*Kwakwala*] names is based on the International Phonetic Alphabet. There are some exceptions, however. For ease of typing, ǧ is written as G, and *dᶻ*, as dz. The x̌ sound is written as x.

2. Daisy Sewid-Smith explains the meaning of the commonly used term Kwakiutl (*Kᵂagulh*), and why she prefers to use the name Kᵂakᵂaka'wakᵂ for herself and her people:

"We have, or did have, about 19 tribal groups . . . within what we call the Kʷakʷaka'wakʷ, meaning 'those that speak the Kʷak'ʷala language.' And, in the early days, we never referred to ourselves as a Nation. We always referred to ourselves by our tribal names. You're either a *Gusgimukʷ*, *mamaliliqǝla, lhawits'is, nemGis* . . . but we never referred to ourselves as a Nation in a whole; we referred to our tribal names. And then, when Hudson's Bay came along, they went and lived among the Kwagulh people, and that [Kwakiutl or *Kʷagulh* is for] Fort Rupert, that's the tribal name of Fort Rupert. . . . they are called *Kʷagulh*. And that is where the first Hudson's Bay fort was built, in 1845, I believe. And, so, when letters were coming out, or going to the government, or England, etc., they started referring to us as the Kʷagulh Nation, simply because these were the people they were familiar with. But when we talk among ourselves, if we say *Kʷagulh*, people would think we were talking about Fort Rupert, so we have to distinguish that, and now we do it. We now call ourselves Kʷakʷaka'wakʷ, those that speak the Kʷak'ʷala language."

3. See James P. Spradley, ed., *Guests Never Leave Hungry: The Autobiography of James Sewid, a Kwakiutl Indian* (Montreal: McGill-Queen's University Press, 1972). The title is a translation of Jimmy Sewid's name, Pugleedee.

4. Pacific yew (*Taxus brevifolia*) is important for its tough, resilient wood, which was used in making implements requiring strength and flexibility, such as bows, wedges, digging sticks, and harpoon shafts. Today, it is well known as the source of the anticancer drug, taxol.

5. Sitka spruce pitch (*Picea sitchensis*) is described later in the interview by Chief Adam Dick.

6. This discussion actually took place later in the original interview, but the information seems to fit more appropriately here.

7. For a discussion of Kʷakʷaka'wakʷ social organization, see Franz Boas, *Kwakiutl Ethnography* (Chicago: University of Chicago Press, 1966), chapter 3, "Social Organization."

8. Daisy Sewid-Smith elaborated further on the mountain goat fur: "It was coveted by all the tribal groups. And then . . . China really wanted them, and . . . that's what Hudson's

Bay really wanted as well. . . . We called these hides *p'əlxalasGəm* because it's so white. *p'əlxala* means "fog," so it actually means "fog mat or garment"; that's what *p'əlxalasGəm* means. And so when Hudson's Bay . . . started coming out with their Hudson's Bay blanket to take the fur off our hands, our people named those Hudson's Bay blankets *p'əlxalasGəm*, [the] same name as the mountain goat fur, because it was equivalent to the mountain goat fur as trade; . . . it was used actually for cash. Like, a canoe might be worth a thousand mountain goat fur. And that's how our people purchased things with it. . . . Later that would be a thousand Hudson's Bay blankets. . . . I used to tease my grandparents, my mentors: 'what on earth would people be doing piling up all these blankets?' But they were counting their cash, that's what they were doing!"

9. Franz Boas, *The Religion of the Kwakiutl Indians*, vol. 2 (New York: Columbia University Press, 1930).

The Kʷakʷakaʼwakʷ words used in this article are reproduced in the English alphabet and therefore are not entirely accurate. Many of the sounds can only be represented with linguistic symbols which were not available in typesetting.

11

Corn Man and Tobacco Woman in Pima Cosmology

AMADEO M. REA

WHEN THE SUN at its setting on the Sierra Estrella was about
to approach that southernmost point where it stopped for
four days, that time when the People said that the Sun was
in its stopping place, someone from the village went out with
a handful of cornmeal and gave it to the storyteller. This was
an invitation for him to come to the large community lodge,
the smokehouse, and to narrate during the four longest winter nights the Creation Epic, the story of the cosmology and
history of the People.[1]

By this time the velvet mesquites throughout the alluvial
lowlands had dropped their fine dull-olive leaves, giving the
bosques a nondescript color. Killing frosts were driving the
last deep-yellow leaves from the cottonwood forest that
marked the course of the Gila, the big river running the
length of Pima country. The trees were now briefly bare.
Willows, carrizo, and cattails at the river's edge took on paler
yellows and tans, leaving only the thickets of bulrush in deep
dark green. Now that the poisonous animals were all safely in
hibernation, the People were ready for their Creation Story to
be recalled, to be recounted once again.[2]

During four long nights the People, from the youngest to
the oldest, would sit awake, listening, pondering. If they
slept, it was just during daylight, a few hours here and there.
These nights were too sacred for anyone to sleep. The story
began with the creation of the world: how Jewed Maakai,

Earth Doctor or Earth Maker, first made land, then made a helper called Ñui, the Turkey Vulture or Buzzard.[3] Ban or Coyote, the third culture hero, is conceived when Sun and Moon meet in the darkness of the new moon. And finally they are joined by Se'ehe or I'itoi, a being from the north, who insists on being called Elder Brother, though he is the youngest of the four. The main narration in free prose was interspersed with songs—tightly structured poems sung four times through—marking the major events of the narration, and with archaic speeches—difficult prose poetry delivered verbatim.

Night by night the stories continue: the peopling of the Earth, the great flood, locating the center, an exodus, the conquests by the Pima of those who built the great ruins and irrigation system in their land. One story in particular captures the intricacies of the how the Pima lived in this Sonoran Desert environment and the origin of their major ceremonies. The story is deceptively simple, yet it is exceedingly complex, highly structured like a Chinese puzzle.

The long unmarried daughter of a powerful shaman asks to be buried. From her grave grows the tobacco plant, new to the People. Tobacco Woman, the person, returns from her grave. She gambles with Corn Man. They quarrel when she loses but refuses to pay up. Snubbing him, she challenges him to leave saying, "Nobody cares for you, now, but they care a great deal for me, and the doctors [rain shamans] use me to make rain, and when they have moistened the ground is the only time you can come out." Corn Man retorts that, on the contrary, everyone likes him. The neurotic Tobacco, imagining that everybody is laughing at her, leaves secretly for the west, taking up residence on a mountain within the territory of another tribe on the Colorado River.

Without Tobacco, the People can no longer make rain. The two summer planting seasons pass

Taatkam (Picacho Mountain), the place to which Corn Man first returned X and has his shrine

PHOTO BY AMADEO M. REA

and the People scold Corn Man for sending Tobacco Woman away, saying he himself should leave. So, taking his companion, Pumpkin or Squash Man, he departs, singing, toward the east, in the direction of the San Pedro River and the Gila uplands.

Next year, still without water, the community sends Verdin, a little desert bird, who is a powerful shaman, with four votive offerings to entice Tobacco to return. Tobacco sarcastically refuses, but gives Verdin four balls of seed and some droppings of the tobacco horn-worm with these instructions: "Take the dirt of the tobacco-worm, and roll it up, and put it in a cane-tube and smoke it all around, and you will have rain, and then plant the seed, and in four days it will come up; and when you get the leaves, smoke them, and call on the winds, and you will have clouds and plenty of rain."

Verdin Shaman takes the dried leaves to the communal meeting house in the evening and initiates a formal smoking ceremony where each person passes the cane tube pipe to the person next to him, addressing him with some relationship term.

The People endure many years without crops. Finally Corn Man returns to Taatkam (Picacho Mountain) for a while, then to White Thin Mountain in the Santans, and finally to the Superstition Mountains. Here he encounters a nephew with a niece who is gathering and pit-roasting a starvation food, chain-fruit (jumping) cholla. With his arrow he impregnates her roasting pit, and upon opening it she discovers not cactus but corn and squash, nicely cooked together.

Chain-fruit cholla (Opuntia fulgida), *ladened with fruit*

PHOTO BY AMADEO M. REA

Navichu ceremonial mask

PHOTO BY TOM BARR.
COURTESY OF
AMADEO M. REA

Corn Man inquires about Tobacco Woman, and when he learns that she has returned and is still unwed, he sends his young nephew to the village to propose to her shaman father on his behalf. Upon acceptance, Corn Man instructs the father to build a special structure for the nuptial couple, a ceremonial house of sleeping mats reserved for sacred beings such as the masked Navichu and his attendants, a borrowed *katsina* cult.[4] Throughout the night it rains pumpkins and corn into containers the People have set out in swept yards.

In time Tobacco and Corn have a baby, who is a crook-necked squash. One day while they go out to work in their fields, some children come into the house, finding the baby. While playing with it they accidentally drop it, breaking its neck. In anger, Corn Man leaves his wife and goes east for a while. Then he remembers his pets, the Red-winged Blackbirds, which he has left behind, so he returns to his wife. When he leaves again, he scatters corn kernels so the blackbirds will follow him east.

Squash Baby lay broken for a while, then sank under the ground, coming up at Superstition Mountains, where it grew

Saguaro harvest carving

DANNY FLORES, TOHONO O'ODHAM, ARIZONA, 1991
CMNH 35154-2

into a Saguaro. The mother and maternal grandfather, unable to find the Squash Baby, called the People together to search. Coyote was asked to look for it. He smelled around where the baby had lain on the ground, then ran around in circles, searching. He came to where the Saguaro was and thought that it might be the baby, but was not sure. When he returned, he told the People he could not find it. Then they asked if Buzzard would search. Coyote confided to Buzzard, "I did see something, but I was not quite sure, but I want you to examine that Giant Cactus."

Buzzard flew in great circles, examined the Saguaro, then returned. When the People questioned him, he said, "I have found it and it is already full-grown, and I tell you I think something good will happen to us because of it."

When the Saguaro fruit was ripe, the People gathered it, making wine from the sweet, deep red pulp and spreading the small black seeds out in the sun to dry. Badger stole the seeds. When the People discovered this, they sent Coyote after the thief. Circling, Coyote got ahead of Badger on the trail, and when they approached, Coyote tricked him into opening first one long finger then another so he could see what he was carrying in his hand. Suddenly Coyote slapped Badger's hand from below, knocking the seeds into the air. The wind scattered the seeds on the south slopes of the mountain *bajadas* or piedmonts, where you find the Saguaros still growing today.

This is the story line very briefly. But the episode contains, both stated and implied, an entire outline of River Pima cultural ecology and ceremonialism. The narrative encodes the Piman way of looking at resources and living in a specific desert environment. Much of the story is allegory or complex metaphor that was understood to the original listeners, the people of this farming, gathering, fishing, and hunting culture, but which may be obscure to readers from an industrialized society who live essentially outside the confines of nature. We can begin to understand some of the Piman relationship to environment through an analysis of the structure of this epic segment.

Until the early twentieth century, the major crops of the Pima were maize or corn, several species of pumpkin or squash, several species of beans (at least the desert-adapted little tepary and lima), grain chenopod, grain amaranth, cotton, and at some point the white-seeded devil's claw or martynia. These are all warm season crops. The highly productive cool-season wheat was a post-European addition.

Basket with mesquite pods

Symbolic evidence suggests that corn was a major cultivated crop, though it was at least equaled if not exceeded in importance by a wild crop, mesquite. According to the oldest Pima now living, pods of this abundant floodplain tree were harvested by the ton until quite recent times. Mesquite pod products found a place at every meal. But it is maize that is mythically embedded in ceremony. It is the white spots painted on dancers' dark brown skin as well as the white dots on the gourd masks of Navichu singers. Cornmeal marked the sacred trails for dancers and was sprinkled in blessing. It was an offering at shrines.

Ruth Giff, a Pima woman, making a mesquite pod basket from arrow-weed

PHOTO BY AMADEO M. REA

But this mythic episode shows that corn was a temperamental crop, with variable productivity. Three times Corn leaves the People. Germination, growth, pollination, and seed set could be affected by soil moisture, air temperature, and humidity. While everyone *likes* corn, they dare not depend on it. Even Corn's sidekick, Squash Man, is not dependable. Conditions may affect squash plant growth, pollination, and fruit set as well.

Tobacco, while not a food crop, is a fickle and neurotic person who holds the key to the Piman system of agriculture: she is essential in rain-making activities. The story tells how the tobacco plant emerged from Tobacco's grave. (This is but one of several tobacco origin stories.) Her leaves serve two ceremonial functions, both encoded in this myth.[5] The first, the communal smoking ritual in the big lodge, is described in the story. This ritual fosters consensus building in an essentially egalitarian society. The other use of tobacco is shamanistic and individual. Shamans diagnosing sickness blew tobacco smoke over the patient. Other shamans, those involved in rain-making activities, used the smoke to initiate a cycle: smoke produced wind which brought clouds which thundered and produced rain.

This last is the critical role played by Tobacco Woman in the story. Only Tobacco (at this point in mythic time) can make the rain that will permit germination and growth of crops. By withholding rain she can hold both corn and the community hostage. So Corn Man and Squash Man depart to the uplands of the east where there is more natural moisture. During the drought described in this story, Verdin Shaman must first smoke tobacco hornworm droppings so the tobacco seeds she gave him will sprout; then he must smoke some of the early leaves in order to have rain for the tobacco to grow on to maturity. It is like priming a pump.

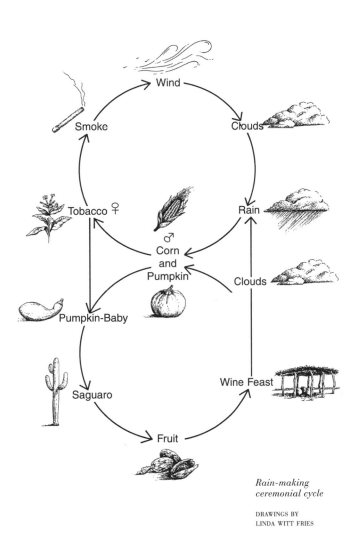

Rain-making ceremonial cycle

DRAWINGS BY
LINDA WITT FRIES

River Pima had two main agricultural strategies available to them, and both are encoded in a speech Corn Man delivers at the nuptial ceremony structure. First, they could plant along the river. The water rose once in the spring from snowmelt, flooding and fertilizing the islands and lower terraces. Then, about midsummer, the river rose again from monsoonal rains in the uplands, once more flooding the farmlands. The double-cropping Pima constructed brush weirs to direct the flow into ditches and onto their fields.[6] The other strategy was to farm the fertile mouths of washes that emerged from the *bajadas* at the bases of the desert mountain ranges such as the Sierra Estrella. If the summer storms hit these relatively low watersheds, water swept through the arroyos, carrying nutrient-rich detritus from rodent and rabbit droppings and nitrogen-rich leaves of leguminous trees, and deposited them at the mouths of washes where the water soaked in. This is called *aki chiñ* farming.

Corn Man's poetic speech obliquely recalls this: "Every low place and every valley was crooked, but the force of the waters straightened them out, and there was driftwood on all the shores [of the river]: and after it was over every low place and every valley *[arroyo]* had foam in its mouth." In the poetry, driftwood indicates the risen river and foam signifies the detritus-laden floodwater rolling down the normally dry washes and other places. The rainmaking doctor (shaman) now takes seeds from his breast and plants them in these wet places, according to the oration.

Corn Man's other nuptial speech is an exquisite piece of poetry.[7] In the east in a shining lodge lives Kingfisher and in the west Bluebird. They fly up and toward each other, meeting at the *hik*, the navel, the middle of the Earth. This is a brief recapitulation of an earlier episode when two birds are sent out after the flood to fly toward each other four times in order to locate mathematically the navel, the center of the world where the Pima are to live. The Pimans, then, are centered people, both geographically and psychologically, and have been so since mythic times.[8]

One of Corn Man's speeches ends: "So everything came up, and there was plenty to eat, and the people gathered it up, and the young boys and girls ate and were happy, and the old

men and old women ate and lengthened even their few days."
The other tells of boys and girls shouting and whistling among
the growing crops. Both finish: "So think of this, my relatives,
and know that we are not to suffer with hunger always."

The story of Corn Man and Tobacco Woman includes the
origin of the Wine Feast, an elaborate communal liturgical
celebration associated with rainmaking. In an episode quoted
above, Buzzard predicts, "I think something good will happen
to us because [of the Saguaro]." The story says simply that
the People gathered its fruit and made *navait*, a ciderlike
wine; the listeners knew the rest.[9] In midsummer, when the
Saguaro fruit ripened, they gathered it, strained out the seeds,
boiled the juice down to a syrup, some of which was mixed
with water and brewed. During the fermenting there was formal singing and dancing by the community. The songs refer
to rain and things associated with rain: toads, mockingbirds,
red velvet mites, black clouds, down feathers, eagle primary
feathers, horned lizards, centipedes, swallows, rainbows,
algae, driftwood, flood foam, wash debris. (This may seem a
strange list, but it is not to those familiar with the summer
rainy season in the Sonoran Desert.)

The People of each visiting village are invited to sit and
drink. The function of the ritual is explained to everyone: to
drink, get drunk, vomit, and hence symbolically to draw the
winds that produce the clouds and ultimately the rains.
Mockingbird speeches describe what the People hope will
happen: rain and growth, particularly of Corn:

> And a thick root came forth,
> And a thick stalk came forth;
> Great broad leaves came forth;
> And well they ripened.

Wine Feasts, held asynchronously in Piman country
throughout the monsoonal season, are intended to *continue*
the rain so that the crops may grow and, most importantly,
mature during this "short planting" season, before the
killing frosts of fall. For the Tohono O'odham, or Papago,
the *aki chiñ* farming with summer rains was the major (usually the only) method of agriculture before the advent of

ground-water pumping. For the Gila Pima it was an alternate strategy, but summer rains in the eastern watersheds were still necessary to provide floodwater in their river for their second planting.

Among the Gileños there was an additional rainmaking or "rain-calling" ceremony, the *jujkida*. This involved a number of shamans and singers in an intervillage event during times of drought.[10] The smoking of ceremonial cigarettes, the formal seating arrangement, and the recitation of orations similar to (or the same as) Mockingbird speeches suggest the ceremony was an abbreviated version of the Wine Feast, though Saguaro is nowhere mentioned. The prominent plant, instead, is greasewood, used to make the sacred scraping sticks accompanying the songs.[11] This bush, with its pale, bluish green, needlelike leaves, is for some reason associated with rain. "So important are these instruments in Pima rain ceremonies," wrote Frank Russell, "that they are usually spoken of as 'rain sticks.'"[12]

Both the corn and tobacco, in nuptial union, are prominent in the *jujkida* oration, however:

Scraping sticks, made from greasewood (Sarcobatus vermiculatus) and played in Pima rain ceremonies.

PHOTO BY TOM BARR

COURTESY OF
AMADEO M. REA

He placed a brand of fire down before me and a cigarette also. Lighting the cigarette he puffed smoke toward the west in a great white arch. The shadow of the arch crept across the earth beneath. A grassy carpet covers the earth. Scattering seed, he caused the corn with the large stalk, large leaf, full tassel, good ears to grow and ripen. As the sun's rays extend to the plants, so our thoughts reach out to the time when we would enjoy the life-giving corn. With gladness we cooked and ate the corn and, free from hunger and want, were happy.[13]

Conclusion

Children of the Industrial Revolution are ill-equipped to understand the Piman cosmological perspective. In modern, urban America, one may step out of the condo in the morning, walk a few yards across pavement to the car, rush off to work in an office with an artificially controlled environment, and at the prompting of a seasonless clock return home over paved roads; or one drives to the mall, picks up chicken and beef in plastic wrappers, milk in waxed containers, cereals in boxes, never seeing the soil the fruits and vegetables must have grown in. Back home a flick of a switch produces light, a twist of a knob produces water, and another flick supplies an evening's entertainment. Ritual is the ten o'clock news, nature is through the eye of a video cameraman, and even sex may be largely voyeuristic. One goes to sleep with the conviction that when needs arise, technology will be there, the ultimate savior.

Through the images and metaphors of the Corn Man and Tobacco Woman episode of the midwinter Piman Creation Epic, we can glimpse quite a different perspective held by a desert tribe. The Piman view of history and economic activity is circular and cyclic, not linear. A harvested plant that is smoked produces wind, which makes clouds, which drop the rain that makes plant growth possible. Squash Baby became the Saguaro whose fruit provides the essential ingredient for the Wine Feast, which brings the rain clouds that water the earth to grow crops and insure that the Saguaros will produce fruit the following year.

The People are not passive participants in this cycle; both as a community and as individuals, they must play an active role in it. The communal celebration of the wine liturgy and the *jujkida* rainmaking have already been discussed. But the farmer also has a responsibility, as an individual, to sing in the fields to promote the growth and development of his crops. This was considered just as important as other farming activities— irrigating, weeding, or cultivating. There were specific songs for planting, for germinating and emerging plants, for growing plants, and for plants in flower and tassel. There were other songs that spoke of the swaying green corn leaves that prefigured the wind and the squash leaves with their white blotches that prefigured the clouds. The beating of the drum baskets and the reverberations of the rasping sticks symbolized the thunder before the rain. There was a series of songs honoring Corn's sacred refuge, Taatkam (Picacho Mountain).

Groups of singers might get together to sing all night in the fields. One Pima song says:

> The darkness of evening
> Falls as we sing before the sacred prayer sticks
> About us on all sides corn tassels are waving. . . .

> The white light of day dawn yet finds us singing
> While the squash leaves are waving.

Prayer sticks, made of arrow-weed and a few feathers tied with native white cotton, were planted in the fields as votive offerings. Wing and tail feathers of the Golden Eagle represented the heavy dark clouds lying in the east, while its white down feathers were the small clouds sailing in the west. But it was always the People who were responsible for putting themselves into the cycle, turning it. They were not outside it or above it, but actively within it.

The individual Piman person perceived an intimate connection between himself or herself and the rest of the created world. Objectively, singing to the corn and squash plants growing in fields does not provide nourishment or other essentials to the plant. But the songs confirm and reinforce the relationship between the singer/farmer and the natural world.[14]

Finally, sharing resources went beyond the confines of one's immediate community. Corn Man's oration at the sacred mat house contains this reminder: "And the relatives heard of those good years, and the plenty to eat, and there came a relative leading her child by the hand, who said, 'We will go right on, for our relatives must have plenty to eat, and we shall not always suffer with hunger.' So these came, but did not eat it all, but returned." The story's listeners understood. There was no need to say specifically that the woman and child represented the Tohono O'odham or Papago. These relatives, with fewer resources, regularly came to the River People to help in the fields, especially at harvest time, or to provide entertainment with singing and dancing. When rain supplied water on the river banks and arroyos, the River People in turn were bound to return a part of their harvest to the Desert People. Even Corn Man or Corn God, when he had abandoned the People, recalls that he had left behind his pets, the blackbirds, and returns to get them, sprinkling his precious kernels for them to follow him back. They were not pests, but his special companions.

Sitting in the large smokehouse throughout the four longest nights of the year, the entire O'odham community was reminded once again in story, song, and formal oration of its intimate relationship with the natural world. In the Corn Man and Tobacco Woman story, the epic told of the People's role in keeping a cultural ecosystem functioning properly in a seemingly harsh desert environment. Simple things were sacred: crop seeds and wild harvests, tobacco smoke and fluffy white feathers, wind and summer rain clouds. With them the community could live comfortably, free from want, with surplus to share.

Appendix: Biological Species Mentioned in the Text

Arrow-weed, *Pluchea sericea*
Badger, *Taxidea taxus*
Belted Kingfisher, *Ceryle alcyon*
Carrizo, *Phragmites australis*
Chain-fruit cholla, *Opuntia fulgida*
Coyote, *Canis latrans*
Devil's claw, *Proboscidea parviflora* var. *hohokamiana*
Frémont cottonwood, *Populus fremontii*
Golden Eagle, *Aquila chrysaetos*
Greasewood, *Sarcobatus vermiculatus*
Red-winged Blackbird, *Agelaius phoeniceus*
Saguaro, *Carnegiea gigantea*
Tobacco hornworm, *Manduca sexta*
Turkey Vulture, *Cathartes aura*
Velvet mesquite, *Prosopis velutina*
Verdin, *Auriparus flaviceps*

Notes

1. The Piman word *O'odham* means "person" or "people." It is used polysemously at various levels of inclusion. In its strict sense, as used here as "the People," it means

Pimans (River Pima, Koahadk, Pima Bajo, Papago). *O'odham* includes as well a southern segment called by outsiders Tepehuan. (Anthropologists refer to the two segments jointly as Tepiman.) The self-designation for Mountain Pima is *Oob*. In distinguishing between themselves, River Pima are Ákimel O'odham and Papago are Tóhono O'odham. *O'odham* may be used in a looser sense to include other Indians. In its broadest sense it can mean "man" or "person." This can include even Europeans, though they are not "true" humans, strictly speaking.

Historically, River Pima were known as Gileños or Pimas Gileños. Those formerly living on the San Pedro and upper Santa Cruz rivers were known as the Sobaípuri.

The Corn Man and Tobacco Woman story is included in a full English transcription of the Gileño Creation Epic made by J. William Lloyd in 1903 through the assistance of a monolingual keeper of the legend, Thin Leather, and a bilingual Pima, Edward H. Wood. Several other shorter and somewhat attenuated versions have been recorded from Pimans. Probably no one now living knows the epic in its original language, only a few isolated episodes surviving in Pima oral tradition. See J. William Lloyd, *Aw-aw-tam Indian Nights* (Westfield, NJ: The Lloyd Group, 1911.) All quotations are from this edition.

2. The winter solstice was not the only four-day period when the story could be told, but it was the ideal time. The story could be narrated in full at other times in midwinter, but at other seasons only individual episodes might be recalled.

3. It is appropriate and minimally respectful that species names of organisms be capitalized (Red-tailed Hawk, Foothill Paloverde) while generic names are not (woman, boy, tree, hawk). Furthermore, elderly Pima have explained to me that Coyote, Buzzard, and Saguaro are *people*, hence demanding respect from their inherent dignity conferred at the time of creation, in contrast to mammal, bird, or cactus, which are just concepts. In the Western written tradition we accord respect by capitalizing proper names.

4. The Navichu was a ceremonial dancer who wore a case mask, kilt, and sash, and who was responsible for healing

certain ailments as well as for entertainment. He was accompanied by various other performers, dancers and singers, most wearing painted half-gourd masks with rows of small holes through which they could see. The Navichu and his attendants bear the unmistakable imprint of katsina figures from the Pueblos, particularly the Zuñi and Hopi. Like the episode of Corn Man and Tobacco Woman, the origin of Navichu is encoded in the Pima Creation Epic.

5. The role of smoking as self-indulgence outside these sacred contexts appears to be of very recent origin and is still relatively uncommon among Pimans.

6. See Joseph C. Winter, "Cultural Modifications of the Gila Pima: A.D. 1697–A.D. 1846," *Ethnohistory* 20 (1973): 67–77. Winter argues that the Gila Pima conducted no ditch irrigation in precontact times because the practice is not mentioned in *relaciones* until 1744, fifty years after the beginning of the Hispanic period in northern Pimería Alta. One version of the Creation Epic confirms this. Be this as it may, those Pimans, called Sobaípuri, living to the east on the San Pedro River, a smaller stream, were indeed ditch irrigationists at contact. Before the 1690s the Gileños, with a broad and biannually inundated floodplain, may have had no need to do this.

7. Although given in the context of Corn Man and Tobacco Woman's nuptials, these two elegant speeches have nothing to do with weddings as such. Both are formal rain-making orations, petitions describing the hoped-for results.

8. Even today, in speaking English, the Piman native speaker refers to all other geographic places, regardless of elevation or direction, as "up there" as if Pimans lived in the bottom of a huge bowl or basin.

9. The ceremony has long been lost among the River Pima, but the evidence is clear that they practiced it in the same complexity as is found among Papago. See Amadeo M. Rea, *At the Desert's Green Edge: An Ethnobotany of the Gila River Pima* (Tucson: University of Arizona Press, 1997); Ruth M. Underhill, *Singing for Power: The Song Magic of the Papago Indians of Southern Arizona* (1938; reprint, Berkeley and Los Angeles: University of California Press, 1976), and *Papago Indian Religion* (New York: Columbia University Press, 1946); Ruth M. Underhill et al.,

Rainhouse and Ocean: Speeches for the Papago Year, vol. 4 of American Tribal Religions (Flagstaff: Museum of Northern Arizona Press, 1979).

10. Frank Russell, "The Pima Indians," *Twenty-sixth Annual Report of the Bureau of American Ethnology* (Washington, D.C.: U.S. Government Printing Office, 1908; reprint, Tucson: University of Arizona Press, 1975), 108, 167, 347–52; Aleš Hrdlička, "Notes on the Pima of Arizona," *American Anthropologist* (n.s.) 8 (1906): 41; Rea, *At the Desert's Green Edge,* 1997.

11. This bush, in the family Chenopodiaceae, is not to be confused with another bush, the creosote-bush, *Larrea tridentata* (Zygophyllaceae), often called by the misnomer "greasewood." Creosote-bush is of high cultural salience among northern Pimans and is carved into rasping sticks used in other ceremonies. The true greasewood is essentially a northern species of the Great Basin deserts, with an isolated outlier in Pima country (the middle Gila and lower Salt River valleys).

12. Russell, "The Pima Indians," 167.

13. Ibid., 352. The antecedents in this oration are ambiguous. "He" may refer to the mythic character, Blue Gopher, mentioned some lines earlier or to some divine power. When these speeches are read in English translation, the ambiguous pronoun conveys a numinous sense. The first person singular represents the orator, repeating the words of some undisclosed ancient. But the first person plural, the "we" at the beginning and end of the liturgical address, are the audience and participants, the ones imploring rain and the ones who will ultimately benefit, communally, from the rain.

14. Little remains among River Pimans of these practices or the overriding cosmology from which they originated. However, in the summer of 1994 an elderly Pima traditional singer who still farms a small plot told me that, although he didn't know any of the actual growth songs, he still goes out and sings other songs to his growing plants.

Recommended Readings

Curtin, Leonora S. M. *By the Prophet of the Earth: Ethnobotany of the Pima.* Reprint, with a new foreword by Gary Paul Nabhan. Tucson: University of Arizona Press, 1984.

Nabhan, Gary Paul. *Gathering the Desert.* Tucson: University of Arizona Press, 1985.

Rea, Amadeo M. *At the Desert's Green Edge: An Ethnobotany of the Gila River Pima.* Tucson: University of Arizona Press, 1997.

Shaw, Anna M. *Pima Past.* Tucson: University of Arizona Press, 1974.

Webb, George. *A Pima Remembers.* Tuscon: University of Arizona Press, 1959.

Nature and Society

Corn-grinding Song

*Oh, for a heart as pure as pollen on
corn blossoms
And for a life as sweet as honey
gathered from the flowers,
And beautiful as butterflies in
sunshine.
May I do good, as Corn has done
good for my people
Through all the days that were.
Until my task is done and evening
falls,
Oh, Mighty Spirit, hear my grinding
song.*

—HOPI, SOUTHWEST[1]

12

Nature as a Model for American Indian Societies: An Overview

MARSHA C. BOL

ON JANUARY 13, 1998, Rosalie Little Thunder wrote a letter to William Clinton, the president of the United States:

> My name is Rosalie Little Thunder. I am of the Sicangu band of the Lakota Nation. I hold no position of power and I hold no wealth, but I do have an important message for you.
>
> Historically, the buffalo were critically essential to our survival and were the center of our culture. We hold them sacred (we, who hold fast to the laws and sacredness of the natural world). . . .
>
> Like the two sides of the buffalo/Indian-head nickel, we are synonymous; two sides of a single coin. We, and the buffalo, share a common history that we dare not forget. We may be generations and miles removed from the buffalo, but according to the wisdom and interdependence with the buffalo, we hold a belief; a prophecy of an inseparable destiny.[2]

Models for Living

Throughout their history the Lakota people of the Great Plains have been intimately linked with the American bison, popularly known as the buffalo. The people relied on the buffalo as their primary resource for meat, housing, tools, and clothing. In practical terms the bison provided nearly all the things that the Lakota needed for daily living. Over 100 different uses, in addition to food, have been recorded for the various buffalo parts—parts such as horns, hides, hair, bones, hooves, stomach, and even dung. (See figure on page 142.)

Woman's workbag and girl's moccasins

Buffalo hide with its hair intact makes a sturdy woman's workbag and a warm lining for a pair of winter moccasins.

BAG: CROW,
COLLECTED 1904
CMNH 2418-77

MOCCASINS: CHEYENNE,
CA. 1880
CMNH 3179-29 a & b

As Ernie Robinson, vice-president of the InterTribal Bison Cooperative, an organization dedicated to restoring buffalo herds on the reservations, says: "We use all the parts of the buffalo, just like in the old days. An hour after we butcher a buffalo, all you'd find would be the grass that had been in its stomach."[3]

The Great Plains teemed with millions of buffalo at the beginning of the 1800s. The Lakota changed their living habits after they acquired a sufficient number of horses to permit men to hunt more advantageously. They moved permanently onto the Plains from the woodlands of Minnesota, following the roaming buffalo herds from place to place across the great grasslands.

The buffalo was much more than a "grocery store." It was a life-giver in the fullest sense. As Black Elk expressed it: "The bison is the chief of all animals, and represents the earth, the totality of all that is. It is the feminine, creating earth principle which gives rise to all living forms."[4]

Lakota people repeatedly connect buffalo with womanhood. Both represent the "creating principle" as both are fecund and reproduce new generations. Through them both the survival and continuity of the Lakota people are assured. In the past this special relationship between women and buffalo became most visible when a girl underwent her puberty ceremony. After being isolated for four days in a separate tipi, the girl was readied for her Buffalo Ceremony.

Nellie Star Boy Menard told about the events of her ceremony in 1925 on the Rosebud Reservation: "They have a ceremony. They got a man to sing over you. And they pray for you and from there you're not a girl anymore. You're going to the womanhood. So they pray for you that you'll lead a good life and . . . , prepare to be a wife and a mother."[5] Observers of this ceremony around the turn of the twentieth

Girls' balls

These beaded balls were made for Lakota girls' puberty ceremonies. At the end of the four days of seclusion and the Buffalo Ceremony, which marked a girl's transition into womanhood, the initiate performed the Throwing-of-the-Ball.

LAKOTA, COLLECTED CA. 1890 CMNH 14526-81, 82, & 83, GIFT OF EARLE SIDNEY CRANNELL

century noted that the ritual leader performed a series of activities impersonating a buffalo bull during rutting season and approached the girl as though she were a buffalo cow.[6]

Emerging from this series of rituals as a completed woman, the young woman was henceforth called a buffalo woman and had the right to paint her face in a particular way. Throughout her lifetime as a buffalo woman, she had a special relationship with the buffalo.

According to Lakota stories of long ago, all the people were once buffalo, members of the Buffalo Nation that lived in the underworld. Tom Haukaas, a Sičangu (Brulé) Lakota/Creole, tells the story: "Originally we [humans] were Buffalo Nation members. We lived in the crystal caves in the Black Hills. One day we were deceived into leaving these caves. . . . Upon being introduced to the outside world we were transformed to our present human configuration."[7] To the present day, some Lakotas cite the social organization of the buffalo herd as the model for the Lakota people's extended family organization, or *tiyošpaye*.[8]

As Rosalie Little Thunder wrote in her letter to President Clinton: "We, and the buffalo, share a common history that we dare not forget . . . an inseparable destiny." In the views of many Lakota and other Plains people, the buffalo and the people have suffered the same fate.

By the end of 1883, because of overhunting largely to satisfy non-Native market demands, not one buffalo remained to be hunted anywhere on the Plains, although a few were protected in Yellowstone National Park and in some small privately owned herds. The loss of this animal that was central to the Lakota's economic and religious life devastated them. About the same time Lakota people were confined to reservations, denied the right to practice their annual Sun Dance, and often faced starvation with no game to hunt and unreliable annuities (supplies) that were promised as part of the treaty settlements but never delivered.

Today, in an effort to reintroduce bison herds into tribal lands and nurture them to thrive, Plains groups are by implication strengthening their own future as a people. Fred DuBray, president of the InterTribal Bison Cooperative, says: "Bringing the buffalo back is an idea with special resonance for the Lakota; attempts to exterminate the buffalo in the 1800s went hand in hand with the attempts to exterminate Indians. Restoring the buffalo is part of reversing that process. If we bring these buffalo back into a healthy state, with that comes a healthier state of the people."[9] Les Ducheneaux explains the healing process in another way: "When the Creator made the buffalo, he put a power in them. When you eat the meat, that power goes into you, heals the body and the spirit."[10]

Whereas the Lakota people traditionally made their living as hunters of the buffalo, the Hopi people of Arizona chose to sustain themselves by farming. Corn is their staff of life. The Hopi place high value on traditional techniques of corn horticulture and continue to exert great effort in the application of these centuries-old practices. Using native seeds and specialized farming methods in their inhospitable environment, which yields only eight inches of rainfall annually, they successfully cultivate corn crops year after year and century after century. Farming has more than economic significance. Working the corn is an act of faith.

Embedded in the Hopi's origin story is the charter for how life is to be lived. As Hartman Lomawaima explains:

> Part of the Hopi origin story recalls the time of emergence from a previous world into the present world. Those who emerged were invited to choose from a number of ears of corn. Some ears were large and hearty, indicating a life of bountifulness and material prosperity on this earth. Some were short, indicating that lessons in life would be learned from hardships but that overcoming hardships would make the people strong and enduring. Hopis chose to live the life of the short ear of corn and migrated to the lands upon which they built their enduring villages and culture.[11]

Corn effigy

Corn is the metaphor for the life of the Hopi people. "We are rooted in our cornfields," says Fred Kabotie.[12] Corn appears in some form—as whole ears, pollen, ground meal, or *piki* bread—in every passage of life and ritual occasion. Hartman Lomawaima points out: "It is the first solid food fed to infants at their clan naming ceremony. It is also prepared for the deceased, to sustain their essences as they journey into the spirit world."[13]

A newborn baby spends the first nineteen days of its life secluded indoors, where it is cared for by the elder women of the family. It is wrapped in a blanket alongside one or two ears of perfectly formed corn, referred to as its mother. On the twentieth day the baby receives its Hopi name in a sunrise naming ceremony.

This ceramic ear of corn emphasizes the singular importance of corn to the Hopi people. Archaeologists say that cultivated maize was carried from Mexico into the American Southwest about 4,000 years ago and became the staple food crop through adaptive breeding. According to Hopi origin stories, corn and the digging stick were gifts from Maasawu, the Earth deity, as he greeted people on their emergence into this world, the Fourth World.

ELMER TOOTSIE, HOPI-TEWA, CA. 1995
CMNH 36078-1

The Lakota consider the buffalo to be the creative principle of life. Similarly, the Hopi refer to corn as their mother. As one Hopi man expresses it, "We call the corn 'mother.' It nourishes us, it gives us life—is it not our mother?"[14]

Hopi brides, as potential mothers, are linked with corn. Both are fruitful and bear children, thus assuring the continuity of life. Cornmeal and its preparation appear repeatedly in the wedding activities. Helen Sekaquaptewa recalled her own wedding: "After we decided to get married, I spent every minute that I could grinding in preparation for feeding the wedding guests. Women and girls of my relatives who wanted to help started grinding too."[15]

Hopi bride

A Hopi bride named Masawunsy prepares to lead the wedding procession to her mother's house in 1901, dressed in her new trousseau with cornmeal dusted on her face.

PHOTO BY FRANK D. VOORHIES, 1901 CARNEGIE MUSEUM OF NATURAL HISTORY, CMNH 1828-5

The bride is joined by female relatives and friends, who help her grind a vast amount of cornmeal—as much as 800 to 1,000 pounds. The meal is mounded high in bowls and tubs, the higher the better.

The bride's family then takes her to the house of the groom's family to stay and grind corn for four days until the wedding begins. Helen Sekaquaptewa remembered: "As a bride I was considered sacred the first few days, being in a room with the shades on the windows, talking to no one. All this time I was steadily grinding corn which was brought in by Emory's kinswomen."[16] On her wedding day, the bride is dressed in her newly woven clothes, and her face is patted with cornmeal.[17]

Models for Social Organization

Among another group of Pueblo people, the Tewa-speaking Pueblos of north central New Mexico, corn is also the mother of the people. Alfonso Ortiz explains: "The Tewa speaking Pueblos speak of two corn mothers . . . a white corn mother and a blue corn mother. The white corn mother is spoken of as being nearer to ice, as the mother of the winter people, and the blue corn mother as being nearer to warmth, as the mother of the summer people."[18]

In each of the six Tewa villages, the people are divided into two groups, or moieties—the Winter People and the Summer People. A child is born into the moiety of its father and spends its lifetime as a member of either the Summer people or the Winter people. Ortiz continues:

> There is no residential segregation of the moieties, but each group has a head who rules the village for a part of the year—the Winter Chief from about the autumnal equinox until a month before the vernal, and the Summer Chief for the remainder of the year. . . .
>
> The division of the year corresponds in a general way to the subsistence activities of the Tewa. The transfer of authority to the Summer Chief in February is seen as initiating the agricultural season. . . . After his Autumn work, the Summer Chief "gives the people back" to the Winter Chief. This ushers in the period of intensified hunting, which begins after all of the late crops are in storage.[19]

Other Indian nations also organize themselves into divisions modeled after the natural world. The Tlingit, who live in southeastern Alaska, base their divisions on the world of animals. According to Tlingit mythology, animals were once humans who were frightened into the woods and the sea by the daylight that Raven let out of a box. In this and other Tlingit stories, people and animals are relatives who may cross into each other's worlds. Animals have the ability to appear before people in human form, just as humans can be transformed into animals in supernatural encounters. Animals and humans even marry and raise families.

Tlingit society is divided into two moieties named the Ravens and the Eagles (or in some regions, the Wolves).

Every Tlingit person belongs to one side or the other. Children are taught the phrase "The eagle flies higher, but the raven flies faster." (See figure on page 34.)

Within each Tlingit moiety there are numerous clans. When introducing themselves, individuals identify their moiety and clan. The clan is the broadest family group, and members are related through a legendary ancestor. Clans own an assemblage of emblems, or crests, that represent creatures with whom an ancestor has interacted in the ancient past.

Through purchase by the ancestor, often in exchange for his or her life, the descendants receive from the creature the right of ownership to the crest and the accompanying story, song, name, and other rights. One clan, for example, owns the story of the creation of the killer whale and has the right to use its image as its crest.

Drum

This drum has a painted image of either a thunderbird or a Golden Eagle on its interior, where the painting is protected from the beating of the drumstick.

TLINGIT, PRE-1949
CMNH 24386-34, GIFT OF
DR. OSHIN AGATHON

The list of crest creatures reads like a *Who's Who* of the inhabitants of the land, sea, and air of the Tlingits' environment in southeastern Alaska. Sea inhabitants include several varieties of salmon, whale, sea lion, halibut, porpoise, and shark. Land and river animals include the wolf, bear, land otter, and frog; some important bird crests are the raven, owl, eagle, tern, and petrel.

The Tlingit people continue to carve, paint, and weave crest animals into their art objects. One commented:

> When you look at these totem poles, Chilkat blankets, and carved wooden hats, do you wonder . . . what they mean to the people who made them? To my people, the Tlingit of Alaska, they record the history of our families and tribes. They document our relationship with the land, with the fish, with the game that has sustained us throughout the ages. When we wear them and put them in our houses,

they tell people who we are, what is our lineage—
they give us self respect.[20]

On the other side of the continent, the Iroquois (living
today primarily in New York State, Ontario, and Quebec) also
organize themselves according to the model of the animal
world. Everyone belongs to the clan of his or her mother, and
every clan is named for an animal. As Kawenniiosta "Yosta"
Boots says, "I was born a member of the Wolf clan, just like
my mother and my grandmother."[21]

Three basic clans—Bear, Turtle, and Wolf—exist at each
of the Iroquois nations. The number of additional clans varies
depending upon the nation. The Mohawks have only the
three original clans; the Onondaga have nine. (See the clan
animals on page 51.) Yosta hung a poster of a wolf in her college dorm room as an identifier of her clan membership.
These animals define and guide people's relationships with
one another.

Among the Winnebago people of the western Great
Lakes, society is also divided into two moieties. One half are
"those who are above," or the Sky moiety, and the other half
are "those who are on earth," or the Earth people. The nature
of the clan names within each moiety depends upon this division of the universe. The Earth people took the names of only
land and water animals, while the Sky people's clans are usually named after birds.

This division of the world was mirrored in the organization of the Winnebago's villages. In the past each village was
divided into halves by an imaginary line running from the
northwest to the southeast. The Sky people, comprising the
Thunderbird, Eagle, Pigeon, and War People clans, lived on
the southwest side of the village, while the Earth clans of
Bear, Wolf, Water Spirit, Deer, Elk, Buffalo, Fish, and Snake
lived on the northeast side.[22]

The Cosmos as a Model for Space

Many Native people have planned and constructed their
dwellings as a microcosm of the universe. They aligned their
houses with the cardinal directions, used lodge poles as

pathways linking the heavens to the Earth, and built domed roofs in the image of the bowl of the sky.

Thomas Tyon, a Lakota from the Plains, explains:

> The Oglala [Lakota] believe the circle to be sacred because the Great Spirit caused everything in nature to be round. . . . The sun and the sky, the earth and the moon, though the sky is deep like a bowl. Everything that breathes is round. . . . Everything that grows from the ground is round like the stem of a tree. . . .
>
> For these reasons the Oglala make their tipis circular, their camp circle circular, and sit in a circle in all ceremonies.[23]

The principal architectural structure of the Lakota, as well as the majority of the other nomadic peoples of the Plains, was the tipi. This circular, portable dwelling suited the lifestyle of a people in pursuit of roving buffalo herds. When Lakota women set up their families' tipis at a new site, they arranged the tipis in a circle, thus creating circles within a circle. They made sure that the camp opening faced to the east, the direction of the rising sun. The women, consequently, were replicating an image of their universe.

Norbert Running from Rosebud Reservation explains: "When they build a tipi, those three poles come first. That three pole triangle is a star. . . . Then seven more poles, that's the directions—west, north, east, south, above, below, and center. Fire at the center. That makes ten poles. Those ten are the laws of this whole world and for the Lakota people."[24] The tipi poles link the sky to the Earth and transmit powers from the heavens down into the dwelling.[25]

Some of the tipis within the camp circle had specially painted covers, a few of which had painted designs given to the owner in a vision or a dream. Lakota men received much of their power and capabilities through communication with the supernatural by means of vision quests or dreams. The dreamer followed the instructions revealed in his dream. These sometimes entailed the reenactment of the vision, which could mean painting the images in his dream on his tipi.

Anthropologist Alice Fletcher described the return of a vision quester and the process of acting out his vision.

> In 1882 I witnessed the acting out of a vision of an elk by an Ogallala Indian. The man was apparently about 22 or 23 years old. . . . Early in the morning the members of the elk society gathered at the invitation of the neophyte. A new tent had been expressly prepared and was set up to the west of the camp, on an open space quite apart from the village. The door of the tent faced the east. . . . Around the top part of the tent were painted four blue bands; across the entrance an elk was drawn in red in such a manner that whoever entered the lodge passed through the body of the animal.[26]

For the Lakota, the cosmos is conceived as a series of disks, one above the other. The paintings on vision tipis are generally organized into horizontal registers representing levels of the cosmos. The upper registers signify the Upper World; the lower registers, the Earth. The predominating motifs on vision tipis are those associated with the Upper World, such as the sun, stars, hail, thunder, and birds. Also prevalent are the earthly but supernaturally powerful animals, particularly the buffalo, the elk, and the horse. Rainbows often appear, perhaps serving as mediators stretching between the Upper and Lower Worlds.

If the vision tipi was a metaphor for the universe or cosmos, then the people occupying the tipi were living within the spirit world. It is understandable, therefore, that strict behavior applied to residing in such a space. For example, when sitting in the tipi no one should lean against its wall. Fire from the tipi could not be taken to another place.[27]

In order to enter a Lakota vision tipi, one often entered through or under the body of an animal or a cosmic sign such as a rainbow. In Fletcher's 1882 description above, for example, those who entered the tipi passed through the body of an elk.

Such positioning of images at the entrance of the tipi suggests protective guardianship. However, to walk through an animal's midsection into the vision tipi suggests power beyond that of guardianship. The significance of the threshold as a transition area is widely recognized. Whoever crosses the threshold passes from one zone to another. In the case of the vision tipi, itself a metaphor for the cosmos, the visitor steps out of the everyday camp circle into the sacred world.

In contrast with the Lakota, the Pawnee people built permanent earth lodges on the central Plains of Kansas and Nebraska. (See the earth lodge on page 82.) The Skidi Pawnee, a tribal subgroup, looked to the stars for much of their religious direction, receiving a ritual blueprint for constructing their lodges.

Pawnee James R. Murie recorded the ritual events in the construction and dedication of an earth lodge in 1905: "The simple dwelling is full of beauty to him who knows its meaning. There is no part of it that is not symbolic. The entrance must always face the rising sun, the domed roof is a symbol of the sky, and each post represents a star which tells the Pawnee of some divine being. . . . Within his walls . . . the Pawnee lived in conscious recognition of the universe about him, ever in the presence of Tirawa, the One Above."[28]

The earth lodge, built to reflect the cosmos, incorporated the essential features of the celestial realm. The domed roof represented the sky. Four central pillars supported the roof in the same way that four world-quarter stars supported the dome of the sky.[29] The doorway faced east toward the Morning Star and the rising sun. The circular smoke hole in the dome represented the circle of stars in the sky. Pawnee holy men used the earth lodge like an observatory. They watched for the Pleiades through the smoke hole in the central dome to time their planting, harvesting, and ceremonies.

In the southwest, the Navajo built hogans, another type of basically circular, earthen and log dwelling. (See the hogan on page 86.) Today modern hogan construction ranges from the traditional peeled-log, polygonal structure with an earth-covered roof to a stud-framed, multisided dwelling roofed with shingles.

The hogan is a central feature in the Navajo origin story. When the first people emerged into this world through four layers of the Underworld, one of the Holy People's first acts was to build a dwelling where they could meet and plan the creation of the world. The structure intended for this important meeting was constructed according to specifications based on the cardinal directions. Four main support poles were placed in position, beginning with the east and moving from south to west to north, following the circuit of the sun.

The Navajo have continued to follow this model when they build their hogans. Conceptually, the single-family dwelling is divided into four sectors according to directional orientation. The four supporting posts are named for each of the directions, and the interior space is divided into areas dedicated to each of the four directions. Facing to the east, the doorway receives the rays of the rising sun. According to ritual prescription, as family members move within the hogan, they proceed around the central hearth in a clockwise direction, mirroring the sun's daily movement from east to west across the southern sky.

In following these construction specifications, Navajo people rebuild the basic tenets of their system of values, based on world order and harmony, into every hogan.[30] The celestial sky offers a model for life as it should be lived, a life filled with order and harmony. The cosmos projects a visual model of the nearly perfect order in the universe, a predictable regularity that appears daily as stars rise in the east and set in the west.

A Model for Time

Many Native people speak of time, or the cycle of regularly recurring events, as circular or cyclic. This includes all components of time—daily, monthly, seasonal, annual, and beyond. For the Lakota, "it is the symbol of the circle that marks the edge of the world and therefore of the four winds that travel there. Consequently, it is also the symbol of a year. The day, the night, and the moon go in a circle above the sky. Therefore the circle is a symbol of these divisions of time and hence the symbol of all time," says Thomas Tyon.[31]

Barre Toelken reflects on the Navajo vision of time: "The Navajo see things as essentially cyclic, circular. The individual craftswoman, instead of standing on a straight ribbon of time leading from the past to some future point, stands in the middle of a vortex of forces exerted in concentric circles upon her by her immediate family, her extended family, the clan, the whole living ecological system within which she lives and functions. . . . Time *surrounds* her, as do her dwelling place, her family, her clan, her tribe, her habitat, her dances, her rituals."[32]

The revolving, cyclic patterns of nature provide the model for life's patterns of activities among traditional Native people. Hopi farmers for example, have developed a specialized system for precisely timing agricultural activities based upon the daily shift of the rising sun on a predetermined horizon. (See the Hopi planting calendar on page 76). With the worrisome potential for killing frosts in both late spring and early fall, correct timing for planting is essential. The village Sunwatcher observes the position of the sun at daybreak against known landmarks on the horizon to determine the optimum times to plant and to harvest crops. Crow-Wing recorded the following entry in his journal.

> May 4. The Sun-watcher went around town to tell people that it was time to plant watermelon. He said that the sun had come out of *neuekchumuvayama* [two buttes standing together], that is between two hills. So the men who want to plant on the right day plant their watermelons. Some may plant tomorrow and the next day. After five days the next watermelon planting time comes. We have to watch carefully to plant on the right day.[33]

According to Iroquois cosmology, the Earth lies on the back of a great turtle. On the turtle's carapace is a pattern of thirteen large plates that the Iroquois equate with the new moons. They counted the moons of the year starting above the turtle's left front leg and moving counterclockwise.[34] The Iroquois people scheduled their activities in tandem with the cycles of the new moon. The people named each new moon according to the concurrent seasonal event. There was, for example, the Maple Sugar Moon, the Planting Moon, the Green Corn Moon, the Harvest Moon, and the Hunting Moon.[35]

The Lakota also calculated increments of time by watching the new moons. They named the moons, however, according to observable natural events rather than human activities.

Carnegie winter count

In this unique contemporary winter count, Tom Haukaas depicted 125 yearly events, from 1868-1869 to 1992-1993, for the Sicaṅǧu Lakota people on the Rosebud Reservation in South Dakota. Haukaas began the winter count with the creation of the reservation in 1868-1869 and ended it with the 500th anniversary of Columbus's encounter with Native Americans.

THOMAS RED OWL HAUKAAS, M.D. (1950–), SICAṄǦU (BRULÉ), LAKOTA/CREOLE, 1995 CMNH 36025-1a

The Moon of Frost in the Tipi, the Moon When the Ponies Shed, the Moon of Red Grass Appearing, and the Moon of the Falling Leaves all relate to the natural cycle of events.[36]

The Lakota recorded both human and natural events annually on winter counts, pictorial records on animal hides or muslin cloth. Every winter, when the year was completed, the community council of each Lakota band reviewed the important events of the year and together selected the most significant one. The keeper of the winter count added this event to the long list of annual pictographs, sometimes consisting of as many as 200 entries. He could recite the story of each successive winter on this lengthy calendar of events, thereby passing on history orally.

Such memorable events as smallpox epidemics, wars, school attendance, and the move from tipi to cabin were noted on the winter counts. Tribal members recalled the year of their birth by the event associated with their birth date. As Afraid of Bear says: "I was born the year When They Brought in the Captives (1843). My father told me these things. He was born the year When the Good White Man Came (1802)."[37]

LEFT TO RIGHT:
Trinket basket, small basket, large basket, and berry basket

Tlingit women developed a technique for weaving finely twined baskets from the roots of the Sitka spruce tree, one of the most abundant conifers in southeast Alaska.

TRINKET BASKET: TLINGIT, PRE-1923
CMNH 8946-11a & b, GIFT OF H. J. HEINZ

SMALL BASKET: ERNESTINE HANLON, TLINGIT, LEINEIDÍ (RAVEN-DOG SALMON) CLAN, HOONAH, ALASKA, 1995
CMNH 35989-1

LARGE BASKET: TLINGIT, COLLECTED 1904
CMNH 3167-57

BASKET: TLINGIT, COLLECTED 1904
CMNH 3167-16

A Model for Art

When Ernestine Hanlon makes a Tlingit spruce root basket, she spends 75 percent of her time collecting and preparing the materials. As she discusses her baskets, her emphasis is on the process of making the basket, not the end product. "We go out to the old growth [in the forest] with the canopy where the bears sleep and the deer sleep [to collect the spruce roots]. The people who call us tree huggers, they're right. We talk to the trees and we say thank you. It feels good."[38] Hanlon forms a relationship with the trees, conversing with them and expressing gratitude for their collaboration.

According to Tessie Naranjo, Santa Clara Pueblo potters form a similar partnership when making their pottery. "Clay has life and necessarily we develop a relationship with Clay Old Lady. [We say:] Give me good thoughts as I am making this pot. We are in partnership. I can't make it without your help."[39]

Navajo weavers bring together the world of animals, the world of plants, and the human world as they weave their rugs. (See the Navajo dye chart on page 183.) When Barre Toelken discussed rug weaving with his adopted Navajo sister, he observed:

> I found she was quite insistent on the idea that the wool represented in and of itself an interaction between the sheep and the human herder, as well as between the sheep and the shearer, the spinner of the yarn, and the weaver of the rug. In addition to this, nearly all the colors in this rug are taken from plant and herb dyes which had to be gathered over the span of an entire year because some of them are from the same plants, whose roots produce different colors in different seasons. Thus the coloration of the rug itself represents not only the interaction of man with plants, but of man with the continuing cycle of natural seasons. . . .
>
> I found that even in the spinning of the yarn, the spindle must be turned in one direction ("clockwise"), for it represents the direction of the sun's movement; to spin the yarn by turning the spindle "backward" would be to produce yarn which represents the reverse of the normal state, yarn which will "come unraveled," "won't stay in the rugs" and "might cause sickness."[40]

In addition to developing a relationship with the natural world, women artists from several tribes frequently draw upon nature as a source of inspiration for their designs. Virginia Beavert, in telling the legendary origin of Yakima basket weaving, says that the cedar tree taught a young woman how to make baskets. The tree told her:

"Now you must go out in the woods and find some designs. Seek out the things of nature and bring them back pictured in your mind." . . . She walked for many days looking at everything. . . . She was walking down the trail one day when a rattlesnake crossed her path. He spoke to her, "See the designs on my back? Use them to design the edging on your baskets." . . . She continued walking down the trail until she saw Patu (Mountain). He spoke to her, "Look at me very closely; this is the way I am, like a design. The outlines of my peaks are like designs."[41]

She also encountered Grouse, who offered his tracks as a design motif, and finally, as she knelt down to get a drink, the brook gave her his reflections and waves as design sources.

Plains women often selected the environment around them as inspiration for their geometric painting, beadwork, and quillwork on hide. One Arapaho woman painted her universe on her parfleche (a rawhide container), describing her intentions to Cleaver Warden, an Arapaho man who collected the piece:

Six rows of colored designs reproduce the whole appearance of the earth (rough). Two white lines traversing two center designs denote the paths of the sun and moon. White and blue lines at the edge of the parfleche mean the "ocean" and horizon. Blue paint, the sky; red paint, the earth; green paint, the grass; white field, water. This parfleche denotes the winter season.[42]

Rather than painting a series of unrelated motifs, this unknown artist combined selected natural elements from her universe to create a landscape composition.

Lakota women also created unified compositions using various landscape elements. In talking with a Lakota artist, Mable Morrow recorded a painted parfleche with a design she named "the distant view," explaining: "It refers to the revered Black Hills. The blue triangular units of the sides of the panels represented tree-covered hills nearby. The yellow in the Lakota rawhide designs is a symbol for rocks."[43] Other women with whom Morrow talked told her about similar compositions, which sometimes appeared to the artists in dreams.[44]

Parfleche

Plains women were often inspired by the environment around them when creating their geometric paintings. Only each individual artist knew the meaning of her design. An Arapaho woman thought about her world and painted an abstract landscape on this folded, rawhide container, called a parfleche.

ARAPAHO, COLLECTED 1903
CMNH 3179-308

Differentiating Lakota objects that have dreamed designs or landscape compositions from other objects is impossible without the artist's interpretation. Unfortunately, very few museum pieces were collected with artists' statements about their work. Regardless, the arts, including architecture, are expressions of a set of concepts made concrete that Native people hold true about the nature of the universe and their connection to it.

As Rina Swentzell of Santa Clara Pueblo expresses:

These values are embedded into the very structure of Pueblo life. Traditional houses are made of earth, or adobe. The mud walls flow out of the ground, showing an undeniable connectedness to the earth. They are born of the earth and eventually return to the earth. The pottery of Pueblo people, which has been produced since 300 A.D., is also earth-connected.

The designs drawn on the pots tell about our universe and the interrelatedness of life-forms and activities. The mountains, which define and contain the Pueblo world, are shown in stepped patterns. The clouds, which remind us of cycles and movement, are drawn in semicircles with lightning or zigzag lines coming out of them. Birds, deer, and fish are shown turning into humans or vice-versa, another way of showing our interconnectedness.[45]

Conclusion

All Native people have connected to their natural world in a diversity of ways, as the examples in this chapter demonstrate. The Lakotas explicitly and repeatedly state this relationship by ending their prayers and ceremonies with the words "all my relations." Lakota Jenny Leading Cloud sums up their fundamental belief:

> We Indians think of the earth and the whole universe as a never-ending circle, and in this circle, man is just another animal. The buffalo and the coyote are our brothers; the birds, our cousins. We end our prayers with the words "all my relations"—and that includes everything that grows, crawls, runs, creeps, hops, and flies.[46]

Notes

1. Polingaysi Qoyawayma, *No Turning Back: A Hopi Indian Woman's Struggle to Live in Two Worlds* (Albuquerque: University of New Mexico Press, 1964), 5.
2. Rosalie Little Thunder, correspondence with author, January 13, 1998.
3. Jacqueline W. Sletto, "Prairie Tribes and the Buffalo," *Native Peoples* 6(2) (1993):41.
4. Joseph Epes Brown, *Animals of the Soul: Sacred Animals of the Oglala Sioux* (Rockport, MA: Element, 1992), 13.

5. Nellie Star Boy Menard, interview with author, July 26, 1993.

6. To learn about the details of this ceremony, see James R. Walker, *Lakota Belief and Ritual* (Lincoln: University of Nebraska Press, 1980), 223, 241–53. By 1925 Menard's ceremony did not contain this element. Today the girl's puberty ceremony is rarely practiced on Lakota reservations.

7. Thomas Haukaas, correspondence with author, April 23, 1998.

8. *Pittsburgh Tribune-Review*, "Indians Work to Restore Buffalo to Tribal Lands," January 11, 1993, sec. C.

9. Ibid.

10. Bryan Hodgson, "Buffalo back Home on the Range," *National Geographic* 186(5) (1994):69.

11. Hartman H. Lomawaima, "Hopi," in *The Encyclopedia of American Indians*, ed. Frederick E. Hoxie (Boston: Houghton Mifflin, 1996), 253.

12. Pat Ferrero, *Hopi: Songs of the Fourth World* (film) (San Francisco: Ferrero Films, 1986)

13. Lomawaima, "Hopi," 253.

14. Natalie Curtis, *The Indian's Book* (1907; reprint ed., New York: Gramercy Books, 1994), 481.

15. Louise Udall, *Me and Mine: The Life Story of Helen Sekaquaptewa* (Tucson: University of Arizona Press, 1969), 154.

16. Ibid., 155.

17. For a complete description of Hopi wedding activities, see Mary Russell Farrell Colton and Edmund Nequatewa, "Hopi Courtship and Marriage," *Museum Notes* (Museum of Northern Arizona) 5(9) (1933):41–54.

18. Alfonso Ortiz, "Some Cultural Meanings of Corn in Aboriginal North America," *Indian Corn of the Americas: Gift to the World, Northeast Indian Quarterly* 6(1,2) (1989):64.

19. Alfonso Ortiz, "Dual Organization as an Operational Concept in the Pueblo Southwest," *Ethnology* 4 (1965):390–91. To learn more about the Tewa dual organization, see chapter 13 by Ortiz in this volume.

20. *The Box of Daylight* (film) (Juneau: Pacific

Communications, 1990).

21. Kawenniiosta Boots, "Dorm Room Audio Transcript," Carnegie Museum of Natural History, 1995.

22. Paul Radin, *The Winnebago Tribe* (1923; reprint ed., Lincoln: University of Nebraska Press, 1970), 137–44.

23. J. R. Walker, "The Sun Dance and Other Ceremonies of the Oglala Division of the Teton Dakota," *Anthropological Papers of the American Museum of Natural History* 16(2) (1917):160.

24. Ronald Goodman, *Lakota Star Knowledge: Studies in Lakota Stellar Theology* (Rosebud, SD: Sinte Gleska College, 1990), 17.

25. Brown, *Animals of the Soul*, 100.

26. Alice Fletcher, "The Elk Mystery or Festival, Ogallala Sioux," *Sixteenth and Seventeenth Annual Reports of the Peabody Museum* 3(3,4) (1884):282.

27. Ella Cara Deloria, Dakota Texts from the Sword Manuscript, 1879–1909, no. 846, American Philosophical Society, Philadelphia. To read more about the special restrictions of vision tipis, see Marsha C. Bol, "The Painted Tipi of the Lakota People," *Archaeology, Art, and Anthropology: Papers in Honor of J. J. Brody*, vol. 18 (Albuquerque: Archaeological Society of New Mexico, 1992), 23–38.

28. Vol Del Chamberlain, *When Stars Came Down to Earth: Cosmology of the Skidi Pawnee Indians of North America* (Los Altos, CA: Ballena Press and Center for for Archaeoastronomy, 1982), 155.

29. Chamberlain (1982, 101) postulates that the four stars are Capella (northwest), Vega (northeast), Antares (southeast), and Sirius (southwest).

30. Trudy Griffen-Pierce, "The Hooghan and the Stars," in *Earth and Sky: Visions of the Cosmos in Native American Folklore*, ed. Ray A. Williamson and Claire R. Farrer (Albuquerque: University of New Mexico Press, 1992), 110–30. See also Trudy Griffen-Pierce, "The Hogan as a Model of the Navajo Cosmos," in *Earth Is My Mother, Sky Is My Father: Space, Time, and Astronomy in Navajo Sandpainting* (Albuquerque: University of New Mexico Press, 1992), 92–126.

31. Walker, *The Sun Dance*, 160.
32. Barre Toelken, "A Circular World: The Vision of Navajo Crafts," *Parabola* 1 (1976):31.
33. Elsie Clews Parsons, "A Pueblo Indian Journal, 1920–1921," *Memoirs of the American Anthropological Association* 32 (1925):81.
34. The cycle of twelve lunar months falls about ten days short of a complete year. Every three years or so the Iroquois inserted a thirteenth lost moon. See Dean R. Snow, *The Iroquois* (Oxford and Cambridge, MA: Blackwell, 1994), 6.
35. For a listing of the names of the new moons, see Snow, *The Iroquois*, 108.
36. The Lakota months of the year are listed in Raymond J. DeMallie, ed., *The Sixth Grandfather: Black Elk's Teachings Given to John G. Neihardt* (Lincoln: University of Nebraska Press, 1984), 291–92.
37. Walker, *Lakota Belief and Ritual*, 201.
38. Ernestine Hanlon, conversation with author, March 1, 1995.
39. Tessie Naranjo, "Cultural Changes: The Effect of Foreign Systems at Santa Clara Pueblo" (Paper delivered at The Great Southwest of the Fred Harvey Company and the Santa Fe Railway: A Symposium, The Heard Museum, Phoenix, February 10, 1996).
40. Toelken, "A Circular World," 33.
41. Virginia Beavert, "Origin of Basket Weaving," in *A Song to the Creator: Traditional Arts of Native American Women of the Plateau*, ed. Lillian A. Ackerman (Norman: University of Oklahoma Press, 1996), 36, 38.
42. Carnegie Museum of Natural History Collection Notes, 1904, 3179–308.
43. Mable Morrow, *Indian Rawhide: An American Folk Art* (Norman: University of Oklahoma Press, 1975), 43.
44. For more examples of Lakota women's landscape compositions and dreamed designs, see Marsha Clift Bol, "Gender in Art: A Comparison of Lakota Women's and Men's Art, 1820–1920" (Ph.D. diss., University of New Mexico, 1989), 243–58.
45. Rina Swentzell, "Accommodating the World: Cultural

Tourism Among the Pueblos," *Native American Expressive Culture* (Ithaca: Akwe:kon Press and National Museum of the American Indian, 1994), 135.

46. The Editors, *The Spirit World* (Alexandria, VA: Time-Life Books, 1992), 19.

13

Origins: Through Tewa Eyes

ALFONSO ORTIZ

I DO NOT REMEMBER THE DAY, of course, but I know what happened. Four days after I was born in the Pueblo Indian village of San Juan in the Rio Grande Valley in New Mexico, the "umbilical cord-cutting mother" and her assistant came to present me to the sun and to give me a name. They took me from the house just as the sun's first rays appeared over the Sangre de Cristo Mountains. The cord-cutting mother proffered me and two perfect ears of corn, one blue and one white, to the six sacred directions. A prayer was said:

Naming bowl

This bowl held *pikami* (baked sweet cornmeal pudding) for the feast following the naming of a Hopi baby.

HOPI, CA. 1860–1890
CMNH 1579–27

Here is a child who has been given to us. Let us bring him to manhood. . . . You who are dawn youths and dawn maidens. You who are winter spirits. You who are summer spirits. . . . Take therefore. . . . Give him good fortune, we ask of you.

Now the name was given. It was not the name at the head of this story. It was my Tewa name, a thing of power. Usually such a name evokes either nature—the mountains or the hills or the season—or a ceremony under way at the time of the birth. By custom such a name is shared only within the community, and with those we know well. Thus, in the eyes of my Tewa people, I was "brought in out of the darkness," where I had no identity. Thus I became a child of the Tewa. My world is the Tewa world. It is different from your world.

Consider the question of the origin of Native American peoples. Archaeologists will tell you that we came at least 12,000 years ago from Asia, crossing the Bering land bridge, then spreading over the two American continents. These archaeologists have dug countless holes in the earth looking for spearpoints, bones, traces of fires; they have subjected these objects to sophisticated dating analysis—seeking to prove or disprove a hypothesis or date. I know of their work. I too have been to Soviet Asia and seen cave art and an old ceremonial costume remarkably similar to some found in America. But a Tewa is not so interested in the work of archaeologists.

A Tewa is interested in our own story of our origin, for it holds all that we need to know about our people, and how one should live as a human. The story defines our society. It tells me who I am, where I came from, the boundaries of my world, what kind of order exists within it; how suffering, evil, and death came into this world; and what is likely to happen to *me* when I die.

Let me tell you that story:

> *Yonder in the north there is singing on the lake.*
> *Cloud maidens dance on the shore. There we*
> *take our being.*
> *Yonder in the north cloud beings rise. They ascend*
> *onto cloud blossoms. There we take our being.*
> *Yonder in the north rain stands over the land. . . .*
> *Yonder in the north stands forth at twilight the*
> *arc of a rainbow. There we have our being.*

Our ancestors came from the north. Theirs was not a journey to be measured in centuries, for it was as much a journey of the spirit as it was a migration of a people. The Tewa know not when the journey southward began or when it ended, but we do know where it began, how it proceeded, and where it ended. We are unconcerned about time in its historical dimensions, but we will recall in endless detail the features of the twelve places our ancestors stopped.

We point to these places to show that the journey did, indeed, take place. This is the only proof a Tewa requires. And each time a Tewa recalls a place where they paused, for whatever length of time, every feature of the earth and sky comes vividly to life, and the journey itself lives again.

At the beginning of all beginnings our ancestors came up out of the earth, until they were living beneath Sandy Place Lake to the north. The world under the lake was like this one, but dark. Spirits, people, and animals lived together; death was unknown.

Among the spirits were the first mothers of all the Tewa, known as Blue Corn Woman Near to Summer and White Corn Maiden Near to Ice. These mothers asked one of the men present to go forth and explore the way by which the people might leave the lake.

After many adventures and struggles he returned to the people, announcing his arrival with the call of a fox. He came now as Mountain Lion or Hunt Chief. The people rejoiced, saying, "We have been accepted."

They left the lake and entered the land.

That the Tewa see all life as beginning within the earth, like the corn plant that has sustained us for centuries, is manifest in our sacred places: The kiva, the ceremonial center, which represents the primordial home under the lake; the "earth mother earth navel middle place" in every village; and our mountaintop shrines—"earth navels"—shaped of stones and boulders.

These trace back to the first permanent habitations of the Pueblo people.

The canyons, cliffs, and mesa tops of the Four Corners area of the Southwest hold evidence that, at least by the fifth century anno Domini (as the white man reckons time),

Mountain Lion

Predatory animals carved in stone are guardians of the six directions. The mountain lion guards the North.

ZUNI, NEW MEXICO, CA. 1900
CMNH 35416-1, GIFT OF CHARLES FUREDY

the Pueblo people did, indeed, begin life within the earth. The habitations they constructed were circular pit houses, dug wholly or mostly underground and covered with branches and dirt. Entrance ramps opened to the southeast, the direction of the rising sun during the colder months of the year. To enter the pit house, then, was to enter the earth, and to enter the earth was to return to one of the two sources of all life through the opening that connected it with the other source, the sun.

These pit-house people lived within the womb of mother earth while also drawing sustenance from the sun father.

A small round hole was also dug and carefully protected on the floor of their pit house to remind them of their original emergence from within the earth. They termed such a hole "earth germinating mother earth navel middle place"—the origin of the sacred place in the plazas of our villages today.

From the outside these pit houses resembled nothing more than giant rounded anthills. Yet their form would take on profound meaning.

In time the pit-house people emerged to build, aboveground, rectangular house blocks, but they retained the basic shape of their pit house by building kivas, or ceremonial chambers, one of which was always attached to each house block. These were built underground and to the southeast. The kiva was no longer entered through a sloping ramp but through a hole in the roof. The old rampway was now represented by a deeply recessed wall, still located in the southeast part of the kiva. This new structure resembled an old-fashioned keyhole so much that it is called a keyhole-shaped kiva by archaeologists.

Southeast of the kiva was the refuse depositing place, where the dead were buried.

Kiva at San Ildefonso, New Mexico

The kiva is central to Pueblo well-being and spiritual life. Here a stair rather than the usual ladder eases the way to a rooftop entry hole.

PHOTO BY T. HARMON PARKHURST, DATE UNKNOWN. MUSEUM OF NEW MEXICO, 3629

The positioning of the dead closest to the direction of the sunrise reflects a recognition by the Pueblo people that the sun father is both the giver and the taker of life. What he gives he also takes back, eventually. The three parts—house block, kiva, and refuse dump/cemetery—became standard.

And the kiva, in its central position, came to mediate between the living and the dead. Here the living may perform rituals addressed to the dead and, hence, communicate with them. In later times there were great dramatic performances in which the living personified the spirits of the dead in these kivas.

Finally the villages became multistoried house blocks resembling fortresses. This presented a dilemma to the people: The buildings blocked the rising sun's rays from the dead buried outside. The old keyhole kiva must give way.

Today the kiva may be a rectangular room in the house block, but the old form is retained; an opening provides an unobstructed channel toward the sunrise, representing the lifeline into the village.

The people also took the shape of the pit house and old kiva to the mountaintops, creating a keyhole form with stones, with the lower end of the keyhole opened toward the sunrise. Only the form

Early Taos, situated on the valley floor below its sacred mountain

Shown here is the five-story north block of houses.

PHOTO BY JOHN K. HILLERS, CA. 1880. MUSEUM OF NEW MEXICO, 16096

reminded one that it represented what was once an underground habitation and later a religious sanctum. The Tewa continue to make pilgrimages to the mountain earth navels, for these are places of great power: They provide the Tewa with a way of rediscovering who we are and of renewing our ties to our beginnings. They represent ongoing lifelines to sustain all creation. And—through the centuries when the Spanish and other peoples dominated the Tewa—these places have provided a tenacious symbol of survival.

Our genesis story establishes another viable aspect of our lives. Remember my naming ceremony: There were two women attending, two ears of corn offered with me to the sun. This duality is basic to understanding our behavior.

When the Tewa came onto land, the Hunt Chief took an ear of blue corn and handed it to one of the other men and said: "You are to lead and care for all of the people during the summer." To another man he handed an ear of white corn and told him: "You shall lead and care for the people during the winter." This is how the Summer and Winter Chiefs were instituted.

The Hunt Chief then divided the people between the two chiefs. As they moved south down the Rio Grande, the Summer People traveled on the west side of the river, the Winter People on the east side.

The Summer People lived by agriculture, the Winter People by hunting.

From this time, the story tells us, the Tewa have been divided during their lives into moieties—Winter People, Summer People. Still today a Summer Chief guides us seven months of the year, during the agricultural cycle; a Winter Chief during the five months of hunting. There are special rituals, dances, costumes, and colors attached to each moiety. Everything that has symbolic significance to the Tewa is classified in dualities: Games, plants, and diseases are hot or cold, winter or summer. Some persons or things, like healers, are of the middle, mediating between the two. This gives order to our lives.

A child is incorporated into his moiety through the water-giving ceremony during his first year. The Winter Chief conducts his rite in October; the Summer Chief in late February or March. The ceremony is held in a sanctuary at the chief's home. There are an altar, a sand painting, and various symbols; the chief and his assistants dress in white buckskin. A final character appears, preceded by the call of a fox, as in the creation story. It is the Hunt Chief.

A female assistant holds the child; the moiety chief recites a short prayer and administers a drink of the sacred medicinal water from an abalone shell, thereby welcoming the child into the moiety.

The third rite in a child's life—water pouring—comes between the ages of six and ten and is held within the moiety. It marks the transition from the carefree, innocent state of early childhood to the status of adult, one of the Dry Food People. For four days the boys are made to carry a load of firewood they have chopped themselves, and the girls a basket of cornmeal they have ground themselves, to the homes of their sponsors.

A sponsor instructs each child in the beliefs and practices of the village. On the fourth night, the deities come to the kiva, and the child may go to watch. Afterward, the sponsor bathes the child, pouring water over him. From this time, the child is given duties judged proper for his sex.

A finishing ritual a few years later brings the girls and boys to adulthood. For the boys it is particularly meaningful, for they now become eligible to assist and participate in the coming of the gods in their moiety's kiva. Thus the bonds of the moiety are further strengthened.

It is at death that the bond of moiety is broken and the solidarity of the whole society emphasized again. This echoes the genesis story, for after the people had divided into two for their journey from the lake, they came together again when they arrived at their destination.

When a Tewa dies, relatives dress the corpse. The moccasins are reversed—for the Tewa believe everything in the afterlife is reversed from this life. There is a Spanish Catholic wake, a Requiem Mass, then the trip to the cemetery. There the priest completes the church's funeral rites: the sprinkling of holy water, a prayer, a handful of dirt thrown into the grave. Then all non-Indians leave.

A bag containing the clothing of the deceased is now placed under his head as a pillow, along with other personal possessions. When the grave is covered, a Tewa official tells the survivors that the deceased has gone to the place "of endless cicada singing," that he will be happy, and he admonishes them not to let the loss divide the home.

During the four days following the death, the soul, or Dry Food Who Is No Longer, is believed to wander about in this world in the company of the ancestors. These four days produce a time of unease. There is the fear among relatives that the soul may become lonely and return to take one of them for company. Children are deemed most susceptible. The house itself must not be left unoccupied.

The uneasiness ends on the fourth night, when relatives gather again to perform the releasing rite. There are rituals with tobacco, a piece of charcoal, a series of four lines drawn on the floor. A pottery bowl, used in his naming ceremony long ago and cherished by him all his life, is broken, or "killed." Then a prayer reveals the purpose of the symbols.

We have muddied the waters for you [the smoke]. We have cast shadows between us [the charcoal]. We have made steep gullies between us [the lines]. Do not, therefore, reach for even a hair on our heads. Rather, help us attain that which we are always seeking: Long life, that our children may grow, abundant game, the raising of crops. . . . Now you must go, for you are now free.

With the soul released, all breathe a sigh of relief. They wash their hands. As each finishes, he says, "May you have life." The others respond, "Let it be so." Everyone now eats.

The Tewa begin and end life as one people; we call the life cycle *poeh*, or emergence path. As a Tewa elder told me:

"In the beginning we were one. Then we divided into Summer People and Winter People; in the end we came together again as we are today."

This is the path of our lives.

Note

This essay is reprinted by permission of the National Geographic Society from *National Geographic* 180, no. 4 (October 1991): 6–12.